# AMC'S BEST DAY HIKES IN THE WHITE MOUNTAINS

## WELCOME TO THE AMC

Welcome to the Appalachian Mountain Club! Founded in 1876, we are America's oldest conservation and recreation organization. We promote the protection, enjoyment, and wise use of the mountains, rivers, and trails of the Appalachian region. The AMC has twelve chapters from Maine to Washington, D.C., comprised of tens of thousands of outdoor enthusiasts like you.

By purchasing this book you have contributed to our efforts to protect the Appalachian region. Proceeds from the sales of AMC Books and Maps support our regional land conservation efforts; trail building and maintenance; air- and water-quality research; search and rescue; and environmental education programs for school age children, at-risk youth, and outdoor enthusiasts.

The AMC encourages everyone to enjoy and appreciate the natural world because we believe that successful conservation depends on such experiences. So join us in the outdoors! We offer hiking, paddling, biking, skiing, and mountaineering activities throughout the Appalachian region for outdoor adventurers of every age and ability. Our lodging destinations, such as our state-of-the-art Highland Center, are Model Environmental Education Facilities, demonstrating our stewardship ethic and providing a place for you to relax off-trail and learn more about local ecosystems and habitats, regional environmental issues, and mountain history and culture.

For more information about AMC membership, destinations, and conservation and education programs, turn to the back of this book or visit the AMC web site at www.outdoors.org.

# AMC'S BEST DAY HIKES IN THE

# WHITE MOUNTAINS

Four-Season Guide to 50 of the Best Trails
in the White Mountain National Forest

Including Snowshoeing and Cross-Country Skiing

ROBERT N. BUCHSBAUM

Appalachian Mountain Club Books
Boston, Massachusetts

AMC's Best Day Hikes in the White Mountains
© 2006 Robert N. Buchsbaum. All rights reserved.

Cover and Interior Design: Eric Edstam
Cartography: Ken Dumas
Illustrations: Nancy Childs
Front Cover Photographs: *Day hikers near Mt. Washington,* © David Brownell; *Cross-country skiers making their way to Crawford Depot,* © Jeff Scher
Back Cover Photographs (l to r): *Falling Waters Trail* by Pete Harley; *Dayhikers in New Hampshire,* by David McHale; *Child exploring nature,* © Robert N. Buchsbaum
All interior photographs by the author unless otherwise noted.
Published by the Appalachian Mountain Club.
Distributed by the Globe Pequot Press, Inc., Guilford, CT

LIBRARY OF CONGRESS CATALOGING-IN-PUBLICATION DATA

Buchsbaum, Robert.
    AMC's best day hikes in the White Mountains : four-season guide to 50 of the best trails in the White Mountain National Forest, including snowshoeing and cross-country skiing / Robert N. Buchsbaum.—1st ed.
        p. cm.
    Includes index.
    ISBN-13: 978-1-929173-88-4 (alk. paper)
    1. Hiking—New Hampshire—White Mountains—Guidebooks. 2. Hiking—Maine—White Mountains—Guidebooks. 3. Snowshoes and snowshoeing—New Hampshire—White Mountains—Guidebooks. 4. Snowshoes and snowshoeing—Maine—White Mountains—Guidebooks. 5. Cross-country ski trails—New Hampshire—White Mountains—Guidebooks. 6. Cross-country ski trails—Maine—White Mountains—Guidebooks. 7. Nature trails—New Hampshire—Guidebooks. 8. Nature trails—Maine—Guidebooks. 9. White Mountains (N.H. and ME.)—Guidebooks. I. Title: Four-season guide to 50 of the best trails in the White Mountain National Forest. II. Title: Guide to 50 of the best trails in the White Mountain National Forest. III. Title: Guide to fifty of the best trails in the White Mountain National Forest. IV. Title.

    GV199.42.N42N482 2006
    917.42'20444—dc22

                                                                    2005035022

The paper used in this publication meets the minimum requirements of the American National Standard for Information Sciences—Permanence of Paper for Printed Library Materials, ANSI Z39.48–1984.∞

**Due to changes in conditions, use of the information
in this book is at the sole risk of the user.**

 Printed on recycled paper using soy-based inks.
Printed in the United States of America.

10 9 8 7 6 5 4 3 2 1                                    06 07 08 09 10 11

This book is dedicated to all the volunteers who build and maintain the trails, allowing us to enjoy more intimately the wonderful vistas, waterfalls, flowers, and creatures of the mountains.

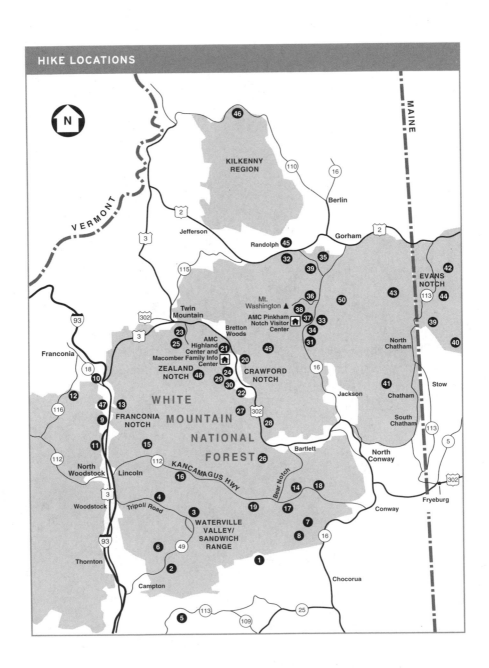

# CONTENTS

# AT-A-GLANCE TRIP PLANNER

| # | Trip | Page | Rating | Distance | Est Time | Elev Change |
|---|------|------|--------|----------|----------|-------------|
| | **SANDWICH RANGE/WATERVILLE VALLEY** | | | | | |
| 1 | Brook Path | 3 | easy | 2.1 mi one-way | 1.5–2.5 hr | minimal |
| 2 | Smarts Brook Trail | 6 | easy | 2.6 mi round-trip | 1.5–2.5 hr | 300 ft |
| 3 | Cascade Path | 10 | easy | 3 mi round-trip | 3 hr | 300 ft |
| 4 | East Pond and Little East Pond | 13 | moderate | 5 mi round-trip | 4–5 hr | 800 ft |
| 5 | Old Bridle Path to West Rattlesnake | 18 | moderate | 1.8 mi round-trip | 1.5–2 hr | 400 ft |
| 6 | The Welch-Dickey Loop | 22 | moderate with some challenging sections | 4.4-mi loop | 3.5–5 hr | 1600 ft |
| 7 | White Ledge Loop | 27 | moderate with some challenging sections | 4.4-mi loop | 3–4 hr | 1400 ft |
| 8 | Carter Ledge | 31 | moderate with some challenging sections | 5 mi round-trip | 3.5–5 hr | 1700 ft |
| | **FRANCONIA NOTCH** | | | | | |
| 9 | Pemi Trail | 36 | easy | 4 mi one-way | 2–3 hr | 500 ft (gradual) |
| 10 | Bald Mtn and Artist's Bluff | 40 | moderate | 1.5 mi round-trip | 1–2 hr | 350 ft |
| 11 | Mt Pemigewasset | 45 | moderate | 3.6 mi round-trip | 4 hr | 1150 ft |

| Great for Kids | Great Views | Waterfall/ Cascade | Wildlife Likely | Wild-flowers | Steep | Trail Running | Snow-shoeing | Xcountry Skiing |
|---|---|---|---|---|---|---|---|---|
| ✓ | | ✓ | | ✓ | | | ✓ | ✓ |
| ✓ | | ✓ | ✓ | ✓ | | | ✓ | ✓ |
| ✓ | | ✓ | | ✓ | | | | |
| ✓ | | | ✓ | ✓ | | | | |
| ✓ | ✓ | | | | | | | |
| | ✓ | | | ✓ | ✓ | | | |
| | ✓ | | | | ✓ | ✓ | | |
| | ✓ | ✓ | | | ✓ | | | |
| ✓ | | ✓ | | ✓ | | ✓ | ✓ | ✓ |
| ✓ | ✓ | | | | ✓ | ✓ | ✓ | |
| ✓ | ✓ | | | | | ✓ | ✓ | |

| Great for Kids | Great Views | Waterfall/ Cascade | Wildlife Likely | Wild-flowers | Steep | Trail Running | Snow-shoeing | Xcountry Skiing |
|---|---|---|---|---|---|---|---|---|
|  |  | ✓ |  |  |  |  |  |  |
|  |  | ✓ |  |  | ✓ |  |  |  |
| ✓ |  | ✓ |  |  |  |  | ✓ | ✓ |
| ✓ |  | ✓ |  | ✓ |  |  | ✓ | ✓ |
| ✓ | ✓ |  | ✓ | ✓ |  |  | ✓ | ✓ |
| ✓ | ✓ | ✓ |  |  |  |  |  |  |
| ✓ | ✓ |  |  |  | ✓ |  |  |  |
|  | ✓ |  |  |  | ✓ |  |  |  |
| ✓ |  |  | ✓ |  |  |  | ✓ |  |
| ✓ | ✓ |  | ✓ | ✓ |  |  | ✓ |  |
| ✓ |  | ✓ |  |  | ✓ |  | ✓ |  |
| ✓ |  |  |  | ✓ |  |  | ✓ |  |
| ✓ | ✓ |  |  | ✓ | ✓ | ✓ | ✓ |  |
| ✓ | ✓ |  | ✓ | ✓ | ✓ | ✓ | ✓ |  |
| ✓ | ✓ |  | ✓ | ✓ |  | ✓ | ✓ | ✓ |
|  |  | ✓ | ✓ | ✓ | ✓ | ✓ | ✓ | ✓ |

| # | Trip | pp | Rating | Distance | Est Time | Elev Change |
|---|------|-----|--------|----------|----------|-------------|
| 28 | Mt Crawford | 120 | moderate with some challenging sections | 5 mi round-trip | 5 hr | 2100 ft |
| 29 | Mt Avalon | 124 | moderate with some challenging sections | 3.7 mi round-trip | 3-4 hr | 1550 ft |
| 30 | Ethan Pond | 128 | moderate with some challenging sections | 5.4 mi round-trip | 4 hr | 1550 ft |
| **PINKHAM NOTCH** | | | | | | |
| 31 | Lost Pond | 135 | easy | 1 mi round-trip | 1 hr | minimal |
| 32 | Waterfall Loop | 139 | easy or moderate | 1.5 mi round-trip | 1-2 hr | 400 ft |
| 33 | Thompson Falls | 143 | easy | 1.4 mi round-trip | 1-2 hr | 200 ft |
| 34 | Square Ledge | 147 | moderate | 1 mi round-trip | 1-2 hr | 500 ft |
| 35 | Pine Mountain | 150 | moderate | 3.5 mi round-trip | 2.5-4 hr | 750 ft |
| 36 | Lows Bald Spot via Old Jackson Rd | 154 | moderate with some challenging sections | 4.2 mi round-trip | 3-4 hr | 850 ft |
| 37 | Tuckerman Ravine | 160 | moderate with some challenging sections | 4.8 mi round-trip | 4.5 hr | 1850 ft |
| 38 | The Alpine Garden | 164 | moderate with some challenging sections | 0.6-2.4 mi round-trip depending on route | 2-3 hr | 300 ft |
| **EVANS NOTCH** | | | | | | |
| 39 | Deer Hill and Deer Hill Spring | 173 | easy to moderate | 4 mi round-trip | 3-4 hr | 850 ft |
| 40 | Lord Hill | 177 | easy | 2.8 mi round-trip | 2-4 hr | 650 ft |
| 41 | Mountain Pond | 182 | moderate | 2.7-mi loop | 2-4 hr | minimal |
| 42 | The Roost | 187 | moderate with some challenging sections | 2.1 mi round-trip | 1-1.5 hr | 550 ft |
| 43 | Basin Trail to Basin Rim | 191 | moderate with some challenging secions | 4.6 mi round-trip | 4-6 hr | 800 ft |

| Great for Kids | Great Views | Waterfall/ Cascade | Wildlife Likely | Wild- flowers | Steep | Trail Running | Snow- shoeing | Xcountry Skiing |
|---|---|---|---|---|---|---|---|---|
|  | ● |  | ● | ● | ● |  |  |  |
|  | ● | ● |  |  | ● |  | ● |  |
|  | ● |  | ● |  | ● |  | ● |  |
|  |  |  |  |  |  |  |  |  |
| ● |  |  | ● | ● |  |  | ● | ● |
| ● |  | ● |  | ● |  |  |  |  |
| ● |  | ● |  | ● |  |  |  |  |
| ● | ● |  | ● |  | ● | ● | ● |  |
| ● | ● |  | ● | ● | ● | ● |  |  |
|  | ● |  | ● | ● |  |  | ● | ● |
|  | ● |  |  | ● | ● | ● | ● |  |
|  | ● |  |  | ● | ● |  |  |  |
|  |  |  |  |  |  |  |  |  |
| ● | ● |  |  | ● |  |  | ● |  |
| ● | ● |  |  |  |  |  | ● |  |
| ● |  |  | ● | ● |  |  | ● |  |
| ● | ● |  |  |  |  |  |  |  |
| ● | ● | ● | ● |  |  |  |  |  |

| Great for Kids | Great Views | Waterfall/ Cascade | Wildlife Likely | Wild-flowers | Steep | Trail Running | Snow-shoeing | Xcountry Skiing |
|---|---|---|---|---|---|---|---|---|
|  | ✓ | ✓ |  | ✓ | ✓ |  |  |  |
|  |  |  |  |  |  |  |  |  |
|  | ✓ |  |  |  | ✓ | ✓ | ✓ |  |
| ✓ |  | ✓ |  |  |  |  |  |  |
|  |  |  |  |  |  |  |  |  |
| ✓ | ✓ |  | ✓ | ✓ |  | ✓ | ✓ |  |
| ✓ | ✓ | ✓ | ✓ | ✓ |  | ✓ | ✓ | ✓ |
| ✓ |  | ✓ | ✓ | ✓ | ✓ |  | ✓ |  |
|  | ✓ | ✓ | ✓ |  | ✓ |  | ✓ |  |
|  |  |  |  |  |  |  |  |  |
| ✓ |  | ✓ |  |  |  |  |  |  |
| ✓ |  | ✓ |  |  |  |  |  |  |
| ✓ |  | ✓ |  |  |  |  |  |  |
| ✓ |  | ✓ |  |  | ✓ |  |  |  |
| ✓ |  | ✓ |  |  |  |  | ✓ |  |
| ✓ |  | ✓ |  |  |  |  |  |  |
| ✓ |  | ✓ |  |  |  |  |  |  |
| ✓ |  | ✓ |  |  |  |  |  |  |
| ✓ |  |  |  |  |  |  | ✓ |  |
| ✓ |  |  |  | ✓ |  |  | ✓ |  |

# PREFACE

**MY FIRST MEMORIES OF THE WHITE MOUNTAINS** are of a family vacation when I was seven years old. Since we all liked model trains, we naturally took the cog railway to the summit of Mount Washington. For the first time in my life I looked down on puffy clouds. Trails, marked by mysterious piles of stones, snaked off into the distance over rugged, barren peaks, and signs pointed the way to wondrous-sounding destinations like Lakes of the Clouds and Tuckerman Ravine. Later I would actually hike on those trails and visit those destinations many times, but nothing can replace that first impression.

To me the Whites have always been a fantasyland of bald mountain summits; extensive views; exotic plants; dark, mossy, enchanted evergreen forests; and cold mountain streams tumbling over boulders in fantastic patterns. My fondness for this region provided the original inspiration for this book. A second inspiration was my many years of hiking, first with friends, then with family. A third was my experiences leading nature walks in the White Mountains, many as an AMC naturalist, where I enjoyed watching kids and adults discover the natural world. And a fourth, very compelling inspiration was becoming a parent. My wife and I had new companions on our hiking trips, companions who did not yet have our abilities or interests but whom we definitely wanted to brainwash into loving the outdoors. It worked too, because by the time we finished researching the hikes for the first edition of this book, our daughter was running along the trails, throwing stones in the water, talking to the gray jays, and trying to pick the wildflowers (our first conservation lesson). Our son followed suit and thrilled us with his enthusiasm for mosses, insects, and other small denizens of the forest. With this third edition of the book, our children's hiking abilities are more than the equal to that of their parents, so additional trails have opened up to us.

As the book developed, I was encouraged by parents who wanted a White Mountain guide directed toward young families and others who wanted an introduction to some of the best nature, hikes, and views at their fingertips. This book describes fifty hikes appropriate for anyone interested in exploring the White Mountains, including adults traveling with children.

## ACKNOWLEDGMENTS

I thank the Appalachian Mountain Club for giving me the opportunity to write this book. I have had the pleasure of working with gifted editors and other staff at AMC Books. Gordon Hardy guided me through the 1st edition of *Nature Hikes in the White Mountains*, and I am particularly grateful for his faith, encouragement, advice, and good humor. Walter Graff and Nancy Ritger at Pinkham Notch provided helpful recommendations on trails appropriate for children and contributed some basic ideas on how to approach this topic. Mark Russell oversaw the 2nd edition. Sarah Jane Shangraw oversaw the development of *Nature Hikes in the White Mountains* into *AMC's Best Day Hikes in the White Mountains*. AMC staff contributed in many ways to this book. The AMC's on-the-ground experts, frontline staff, and volunteers assisted in creating the new mix of trips and were particularly helpful in providing input on cross-country skiing, snowshoeing, and trail-running opportunities. Much of what I have learned about the White Mountains comes from my association with a wonderful group of AMC volunteer naturalists.

Thanks to Lesley Rowse of the White Mountain National Forest and Gary Inman for their advice on trails, particularly in Evans Notch; for sharing their knowledge of the White Mountains; and for letting us invade their home on numerous occasions. Rebecca Oreskes, Patti Dugan, and David Govotski of the White Mountain National Forest also provided valuable information— David contributed the historical information on Lows Bald Spot. I am grateful also to Ed Quinlan, Leslie Nelkin, and their children, Suzanna and Michael, for sharing their house with us and accompanying us on a number of hikes. Suzanna and Michael were two of our primary "field-testers."

E. Dykstra Eusden, Betsy Colburn, Peter Dunwiddie, and Steve Weisman made helpful comments on various sections of the manuscript. Of course the author takes all responsibility for any errors.

Very special thanks are due to my wife, Nancy Schalch, and our children, Alison and Gabriel. Nancy was my chief hiking companion, cheerfully doing more than her share of the child care on our trips so I could concentrate on taking notes and photographs. She provided continual encouragement and logistic support, reading and making useful comments on the entire manuscript. It simply would not have been possible to complete this book without her. Alison went on her first hike when she was two months old and, fortunately for us (and for this book project), instantly took a liking to being out on the trails. Gabriel was not there when the first version of this book came out but has more than made up for it with his running commentary and enthusiasm for the natural world whenever we have walked these trails together since then. I also thank my family for tolerating me on weekends and evenings, when I disappeared to work on the manuscript.

# HOW TO USE THIS BOOK

THIS BOOK INCLUDES TRAIL DESCRIPTIONS grouped by geographic region within the White Mountains. At the beginning of each regional chapter is a summary of local resources, followed by individual trail descriptions for that region. They are ordered by level of difficulty with those rated easy first, those rated moderate next, and those that are moderate with some steep sections last. Each recommended trail is described in detail, with:

- Symbols indicating whether the trail is appropriate for snowshoeing and/or cross-country skiing as well as hiking.
- A chart containing the degree of difficulty, the length of the trail, elevation gain, how long it should take, and where to locate the trail on AMC maps.
- A brief summary of highlights of the trail, such as outstanding natural features, special activities, and what to expect along the trail and at the destination.
- Directions—how to get to the trailhead from major roads and towns.
- Detailed hiking directions for the trail.
- A general trail map showing the locations of various features.
- Nature Notes—natural history, scenery, human history, and special activities such as swimming or exploring a quarry.

Also included in this book is an illustrated glossary of flora and fauna in the White Mountains, advice on planning a hike in the Whites, and an appendix on hiking with children. The appendix on natural history in the White Mountains emphasizes things that are visible on most trails.

To use this book we recommend that you refer to the At-a-Glance Trip Planner to see if there's something you and your hiking companions might especially like. This chart summarizes each trail according to its features: running water, great vistas, especially notable wildflowers, and so on. This chart will give you a "snapshot" view of the trail so you can match its features to your favorite trailside pastimes.

Before starting out, read through the trail descriptions to decide if the hike is right for you. Remember that the advice in the trail description on "degree of difficulty" and the length of time a hike should take naturally involves some subjectivity. "Easy" means the terrain is relatively level and the hike is less than 3 miles long, or the hike is somewhat steep but very short. "Moderate" means the terrain may be rocky or there is a steeper grade. The hike may be 2–4 miles long. "Moderate with some challenging sections" means the terrain can be difficult, especially for children, and the hike may be 4–6 miles long. None of the hikes in this book are rated "difficult" because our frame of reference is the AMC's *White Mountain Guide*, which includes many steeper and longer hikes. The estimated times are based on the assumption that you'll take your time and make some stops—they do not factor in additional time for picnics, blueberry-picking, or other activities.

The AMC's *White Mountain National Forest Map and Guide* provides a wonderful lay-of-the-land overview and is a good reference for getting to the trailheads indicated in the book. Its numbered icons correspond to the hikes in this book—it is an invaluable companion for both someone getting to know the White Mountain landscape, with its ranges and notches, as well as an experienced hiker who is planning a multiday hike replete with backcountry lodging or camping, drop-off and pick-up points, shuttling via the AMC Hiker Shuttle, and more.

We hope you enjoy this book and that it is a useful companion on many great hikes in the White Mountains. If you are bringing children along, we hope the children experience the same sense of wonder about this special region that has inspired you and us.

# TRIP PLANNING AND SAFETY

## hikeSAFE

The U.S. Forest Service and New Hampshire Fish and Game Department have developed "hikeSafe," a program to encourage hiker responsibility in the White Mountain National Forest. The hikeSafe "Hiker Responsibility Code" states: You are responsible for yourself, so be prepared:

- With knowledge and gear. Become self reliant by learning about the terrain, conditions, local weather and your equipment before you start.
- To leave your plans. Tell someone where you are going, the trails you are hiking, when you'll return and your emergency plans.
- To stay together. When you start as a group, hike as a group, end as a group. Pace your hike to the slowest person.
- To turn back. Weather changes quickly in the mountains. Fatigue and unexpected conditions can also affect your hike. Know your limitations and when to postpone your hike. The mountains will be there another day.
- For emergencies, even if you are headed out for just an hour. An injury, severe weather or a wrong turn could become life threatening. Don't assume you will be rescued; know how to rescue yourself.
- To share the hiker code with others.

## WHAT TO BRING

Ten essential items you should carry on every trip include:

- Map
- Compass
- Warm clothing including hat and mittens
- Extra food and water
- Flashlight or headlamp
- Matches/firestarter
- First-aid kit
- Whistle
- Rain/wind gear
- Pocketknife or multitool

Protection from insects is essential for certain hikes all summer and for all hikes during black-fly season (mid-May through mid-June). Bring along insect repellent, or dress in light, long-sleeved shirts and pants if you prefer to avoid using repellents. And if you expect to spend much time in the sun, remember sun hats and sunscreen.

First-aid kits are available from outdoors and sporting goods stores, but you can easily put together your own. It should include Band–Aids and sterile gauze pads, adhesive tape, small scissors, tweezers, an Ace bandage, antiseptic ointment, aspirin or another painkiller, a small bar of soap, moleskin for blisters, and any special medication required.

Carry these items in a comfortable daypack. It is important to fill your water bottle before you start hiking because water in mountain lakes and streams is considered unsafe to drink without purification. Bring at least two liters per person. For trips longer than a few hours, consult the AMC's *White Mountain Guide* for more details.

Good hiking boots are a critical element of a successful hike, especially for the more strenuous ones. Make sure yours have sturdy soles and good ankle support, and are well broken in before you set off.

Dress in layers so that you can peel off or add an item easily. Remember, cotton clothes are very comfortable when dry but lose their insulating properties when wet. Wool or synthetics like polypropylene or pile are better. You'll need windbreakers and extra clothes because summit ledges, even at low elevations, are likely to be cool and windy compared to the forest. All of the hikes in this book except one (Alpine Garden) are below 3,500 feet in elevation, so you are not likely to face the potentially extreme weather conditions that characterize life above treeline. Nevertheless, the weather in the White Mountains can be notoriously fickle, even at lower elevations, and the extra clothes will help you enjoy exposed summits and lunch breaks.

## WHAT TO BRING ESPECIALLY FOR KIDS

First of all, you should bring along all the items necessary for hikes without children. A child who is cold or hungry is not going to be a good hiking companion. Remember that children are more likely to get chilled if you end up carrying them, so have extra clothing, especially for backpack-sized babies.

One important safety item is a whistle. Beforehand, teach the children to stay in sight so hopefully you won't need it. However, each child should have a whistle and know that if they are separated from the group, they should stay put and blow the whistle at regular intervals. Remind them that the whistle is not for play but should be used only when they sense they are lost from the group.

Food is another critical ingredient of a successful hike with kids. Lunch is a great motivator and reward. Occasional snacks such as granola bars, fruit, or cookies can nip the start of any crankiness before it goes too far.

Have kids carry a pack of their own when they are old enough. In addition to extra clothes and perhaps a small canteen, make sure each child's pack has something essential for one of the group's activities—a special snack, bags for blueberries, a lunch treat. If the kids insist they won't need a jacket, suggest that they can sit on it during lunch.

Consider bringing along a child carrier, especially for longer hikes. It is a lot easier than carrying a tired child on your shoulders, and safer too.

Other small items that are good to have: a hand lens or magnifying glass aids in examining small things; binoculars are great if your destination has a view; a tea or soup strainer can make searching for aquatic life along ponds and streams more fun; and a bug box enables a child to examine insects closely. Finally, younger children can bring a favorite toy or stuffed animal in their own day packs.

## PARKING FEES

The White Mountain National Forest Recreational Fee Program has existed since 1998. Your vehicle must display a sticker in order to park at most trailheads within the national forest. At the time of this writing the cost of the sticker was $3 for a one-day pass, $5 for seven days, and $20 for one year ($25 for two cars in the same family). Stickers are available at ranger stations, AMC facilities, and some businesses throughout the region. The fee goes directly to support the White Mountain National Forest. According to WMNF staff, the fee program is under review and may be changed in the near future.

## FOLLOWING THE TRAIL

The trails in this guide are generally well marked with signs and blazes (painted spots on tree trunks or rocks). Nevertheless, always carry a trail map and a compass and read the trail description before you depart so that you are prepared for any quirks. Intersections with logging roads, unmarked trails, and occasional faded blazes might lead to some confusion. The maps in this guide are designed to give a general idea of the trail, but they are not as definitive as a detailed contour map. You should review the maps and trail descriptions in the AMC's *White Mountain Guide* in addition to this book. If you think you are off the trail, the best thing to do is to backtrack until you find the last blaze. Keep track of the blazes as you hike, a job that you might share with children so they feel responsible for the successful navigation of the trip. Remember, too, to stay on the trail, not only for safety but also to protect the plants and other wildlife.

# 1

# SANDWICH RANGE/ WATERVILLE VALLEY

## LAY OF THE LAND

Waterville Valley is a beautiful valley tucked in among 4,000-foot peaks. It still feels secluded and quiet despite the presence of a major ski resort and conference center. If you are coming from the south, you reach Waterville Valley from I-93 by traveling about 11 miles northeast on NH 49 (Exit 28, Campton). This is a well-paved scenic road that parallels the Mad River. If approaching from the north, travel about 10 miles east through Thornton Gap on Tripoli Road, an unpaved road for much of its length. Note that Tripoli Road is not plowed in winter.

The region has the advantage of being a shorter drive from the big metropolitan areas of the East Coast than other parts of the White Mountains and also of warming up earlier in spring and cooling down later in fall. The valley's loop hike to Welch and Dickey mountains is one of the most popular family hikes in the White Mountains (see Trip 6). There is also an extensive network of easy trails along streams.

The Sandwich Range is southeast of Waterville Valley and contains a wilderness area and a number of 3–4,000-foot mountains. Mount Chocorua, in the eastern part of this region, is a striking, cone-shaped peak and one of the most popular hiking destinations in New England. Two of our suggested day hikes take you to ledges with wonderful views of this peak (see Trips 7 and

8). Lower hills in the southwest part of this region provide vistas of Squam, Winnipesaukee, and other lakes. Much of this southwest area is covered in the AMC's *Southern New Hampshire Trail Guide*, as well as *Nature Walks in the New Hampshire Lakes Region* by Julia Older and Steve Sherman (also from AMC Books). Rattlesnake Mountain (see Trip 5) overlooks Squam Lake south of Waterville Valley.

## SUPPLIES AND LOGISTICS

Waterville Valley is a resort community with downhill ski slopes, a convention center, and condominiums. It caters to outdoor activities, so you'll have no trouble buying last-minute supplies. If you are coming from the north, you may find it convenient to get your supplies at the Lincoln/North Woodstock exit, where there are a number of stores.

The Sandwich Range region contains a number of classic, New England villages, such as Center Sandwich, Tamworth, and Chocorua. These small towns are great places to stay, but do not expect to find a great variety of supplies for your hike. There are plenty of places to get supplies along NH 16 if you are approaching the region from the east.

## NEARBY CAMPING

There are two national forest campgrounds off NH 49. The Campton Campground is closer to I-93 and has 58 sites open in the summer season and a group camping area open year-round. The Waterville Campground, open year-round, is 8 miles from I-93 and has 27 sites. Russell Pond Campground is accessible from Tripoli Road. The campgrounds in Franconia Notch and the western part of the Kancamagus Highway are about 30 to 45 minutes from the trails in Waterville Valley.

White Ledge Campground, a National Forest campground with 28 sites, is off Route 16 about 4 miles south of the village of Conway. The White Ledge Loop Trail (Trip 7) and Carter Ledge Trail (Trip 8) leave from this campground.

## TRIP 1
## BROOK PATH

**RATING:** Easy

**DISTANCE:** 2.1 miles one-way

**ELEVATION CHANGE:** Minimal

**ESTIMATED TIME:** 1.5–2.5 hours

**MAPS:** AMC's *White Mountain National Forest Map and Guide*, K9
AMC's *White Mountain Guide*, 27th ed., Map 3: Crawford Notch–
Sandwich Range, K9

**WMNF PARKING FEE:** No

**WINTER NOTES:** Skiing

**OTHER ACTIVITIES:** Swimming

**A beautiful, shady streamside walk, great for a hot summer day or for an early spring outing when higher elevations may still be locked in snow and ice.**

The Brook Path follows the Wonalancet River through a rich forest of hemlocks and northern hardwoods. Many small cascades, pools, and boulders make it continuously interesting, and an intriguing old wooden dam provides an historical element. This flat trail makes a great, low stress family walk, even for those with young children. Mosquitoes could be an issue in early to midsummer so bring repellent. The eastern section of the trail, where it follows Old Locke Road, is an easy cross-country ski trail. The rest of the hike can be skied with a little more care.

## DIRECTIONS

The Brook Path runs east–west with two trailheads on NH 113A in Wonalancet. You can walk it one way and then retrace your steps or leave a car at one of the two trailheads. NH 113A is a winding road between Tamworth and North Sandwich, so it is wise to consult a map, since what is north, south, east, or west relative to this road is constantly changing (see the AMC's *White Mountain National Forest Map and Guide*, section K9). The western trailhead is on the south side of Rte 113A, opposite the trailheads for the Cabin and Big Rock Cave trails and is easier to find. It is 6.2 miles from the intersection of Rte 113 and 113A in Tamworth. Along the way, you pass Hemenway State Forest. There is space for several cars. The eastern trailhead is just off Rte 113A on an

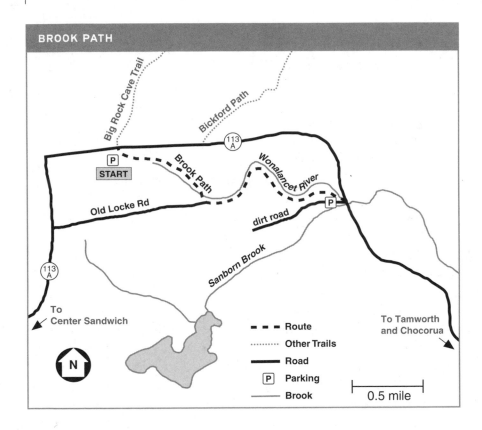

## BROOK PATH

Big Rock Cave Trail

Bickford Path

113 A

Brook Path

Wonalancet River

P

START

Old Locke Rd

dirt road

P

113 A

Sanborn Brook

To Center Sandwich

To Tamworth and Chocorua

N

- - - Route

.......... Other Trails

Road

P Parking

Brook

0.5 mile

unpaved road. This road leaves west from 113A just south of the bridge over Sanborn Brook. There is a large parking area for the trail about 0.1 mile down the road from 113A, but unfortunately, the last we checked there was no road sign or other indicator of the trailhead at its intersection with Rte 113A.

Do not confuse this trail with the Brook Trail, which ascends Mount Chocorua.

## TRAIL DESCRIPTION

This description is from the western trailhead. The trail is marked with blue blazes and has virtually no elevation gain. It starts out through a rich forest of northern hardwoods and very quickly approaches the brook. It follows the north bank with plenty of pools—some deep enough for a swim—small waterfalls, and a few glacial erratics. The hardwoods give way to Canadian hemlock, some of which reach impressive sizes. At 0.9 mile, the trail crosses the brook on a solid, wooden bridge. A glacial erratic just before the wooden bridge is covered with moss and Virginia polypody fern—look underneath the fronds of the fern for the small round dots that contain the spores through which this fern reproduces. Leaving the bridge, the trail turns left to follow the south bank for the remaining 1.2 miles of the hike (to Sanborn Brook). Old Locke Road comes in from the right at this point, so for much of the remainder of the walk, you are on this abandoned section of road. At about 1.1 miles, you pass an old wooden dam that first brought electricity to the region and then hit a short, rocky stretch. If you only have one car back at the west trailhead, this would be a logical place to turn around. The trail then follows the old road for another mile. The trail comes out on the unpaved road at a point where Wonalancet River joins Sanborn Brook. Turn left for the parking area and Rte 113A.

## NATURE NOTES

There are some impressively large hemlocks along the trail, particularly in the same area as the glacial erratic. Counting the annual rings in a few stumps will give you an idea of the age of some of these giants.

Many small cascades form pools where you can wade or swim on a hot summer day. Because of the lower elevation, the water tends to be warmer than in other White Mountain streams, so you do not have to be a polar bear to enjoy a dip. By carefully turning over stones and exploring little pools among the rocks, you may find wood frogs, streamside salamanders such as the very fast two-lined salamanders, and insects typical of flowing waters, such as caddisfly

**Along the Brook Path.**

larvae. These latter build small tubes of bits of leaves and other debris in which they live.

The western end of the trail contains a particularly rich assortment of wildflowers. Look for bloodroot, a relative of poppies, right at the beginning of the trail. Its delicate white flowers are one of the earliest spring wildflowers, so most visitors are not likely to see them. Instead, look for a single, broad leaf that resembles hands clasping its 6-inch high flowering stalk. This plant is named for its red sap, which was used by Native Americans as a dye. Bloodroot contains alkaloids that have been used medicinally in the past to treat a variety of ailments, such as asthma and dyspepsia (i.e., indigestion). Other wildflowers and ferns nearby include Jack in the pulpit, Solomon's seal, Solomon's plume, interrupted fern, and royal fern.

Trailing arbutus (mayflower), another early spring wildflower with an exquisite scent, occurs further along the trail. This low, trailing plant has wiry stems covered with rusty hairs and leathery, oval leaves. Another interesting wildflower is pipsissewa (prince's pine), often found under hemlocks. This plant has shiny, dark green, evergreen leaves that radiate out from a single point along the stem, much like spokes of an umbrella. Its small cluster of white flowers hangs down. Along much of the trail you can find wintergreen (checkerberry), whose leaves release the sweet odor of its namesake when crushed.

## TRIP 2
## SMARTS BROOK TRAIL

**RATING:** Easy

**DISTANCE:** 2.6 miles round-trip

**ELEVATION CHANGE:** 300-foot elevation gain

**ESTIMATED TIME:** 1.5–2.5 hours

**MAPS:** AMC's *White Mountain National Forest Map and Guide*, K6
AMC's *White Mountain Guide*, 27th ed., Map 3: Crawford Notch–
Sandwich Range, K6

**WMNF PARKING FEE:** Yes

**WINTER NOTES:** The Smarts Brook Trail is listed as a "more difficult" cross-country ski trail and connects to a network of cross-country ski trails in the area. The Pine Flats Trail leaves from the same parking area as the hiking trail.

**OTHER ACTIVITIES:** Wading

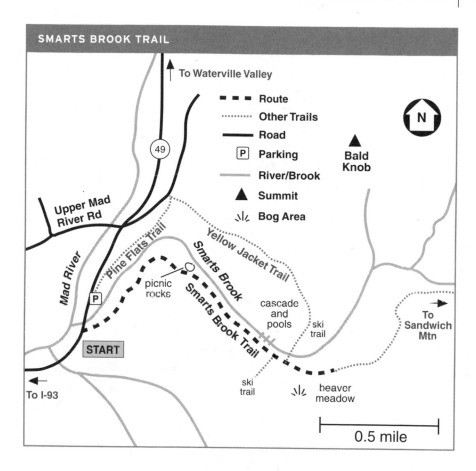

**SMARTS BROOK TRAIL**

To Waterville Valley

- - - Route
.......... Other Trails
—— Road
P Parking
—— River/Brook
▲ Summit
⩘ Bog Area

N

Bald Knob ▲

49

Upper Mad River Rd

Pine Flats Trail

Yellow Jacket Trail

Mad River

P

picnic rocks

Smarts Brook

Smarts Brook Trail

cascade and pools

ski trail

To Sandwich Mtn

START

To I-93

ski trail

⩘ beaver meadow

0.5 mile

**A good choice on a hot summer day because of the dense forest and accessibility of the stream. Wade in a beautiful swimming hole beneath a small waterfall and then explore an open pond and meadow area created by beavers.**

The trail runs for 5.1 miles between NH 49 and the Sandwich Mountain Trail. The first 1.3 miles makes a very pleasant family walk along Smarts Brook on an old logging road. In the right season you will see lots of pink lady's slipper and other wildflowers.

This is a "southern" trail (relative to others in the White Mountains) and is at low elevation, so snow melts and plants bloom earlier in spring than elsewhere. Bring mosquito repellent because it can be buggy.

You can make a loop by walking the Pine Flats and Yellow Jacket ski trails. This intersects the Smarts Brook Trail after 2 miles.

## DIRECTIONS

From I-93, take the Campton/Waterville Valley exit and follow NH 49 toward Waterville Valley. The parking area for Smarts Brook Trail is on the southeast side of NH 49, 4 miles east of its intersection with NH 175 in Campton and just past the bridge over Smarts Brook. The trailhead is at the south side of the parking lot.

From Waterville Valley, the trailhead is 0.5 mile past the intersection of NH 49 with Upper Mad River Road, 5.2 miles from the junction of NH 49 and Tripoli Road.

## TRAIL DESCRIPTION

Begin by walking back across the NH 49 bridge over Smarts Brook. Do not confuse the Smarts Brook Trail with the ski trail that leaves from the same parking lot. After ascending a few log steps, the Smarts Brook Trail picks up the course of an old logging road. Fairly soon the cross-country ski trail marked with blue diamonds runs together with the trail for a while. After another logging road enters from the right (keep this in mind for your return trip), you start picking up the yellow blazes that mark this trail. A number of well-marked cross-country ski trails, which are not on any hiking map, intersect with this trail at various times, so be careful to stay on the main path.

After about 30 to 40 minutes, the trail approaches the bank of Smarts Brook. There are some flat rocks here, so it is a good place for a picnic or to turn around if you have had enough. Continuing along the brook, the swimming "pool" and cascade are only a few minutes farther.

Just beyond the falls, the Tri Town cross-country ski trail comes in from the right, then departs shortly to the left. Where it departs, a sign for the Smarts Brook Trail points you to the left across the stream. This is a loop that eventually rejoins the main trail, but we recommend you ignore it and follow the main path to the beaver meadow a few minutes ahead.

About 0.2 mile beyond the pool, cross a tributary stream over some wooden boards. The beaver dam and meadow will be visible through the woods to the right, but continue a bit past it for easiest access.

Beyond the beaver meadow the Smarts Brook Trail narrows to a path and continues more steeply for another 4 miles to the Sandwich Mountain Trail. Families with children may want to turn back after exploring the beaver meadow. Just remember to follow the trail to the right when you reach the point where the logging road forks to the left about 0.2 mile from the trailhead.

## NATURE NOTES

As you walk along the Smarts Brook Trail, you will encounter a number of aquatic insects that are common in streams, ditches, and temporary woodland pools of the White Mountains. They include the crane fly and mosquitoes, water striders, and whirligig beetles.

The beaver-created wetland at the end of this hike provides a good opportunity to inspect the beaver's handiwork so closely. You can walk right out on one of the old dams. You should be able to see the combination of small branches and mud underneath the new plants that now grow on top of the dam. The dam that you are walking out on is actually one of the oldest in a series. The beaver have

**It's easy to discover where beaver have been.**

moved farther downstream over the years as they have chopped down the more upstream trees. The part of the wetland they have abandoned has since silted in.

The open wetland created by the beaver provides a good lesson on how different kinds of habitats attract different types of plants and animals. The wetland plants, such as marsh Saint John's wort, steeplebush, and sedges, must be tolerant of full sunlight as well as wet soil. Birds attracted to the open spaces of the beaver meadow are tree swallows, flickers, blue jays, and hawks such as the broad-winged hawk. You may also find moose tracks in soft muddy areas of the wetland and hear green frogs calling *glunk* as if someone had just plunked a banjo string.

In contrast to the open beaver meadow, most of the Smarts Brook Trail is within a northern hardwood forest, with yellow birches particularly abundant. Hemlock and haircap moss thrive in the damp areas near the brook, and the understory is dominated by hobblebush and striped maple. Wildflowers are abundant in spring and the most common birds are thrushes and warblers.

About halfway to the falls, you will pass a huge glacial erratic that looks like a boat. Its top is covered with rock fern (Virginia polypody). The overhang provides a great hiding place and rest stop before you continue down the trail.

## TRIP 3
## CASCADE PATH

**RATING:** Easy
**DISTANCE:** 3–4.5 miles round-trip, depending on your route
**ELEVATION CHANGE:** 300-foot elevation gain
**ESTIMATED TIME:** 3 hours
**MAPS:** AMC's *White Mountain National Forest Map and Guide*, J7
AMC's *White Mountain Guide*, 27th ed., Map 3: Crawford Notch–
Sandwich Range, J7
**WMNF PARKING FEE:** None
**WINTER NOTES:** Many ski trails in the area
**OTHER ACTIVITIES:** Swimming

**This is a pleasant, relatively easy walk to a beautiful series of small waterfalls in Waterville Valley near the resort community. It's a perfect family outing, easy except for a few short uphills. In spring (through mid-June) an added bonus is the rich assortment of wild-flowers.**

## DIRECTIONS
Waterville Valley is at the end of NH 49 about 11 miles northeast of the Campton exit of I-93, or about 10 miles east of I-93 through Thornton Gap on Tripoli Road. Tripoli Road is closed in winter. To find the trailhead, continue past the town square and turn right on Valley Road, following the signs to Snow's Mountain Ski Area and WVAIA Hiking Trails. Park in the lot just past the tennis courts and follow sign to Cascade Path.

## TRAIL DESCRIPTION
The Cascade Path begins by climbing up an old ski slope (the steepest uphill of the trail) that is now a road to new houses. The trail enters the woods on the left (north) side after about 0.4 mile. At 0.2 mile the road turns off and you walk up the old slope, then cross the road once more. Do not turn off too soon on the cross-country ski trail. The hiking trail, marked with yellow blazes, passes the Elephant Rock Trail (0.5 mile), crosses over a series of small wooden bridges, and reaches Cascade Brook (about 1 mile). You could turn around here, although the cascades are not much farther and are really worth

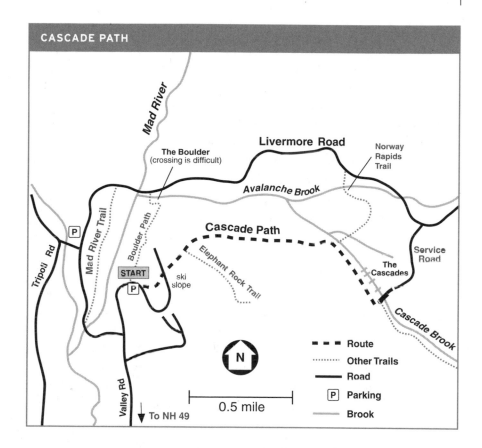

CASCADE PATH

Mad River

The Boulder
(crossing is difficult)

Livermore Road

Norway
Rapids
Trail

Avalanche Brook

Mad River Trail

Boulder Path

Cascade Path

Tripoli Rd

START

ski
slope

Elephant Rock Trail

Service
Road

The
Cascades

Cascade Brook

N

Valley Rd

To NH 49

0.5 mile

■ ■ ■   Route
·········   Other Trails
———   Road
[P]   Parking
———   Brook

seeing. Note the old logging road that angles in from the left at this point, and be careful not to use it if you return by retracing your steps. The Norway Rapids Trail heads left across the brook, but keep walking straight. After about ten more minutes, you reach the first cascade.

The trail then becomes a little rougher as it climbs the right side of the brook. Keep walking until you run out of cascades. When you reach the unpaved maintenance road for the Snow's Mountain Ski Area (1.5 miles), retrace your steps back to your car.

For a longer loop, turn left on the maintenance road, follow for 0.5 mile, then left on Livermore Road (another unpaved road—no motorized vehicles) for about 2 miles, and left on Boulder Path. The boulder, a huge glacial erratic in Avalanche Brook, is reached just a short distance from the turn. The path crosses the brook (difficult in high water) and reaches the parking lot in 0.5 mile. If the crossing of that brook looks too challenging, then complete the loop on Livermore Road instead.

## NATURE NOTES

The series of cascades on Cascade Brook is the major highlight. They go on for a good distance, shooting through small gorges and tumbling into deep pools. Just when you think you've reached the last waterfall, you walk up a little farther and discover yet another. Although pools below several of the cascades may look inviting, care and common sense should be used. Some are difficult to reach because of the steep sides of the bank. Others show signs of erosion where too many people have scurried down the sides to get to them, inadvertently destroying the vegetation.

Much of the streambed around the cascades (and around the Norway Rapids too) consists of flat slabs of granite. A flat slab just below the bridge at the top of the trail is a great lunch rock. Note there and elsewhere how the granite fractured along smooth joints when eroded by streams.

Where the trail runs right along Cascade Brook, try your luck at finding salamanders by turning over some stones along the water's edge. Two species that may be found here are two-lined and dusky salamanders. Although they are more at home in water than on land, both breathe air through their moist skin rather than through lungs. The two-lined is more common and is usually yellowish with two dark lines running the length of its body along the side. It can be quite speedy in beating a hasty retreat if you uncover its hiding place. The dusky is variable but is typically grayish or brownish and somewhat chunkier (and slower) than the two-lined.

The woods along the trail are dominated by northern hardwoods—beech, sugar maple, and yellow birch. Not long after entering the woods from the ski trail, you will walk through a section that has been recently cleared. The giveaway is the growth of spindly young yellow birch, none taller than about 20 feet.

Spring wildflowers abound along the trail. Red and painted trillium, clintonia, Canada mayflower, goldthread, and mountain wood sorrel put on particularly showy displays. In late sum-

**At least one of this pair did not have to work hard to enjoy the cascades.**

mer most of the flowers are gone, but the rich woods are a great habitat for mushrooms. Amanitas, most of which are deadly poisonous, are particularly abundant. There are also boletes, which have tiny pores instead of gills on their undersides.

## TRIP 4
## EAST POND AND LITTLE EAST POND

**RATING:** Moderate

**DISTANCE:** 5.0 miles round-trip

**ELEVATION CHANGE:** 800-foot elevation gain

**ESTIMATED TIME:** 4–5 hours

**MAPS:** AMC's *White Mountain National Forest Map and Guide*, I5
AMC's *White Mountain Guide*, 27th ed., Map 4: Moosilauke–Kinsman, I5, 6

**WMNF PARKING FEE:** Yes

**WINTER NOTES:** The entire loop is classified as a moderately difficult cross-country ski trail.

**OTHER ACTIVITIES:** Swimming

**East Pond and Little East Pond are two gems nestled behind Mount Osceola and Scar Ridge at 2,600 feet. The trails pass through rich woodlands carpeted with wildflowers, ferns, and mushrooms and cross over a number of streams.**

One can easily spend all day at East Pond, picnicking, swimming, enjoying the scenery, and observing the natural history of the pond shores. To enhance your water exploration, bring water shoes since the pond bottom has gravelly and muddy spots (and unfortunately you also need to keep your eye out for broken glass). Little East Pond is smaller, shallower, more remote, and very scenic too. *Ponds and Lakes of the White Mountains* by Steven Smith (Backcountry Press) is a good reference for additional information about the ponds.

The entire loop may be long for younger children, so you can shorten the hike by walking only to East Pond and back, a moderately uphill 1.4-mile walk in each direction.

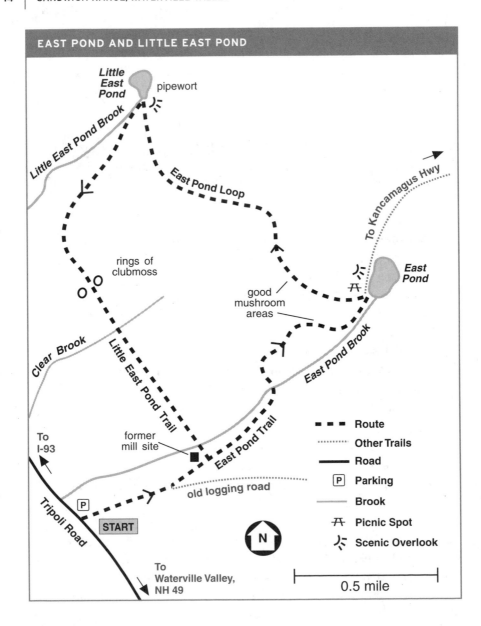

## EAST POND AND LITTLE EAST POND

## DIRECTIONS

The trailhead for the East Pond Trail is off Tripoli Road, about 5.4 miles from its junction with I-93. If you are coming from Waterville Valley, the trailhead is about 6 miles west of the junction of Tripoli Road and NH 49. Stay to the right when the road to the ski area splits off to the left. Turn north off Tripoli Road onto a gravel side road for about 100 yards to reach the parking area. Tripoli Road is closed in winter (November–April).

## TRAIL DESCRIPTION

The East Pond Trail starts out on an old, wide logging road. After a few minutes the logging road swings off to the right, and the East Pond Trail continues straight, still on a wide path. Look for the yellow blazes that mark the trail.

After 0.4 mile, the Little East Pond Trail goes off to the left. At this point it is 1.1 miles to East Pond and 1.7 miles to Little East Pond. This description assumes that you are heading to East Pond. From East Pond you can either complete the counterclockwise loop to Little East Pond or simply return the same way you came.

The trail to East Pond continues along the old logging road straight ahead on a gradual uphill. It remains wide and, for the most part, easy walking. The trail crosses East Pond Brook, which could be difficult if water levels are high, at about 0.7 mile. Even in low water, use care when stepping across the wet rocks. At 1.4 miles, just below East Pond, the East Pond Loop Trail diverges left toward Little East Pond. Take a side path to the right to reach the shore of East Pond at an open, meadowy area. This is the best spot to view the pond, swim, and picnic.

For some additional perspectives of the pond, the East Pond Trail continues along the west side of the pond for a couple of hundred yards. (It eventually swings away and meets the Kancamagus Highway in 3.7 miles.) Explore some short spur paths to informal camping areas near the pond shore.

If you want to hike the entire loop, return to the trail junction and head west on the East Pond Loop. It is about 1.5 miles (one hour) from East Pond to Little East Pond via the East Pond Loop. The trail has a few minor ups and downs but almost no overall change in elevation.

The East Pond Loop passes mainly through a forest of paper birch with an understory of red spruce and balsam fir. There are a number of sunny, open patches caused by blowdowns where you get partial views through the trees of Mount Osceola, Scar Ridge, and the Sandwich Range. After about 0.9 mile from East Pond, you cross a stream bed that is likely to be dry in mid- to late summer. The trail reaches the junction of the Little East Pond Trail at the south end of Little East Pond, which is also the best vantage point.

From Little East Pond return to your car via the Little East Pond Trail (1.7 miles) and the East Pond Trail (an additional 0.4 mile). The Little East Pond Trail descends gradually for the first 0.7 mile, initially along a small ravine. It then makes a sharp left turn, levels out, and follows the grade of an old logging railroad. The trail crosses Clear Brook, East Pond Brook, and other smaller brooks, eventually reaching the trail junction with the East Pond Trail. Turn right to get back to the parking area.

## NATURE NOTES

East Pond is a scenic mountain pond of about 6.5 acres. A saddle in Scar Ridge forms the backdrop of the pond as you look out from the southern end. The pond is shallow by the gravelly "beach" area but then grades off to a depth of 27 feet.

There's much for everyone to enjoy right at the edge of the pond. If you swim, you'll be joining the abundant resident red-spotted newts. These aquatic salamanders have green bodies with red spots and a flattened tail that they use to propel themselves through the water. In an unusual twist for an amphibian, immature newts—just recently graduated from being tadpoles—typically leave the water and live on the forest floor for several years as a juvenile life stage called red efts. You may have seen these brightly colored critters (orange-red bodies with green spots—the reverse of the adult color pattern) on the forest floor of the White Mountains, often a considerable distance from water. They then return to the water and transform into the newts that spend their adult life swimming in places like East Pond.

Newts have a number of companions in East Pond. The tadpoles of frogs are quite abundant at times. Be aware that leeches also inhabit the pond (keep moving—leeches are reportedly less likely to latch onto a moving target). A beaver dam is nearby at the outlet, and a lodge is visible near a big rock on the opposite shore. Dragonflies patrol the shores of the pond for unwary insects, and water striders skim across the pools in the small outlet creek near the informal camping area.

Keep a watchful eye skyward for birds that may fly over the pond. Ravens are likely and hawks a possibility.

Little East Pond (3.5 acres) is shallow and dotted with waterlilies and pipeworts. Pipeworts look like hatpins, with small, white rounded balls on top of thin stalks. The "pinheads" are the flowers. The shoreline of Little East Pond is boggy, with abundant sphagnum, leatherleaf, mountain holly, and marsh Saint John's wort. Right by the trail sign look for a pretty patch of snowberry and bunchberry growing under small balsam fir and red spruce.

There is plenty to see along the trails too. Witch's butter is a bright yellow or yellow-orange fungus that grows on dead logs. It is also called jelly fungus because it looks like a blob of jelly on a log and is somewhat sticky. Like most fungi, witch's butter gets its nutrition by breaking down dead organic matter, such as the log upon which it rests. You will find lots of witch's butter and a variety of brightly colored mushrooms along the upper part of the East Pond Trail and the East Pond Loop.

The forest dynamics are also particularly interesting. Much of the forest

**Shiny club moss grows in circles along the East Pond Trail.**

was logged in the past and is now dominated by paper birch. Look for places where there is a canopy of paper birch and an understory of balsam fir and red spruce, particularly along the upper part of the East Pond Trail and the East Pond Loop. Fir and spruce were dominant before logging and will eventually replace the paper birch. In ten or twenty years, this forest will look quite different than it does now.

There are many small gaps in the forest created by trees that have fallen, particularly along the East Pond Loop. Gaps in the forest are often colonized by hay-scented fern, a large, lacy fern that smells like fresh-cut grass when it dries out in fall. Hay-scented fern grows as a dense colony because new individuals are produced from old ones by underground runners. So the patch you see is really a clone, technically one individual because the ferns are all connected underneath.

On the Little East Pond Trail where it follows the old logging railroad bed you walk through a rich northern hardwood forest. Along with the typical hobblebush and striped maples, notice the many young sugar maple coming up. Unlike many species of trees, which will die if they are kept in the shade too long, sugar maple saplings are able to survive under the forest canopy, biding their time and waiting for their moment in the sun when one of the giants around them falls. Then, finally bathed in full sunlight, the little trees grow fast toward the forest canopy. This is a lesson in natural selection, as slower-growing individuals are shaded out by the faster ones.

A mill once stood at the junction of the East Pond and Little East Pond trails. The mill no longer exists, but it is a good spot for doll's-eye. Doll's-eye, also called white baneberry, has pyramidal clusters of tiny white flowers in spring. Wild sarsaparilla is also common at this spot.

There are striking "fairy rings" of shiny club moss along the Little East Pond Trail. These are almost round patches of a dark-green, low plant with small, dense, needlelike leaves on upright stems. Like the hay-scented fern described earlier, this growth habit is the result of one individual spore germinating and then sending out runners that create new upright plants.

And for our last question: How did Tripoli Road get its name? Tripoli (or tripolite) is a rock, also called diatomaceous earth, that can be made into a fine powder used as a polish in toothpaste and in industry. Tripoli is composed of the silica derived from the skeletons of diatoms, which are microscopic marine algae. The rock was mined from the bottom of East Pond in the early part of the twentieth century and hauled down to the aforementioned mill for processing. So, before East and Little East ponds existed, and before doll's-eye and witch's butter were here, an inland sea covered this region, depositing the microscopic organisms that would eventually give Tripoli Road its name.

## TRIP 5
## OLD BRIDLE PATH TO WEST RATTLESNAKE

**RATING:** Moderate
**DISTANCE:** 1.8 miles round-trip
**ELEVATION CHANGE:** 400-foot elevation gain
**ESTIMATED TIME:** 1.5–2 hours
**MAPS:** AMC's *White Mountain National Forest Map and Guide*, L6
AMC's *White Mountain Guide*, 27th ed., Map 3: Crawford Notch–Sandwich Range, L6
**WMNF PARKING FEE:** None

**Rattlesnake Mountain is a low, 1,200-foot mountain that provides wonderful sweeping views of Squam Lake and points farther south from its two summits. It is a relatively short hike with a moderate elevation gain.**

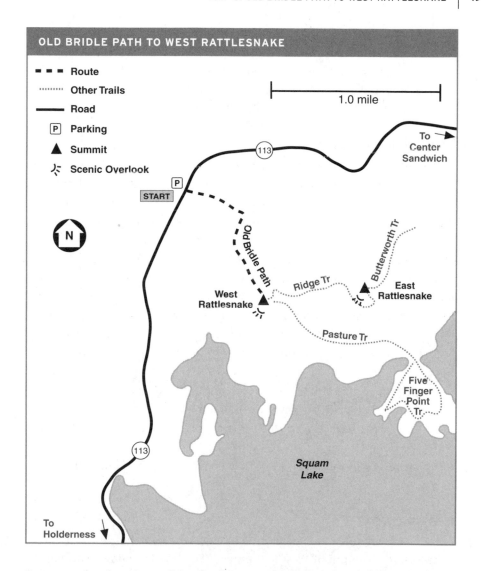

For many families this will be the first mountain that the children climb under their own power. As a low mountain in the southern part of the White Mountain region, this is a good trail to take early or late in the season, when the weather in the more northern and higher areas may be less congenial for hikers.

## DIRECTIONS

The Old Bridle Path is the most gentle of the number of trails that run to the summit of West Rattlesnake. Its trailhead is on NH 113 between the towns of Holderness and Center Sandwich. From Exit 24 on I-93 follow US 3 through

Ashland to Holderness. Make a left on NH 113, go past the Science Center of New Hampshire, and travel northeast. After about 5 miles you pass the road that goes right to the Deephaven and Rockywold camps. The trailhead is on the south side of NH 113, about 0.5 mile farther and opposite the trail for Mount Morgan. The parking area is on the north side of the road.

## TRAIL DESCRIPTION

The Bridle Path grades up the northwest side of Rattlesnake Mountain, following the remnants of an old dirt road to the summit. It is very well traveled, with some heavily eroded sections with exposed roots. The lower section of the trail passes through a northern hardwood forest (beech, sugar maple, and yellow birch). Nearer to the summit, the vegetation shifts to a predominance of oak so you can gauge your progress by the forest transition. You first pass a viewpoint with a more restricted view before reaching the open ledges of West Rattlesnake, 0.9 mile from the trailhead. The summit (1,260 feet) is marked with a plaque that tells you this is the Armstrong Natural Area, donated to the University of New Hampshire in memory of Mary Alice Armstrong and Margaret Armstrong Howe, two "Ladies of the Lakes" by the Rockywold and Deephaven camps.

If energy levels are still high, you could continue to East Rattlesnake (1,289 feet), about 0.7 mile farther down the trail, for another perspective on Squam Lake. Otherwise, retrace your steps. You should be back to the parking area within 30 minutes.

Bring your mosquito repellent, particularly if you are hiking early or late in the day.

## NATURE NOTES

Be sure to leave yourself enough time to enjoy the incredible vista of Squam Lake from the summit of West Rattlesnake. The lake is studded with numerous coves and islands, and its beauty is further enhanced by a heavily wooded shoreline that has largely been spared the scars of civilization. You are too high up to see or hear the loons that inhabit the lake in summer, but from your lofty perch it is easy to see why this lake is a good home for these birds. Dragonflies, mostly darners, will likely be buzzing right around you as you look out in the distance. Look for the metal USGS (United States Geological Survey) marker in the rock telling you that you are at 1,231 feet.

The flat ledges of the West Rattlesnake summit harbor some interesting plants. There are low blueberries and black chokeberries, but the popularity of this trail ensures that you will have lots of competition for the former—the name of the latter does not inspire confidence in its gastronomic value. Choke-berry, close relatives of apple and mountain ash, do have pretty white flowers in May, but their fruits are best left for the birds. Red pine can be identified by its long needles in bunches of two and reddish bark. See if you can figure out the direction of the prevailing winds from their beautiful, sculptured shapes. A few white birches grow on the summit too. Look for three-toothed cinquefoil lining the cracks in the rocks, where a tiny amount of soil has accumulated.

The first part of the trail has many log steps, and many exposed roots due to heavy erosion. Chipmunks will be your constant companions on this trail.

Be sure to note the forest transition from northern hardwoods (sugar maple, American beech, and yellow birch) with some oak to a woodland dominated almost completely by oak as elevation increases. In most other parts of the White Mountains northern hardwoods are replaced by red spruce and balsam fir as you climb uphill. Oak, an indicator of a relatively warm, more exposed, and drier climate, is found on the summits of smaller mountains, particularly those in the more southern part of the White Mountains. The understory plants change too. Look for wild oats, false Solomon's seal, white wood aster, Indian pipe, and rattlesnake root in the northern hardwood forest. Dwarf juniper, trailing arbutus, and bearberry grow near the summit.

There are several species of rattlesnake root, relatives of daisy and aster, in the White Mountains. The name comes from the belief that their roots, which

**Red oak, red pine, and the view of Squam Lake from West Rattlesnake.**

taste quite bitter, provide an antidote to a rattlesnake bite. Their distinctively shaped leaves are likely to evoke your curiosity. Two species you can see on this trail are white lettuce, which has triangular lower leaves, some of which may be divided into three parts, and tall rattlesnake root (also called gall of the earth) with its leaves divided into three definitely pointed lobes. The pale-white flowers of both species bloom in mid- to late summer and are nodding (hang downward).

## TRIP 6
## THE WELCH-DICKEY LOOP

**RATING:** Moderate to challenging
**DISTANCE:** 4.4-mile loop
**ELEVATION CHANGE:** 1,600-foot elevation gain
**ESTIMATED TIME:** 3.5–5 hours
**MAPS:** AMC's *White Mountain National Forest Map and Guide*, J5
AMC's *White Mountain Guide*, 27th ed., Map 4: Moosilauke–Kinsman,
J/K 5, 6
**WMNF PARKING FEE:** Yes

**The single-most "suggested" family hike in the White Mountains. Welch and Dickey summits command excellent views. The hike is substantial enough to give you a feeling of accomplishment, yet manageable.**

The Welch and Dickey Loop Trail is a good choice early in the season, since its lower elevation and relatively southern location ensures that snow disappears earlier here than farther north. For those with less time or energy, a hike up to the first great viewpoint on Welch Mountain requires only about an hour one way.

The extensive open areas of the summits of Welch and Dickey mountains resemble the alpine zones on the Presidential and Franconia ridges. Although not technically alpine habitats because they are too low in elevation, the Welch and Dickey summits have a similar feel: low gnarled trees and shrubs, extensive ledges and boulders, and the presence of some alpine plants. You can see all this without having to worry about the more extreme weather conditions that occur on the higher ridges.

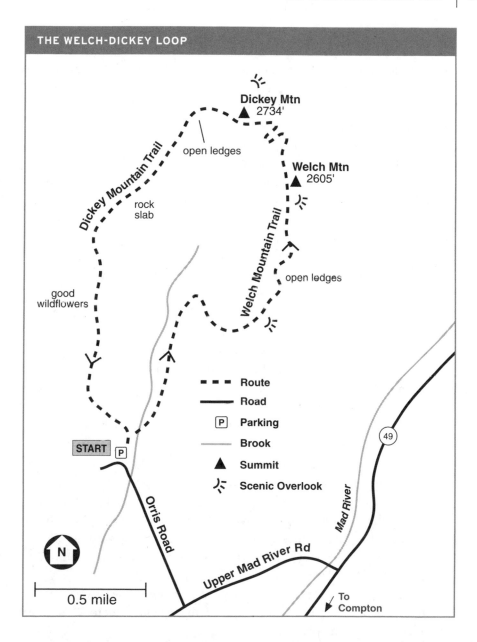

THE WELCH-DICKEY LOOP

Dickey Mtn
▲ 2734'

open ledges

Dickey Mountain Trail

rock
slab

Welch Mtn
▲ 2605'

good
wildflowers

Welch Mountain Trail

open ledges

- - - Route
——— Road
P Parking
——— Brook
▲ Summit
Scenic Overlook

START P

49

Orris Road

Mad River

N

Upper Mad River Rd

0.5 mile

To
Compton

The large areas of rocky ledges near the summits should present no prob-
lems for most hikers; however, we do not recommend this trail for a family
hike if the weather is wet or if walking on rocks makes anyone in the group
anxious. And remember, these summits, despite their low elevations, are still
quite exposed, so do not forget windbreakers and raingear.

## DIRECTIONS

The Welch and Dickey Loop Trail is located off NH 49 at the entrance to Waterville Valley. Take I-93 to the Campton/Waterville Valley exit and follow NH 49 through Campton toward Waterville Valley. Four and a half miles beyond NH 175 in Campton, turn left (northwest) on Upper Mad River Road (second intersection with this loop road) and cross the river. There is sometimes a sign at the turnoff for Welch and Dickey; however, never rely on such signs due to the misguided nostalgia of some hikers for a souvenir. Follow this road for 0.7 mile, then turn right on Orris Road. A newly expanded parking area is at 0.6 down this road. There are rest rooms at the trailhead.

## TRAIL DESCRIPTION

The Welch and Dickey Loop Trail does not connect up with any other trail, so it is hard to make a wrong turn. The biggest decision is whether to follow the loop counterclockwise up Welch Mountain first or to begin by scaling Dickey. We recommend Welch first because it is a shorter walk to a viewpoint. You can turn around there if going farther is just not in the cards.

The trail up Welch Mountain is well marked with yellow blazes. Take the right fork just beyond the display board and lost-and-found box at the trailhead. Although its popularity has led to erosion in some places, the walk is smooth for much of its length.

The hike up Welch follows a stream through a northern hardwood forest for about the first 0.5 mile. There are a number of stream crossings on wooden boards. After about 45 minutes there is a switchback with steps, and the trail then ascends more steeply. The south ledges provides the first vista soon after (0.9 mile). A sign and small stones placed in neat lines urge hikers to avoid stepping on the low vegetation of this and other ledgy areas by remaining on the trail or on exposed rocks. The trail then proceeds upward, past other ledges and through low forests of evergreens, before reaching the summit of Welch (1.5–2 hours).

If you want to go on, the trail descends steeply to the saddle between Welch and Dickey and then ascends to the Dickey summit. It takes 20 to 30 minutes (0.5 mile) to hike from Welch to Dickey.

From Dickey, the trail descends through more ledges with great views and is marked with cairns in a number of places. A half-hour or so beyond the Dickey summit, the trail crosses a particularly impressive rock slab and shortly thereafter enters a forest of beech and maple. It's about another mile to the parking lot. Near the end, make sure to stay on the trail as it passes an abandoned road and a logging road.

## NATURE NOTES

From the ledges and summit of Welch the prominent peaks are Dickey Mountain, the Sandwich Range (southeast), Mount Tecumseh (north—the major ski area for Waterville Valley), and Mount Tripyramid (northeast). You also have an excellent view of the Mad River valley and a breathtaking view down into the saddle between Welch and Dickey. The view from Dickey includes the Franconia Range. When you descend Dickey, the impressive cliff on Cone Mountain is straight ahead (southwest).

You may wonder what has caused rectangular open areas visible in the forest below. These are places where loggers have clear-cut the forest. They are in various states of revegetation, depending on how long it has been since the area was logged. A dense tangle of shrubs, such as raspberry, blueberry, and huckleberry, will grow up within a few years, followed by early successional trees including paper birch, aspen, and pin cherry.

Spring wildflowers and ferns are abundant, especially as you descend Dickey Mountain. Look for Canada mayflower, wild oats, clintonia, Indian cucumber-root, false Solomon's seal, true Solomon's seal, painted trillium, starflower, and goldthread. Around Memorial Day when the leaves are just emerging, wild sarsaparilla appears, a plant with glossy reddish leaves in groups of threes or fives. You might think that you have come into contact with poison ivy. Rest assured.

A plant restoration area marked by stones on Welch Mountain.

Poison ivy does not occur at these elevations. You may also find pink corydalis on the backside of Dickey. It has ferny leaves and small, pink flowers that resemble the heads of birds. Partridgeberry is a small, low plant with paired, dark green leaves that hug the ground and are occasionally punctuated with bright red berries. The distinctive, arrowhead-shaped leaves of the rattlesnake root are present throughout the year, but its flowers do not appear until late summer.

Near the summits, you enter a red spruce forest with some balsam fir. In open areas these species are joined by oak and white pine, species that thrive in sunny locations. Jack pine, a rare tree in the White Mountains (only two other known locations), is abundant on the ledges near the summit of Welch Mountain. You can identify it by its short, stiff needles occurring in bunches of two. Why it occurs on Welch but not in similar habitats on Dickey is a mystery (see also Trip 8).

Recovery areas for small plants on the ledges are delineated by lines of small stones. Two small alpine species protected by this effort are mountain cranberry and mountain sandwort. The thin soil, exposure to the winds, and absence of trees mimic the alpine conditions normally found above about 4,500 feet in the White Mountains, allowing these plants to thrive on Welch and Dickey. Three-toothed cinquefoil, whose small white flowers bloom in June, is probably the most abundant plant in the recovery areas. Each of the three leaflets of this low plant has three teeth on its outer edge.

Shrubs are a major component of the vegetation on the open ledges. Blueberries are a popular midsummer attraction, but please make sure your picking does not destroy them or any other vegetation in this fragile habitat.

In the saddle between Welch and Dickey, there is a particularly attractive example of boreal forest plants. Where the shading from the red spruce is not dense, bunchberry and reindeer lichen grow in patterns that look like they were designed by a rock gardener. Mountain holly, wild raisin, the white form of the pink lady's slipper, clintonia, and haircap moss grow under the spruce canopy as well.

As you hike along notice the glacial erratics scattered throughout the woods. These are often covered with moss and rock tripe, the latter a type of lichen that, although edible, looks and tastes like a piece of shoe leather. Two other particularly interesting geological features are a jumble of rocks that form a cul-de-sac tunnel with a natural bridge, and a very prominent large granite rock slab a mile below the summit of Dickey. This is laced with stripes that are sills of dark gray basalt formed from molten lava that penetrated cracks within the granite.

## TRIP 7
## WHITE LEDGE LOOP

**RATING:** Moderate

**DISTANCE:** 4.4 miles loop

**ELEVATION CHANGE:** 1,400-foot elevation gain

**ESTIMATED TIME:** 3–4 hours

**MAPS:** AMC's *White Mountain National Forest Map and Guide*, J10
AMC's *White Mountain Guide*, 27th ed., Map 3: Crawford Notch–
Sandwich Range, J10

**WMNF PARKING FEE:** Yes

**White Ledge Loop is an excellent family outing that provides views of Moat Mountain to the north and Mount Chocorua to the south.**

The trail takes you through a hemlock forest, along an esker, past stone walls, through an old pasture, then up to a pleasant viewpoint. Part of the loop follows along a mountain stream.

### DIRECTIONS

The trailhead is at White Mountain National Forest's White Ledge Campground off the west side of NH 16, about 6 miles north of the village of Chocorua and 5 miles south of Conway. Park in the day use, picnic area and follow the campground road straight ahead to the trailhead. The Carter Ledge Trail (Trip 8) also starts at this campground.

There is an alternate trailhead 0.5 mile north of the White Ledge Campground off Route 16 opposite Pine Knoll Camp. This follows an old town road for 0.5 mile and reaches the main trail 0.3 mile beyond the loop junction.

### TRAIL DESCRIPTION

The trail, marked with yellow blazes, departs to the right from the campground road and starts out through a dense hemlock forest. In 0.3 mile, it reaches the loop junction. At this point, it is 2.4 miles to the summit ledge going counterclockwise and 1.4 going clockwise. We describe the loop in the counterclockwise direction. Shortly after the loop junction, the trail crosses over a stream (could be an issue when water levels are high). A few minutes later, you will be on a long narrow ridge with steep sides, an esker (see Nature Notes). At 0.6 mile, the alternate access trail comes in from NH 16. The White

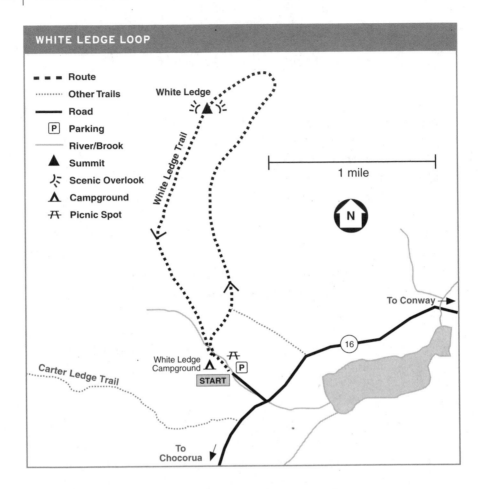

WHITE LEDGE LOOP

- - - Route
·········· Other Trails
—— Road
P Parking
—— River/Brook
▲ Summit
⅄ Scenic Overlook
▲ Campground
🜊 Picnic Spot

White Ledge

White Ledge Trail

1 mile

N

To Conway

16

White Ledge Campground

START

Carter Ledge Trail

To Chocorua

Ledge Loop Trail continues uphill and passes by old stone walls. At about 1.2 miles it levels off, descends for a short distance, and then passes through an overgrown pasture. After leaving the pasture at about 1.9 miles, the trail turns left and elevates moderately steeply. You'll reach the first set of ledges at about 2.3 miles. The best view of Moat Mountain and other peaks to the north is from the ledges below the actual summit, so take time to enjoy the views on your way up. You need to follow the blazes and cairns carefully as you ascend the ledges. When we hiked this trail, some of the blazes were faded and hard to see. At 2.7 miles, you reach the summit where there is a nice view to the east. The trail then begins to descend and very soon passes an excellent vista of Mount Chocorua to the south. At about 3.6 miles, the trail crosses a stream, then follows that stream to the loop junction (4.1 miles). Turn right at the junction to go back to the trailhead.

**Moat Mountain from White Ledge.**

## NATURE NOTES

The first part of the White Ledge Trail follows an esker for a short distance. An esker is a narrow, steep-sided, winding ridge composed of loose rocks and sand. It is formed by a river flowing underneath a glacier. The river deposits the sand and rocks that eventually build up into a hill. The walls of ice on both sides of the river keep the sediment within a narrow path. As you walk along this esker, picture yourself being in a tunnel within the glacier with the river at your feet and ice walls along the banks.

After the glaciers left their mark, humans had a strong hand in landscaping the White Mountain region. The stone walls and the overgrown pasture give a hint that this land was formerly used for grazing cattle or sheep. The New England landscape is peppered with old stone walls, a remnant of its more agrarian past, but there are not many such walls in the White Mountains. Perhaps the countryside was just too rugged to support more than marginal farms.

The old pasture is a laboratory of ecological succession, the process by which cleared land eventually turns back into forest. Look for pin cherry, a tree that is often a pioneer in burned or cut over land (hence its other name, fire cherry). It has reddish, flaky bark speckled with narrow pores called lenticels. These help to aerate the tree. Birds relish the cherries, which aid in its dispersal to other early successional habitats. Blackberry and raspberry are also colonizers of cleared land. Young American beech and striped maples are also coming up in the pasture. The beech will eventually become a tree of the canopy, and the striped maple the understory.

A constant companion of beech along this trail is a small parasitic plant called beechdrops. This is a parasite of beech trees. See Trip 44 for a description.

Moat Mountain is the most prominent feature of the view north from White Ledge. This mountain is unique in the White Mountains in containing volcanic rock extruded from the earth somewhere about the dawn of the Age of Dinosaurs. Other mountains you can see from the ledges are Mount Cranmore, Kearsarge North, and Bear Mountain. The summit of Mount Washington is barely visible just to the east of Moat Mountain. The view of Mount Chocorua on the other side of the summit is particularly attractive.

The ledges have interesting seeps that support growth of sphagnum (peat) moss and other mosses. Common shrubs around the ledges include black huckleberry, lowbush blueberry, and sheep laurel. Three-toothed cinquefoil grows wherever its roots can find enough soil among the rocks. Trees to note at the 2,005-foot summit include red and white pine, red spruce, and red oak.

The loop trail provides a nice illustration of the ecological differences between a north-facing slope and a south-facing one. On your ascent, the boreal (spruce-fir) forest becomes dominant right after you pass the old pasture, an elevation of about 1,400 feet. This part of the loop faces north so it often is in shadow and therefore is relatively cool. On the southern side of the mountain the boreal forests gives way to northern hardwoods, the more "southern forest," almost as soon as you begin your descent, at about 1,900 feet. The southern side of the mountain is bathed in direct sunlight for a much longer part of the day, so the southern forest type occurs higher up on the mountain.

Look for some enormous white pines on your descent just after the trail makes a sharp left turn about 30 minutes from the summit. White pines such as these were characteristic of New England forests at the time European settlers first arrived. These huge, straight trees were sought after by the crown for masts of ships, so most were cut.

# TRIP 8
# CARTER LEDGE

**RATING:** Moderate to challenging
**DISTANCE:** 5.0 miles round-trip
**ELEVATION CHANGE:** 1,700-foot elevation gain
**ESTIMATED TIME:** 3.5–5 hours
**MAPS:** AMC's *White Mountain National Forest Map and Guide*, J10
AMC's *White Mountain Guide*, 27th ed., Map 4: Crawford Notch–
Sandwich Range, J10
**WMNF PARKING FEE:** Yes

**Carter Ledge provides striking views of Mount Chocorua, views of other peaks, and lots of blueberries in season. It is a little bit off the beaten track so if you prefer less traveled trails, the Carter Ledge Trail is for you.**

The Carter Ledge Trail continues beyond Carter Ledge, ending at the Middle Sister Trail on a ridge of Mount Chocorua. You could do a long loop by combining the Carter Ledge Trail with the Middle Sister Trail. We hiked it on a beautiful summer weekend day and spent an hour and a half at the summit without seeing another soul. A singular feature of Carter Ledge is the stand of jack pine, one of only three places in the White Mountains where this tree occurs. The last section of the trail before you reach the ledge ascends steeply on some loose gravel, but aside from that, the trail is not particularly difficult.

## DIRECTIONS
The trailhead is at White Mountain National Forest's White Ledge Campground off the west side of NH 16, about 6 miles north of the village of Chocorua and 5 miles south of Conway. Park in the day use, picnic area and follow the left branch of the campground road to the trailhead. Note these directions differ from those on the AMC's *White Mountain National Forest Map and Guide* (2005 edition). Those directions point you to the Piper Trail, whose trailhead is actually a mile farther south on NH 16. Follow these instead.

## TRAIL DESCRIPTION
The trail leaves from the west side of the campground road and is marked with yellow blazes. The last time we hiked this trail, many of the blazes were faded

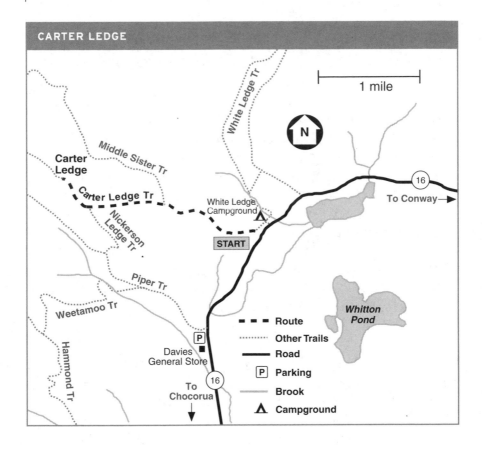

CARTER LEDGE

and resembled lichens that often live on tree trunks. We had to be careful not to get off on some side trails one or two times in the beginning where the forest is quite open. Later on, the woods becomes denser and the location of the trail is more obvious, even if you can't easily distinguish fungus from paint.

The first mile ascends through northern hardwoods and hemlock with some moderately steep sections. After 1 mile (about 40 minutes), the Middle Sister Trail comes in from the right. The forest then becomes dominated by red spruce and balsam fir. At 2 miles (1 hour, 15 minutes), the Nickerson Ledge Trail comes in from the left. This trail connects the Carter Ledge Trail with the Piper Trail. There is a small tree right at this junction that when shaken, the surrounding earth also moves. This brings home how shallow roots are in this rocky area. The trail then ascends more steeply, passes a sloped, open area with views across to Mount Chocorua. Avoid walking out onto this open area because of the loose rocks. The trail turns right and ascends a steep, gravelly section. After a little scrambling on rocks and squeezing through a narrow

**Berry-picking on Carter Ledge.**

passage, the relatively long open ridge of Carter Ledge is reached at 2.5 miles (about two hours).

## NATURE NOTES

Carter Ledge is a very attractive ridge with open views to the south and west to the sharp cone of Mount Chocorua in the foreground and numerous lakes in the distance. By walking to the other side of the ledge, the vista north includes Moat Mountain and North Conway close by and Mount Washington in the distance. In this direction, note how the forest has distinct, rectangular patches of different colors. These represent areas that were previously logged and are regrowing.

Jack pine (*Pinus banksiana*) looks like a small, shrubby evergreen with short (1 inch) needles in bunches of two and cones that are often curved. This is a northern species that grows in poor soils, such as on Carter Ledge. The jack pines on Carter Ledge and the two other locations in the White Mountains (see Trip 6) are likely relics from the last glaciation.

While on the ledge, compare the plants that grow on the open ledge with those that are in hollows. Plants that can withstand the exposure of the ledge include jack pine, lowbush blueberry (very abundant!), black crowberry, poverty grass, and three-toothed cinquefoil. Those that do better with a slight bit of protection from the wind and a little more soil include wild raisin, rhodora, sheep laurel, large-leafed goldenrod, and bracken fern.

Some of the lowbush blueberries at Carter Ledge produce berries that are black, a genetic variation that tastes just as good. Another botanical variation to look for is heart-leaved white birch. This birch occurs at higher elevations and is considered by some botanists to be a separate species, by others a variety of the familiar paper birch.

You are likely to hear the song of the red-eyed vireo as you hike up to the ledge. This small, nondescript bird is rarely seen because it lives in the foliage of the canopy, but it is often heard. It is likely the most abundant bird in the northern hardwood forests of the White Mountains. Its song sounds somewhat like a robin, with paired whistled phrases, the first phrase rising in inflection, and the second descending. It sounds like the bird is asking a question, then answering it, then asking another question and then answering that. It is a very persistent songster.

Partridgeberry forms abundant ground cover, particularly for the first mile along the trail. This tiny plant has two round, opposite, shiny leaves, each with a white vein down the middle. Each plant produces a pair of small white flowers with four petals and eventually a bright red berry. Partridgeberry is one of the few northern representatives of the coffee family, a mostly tropical group of plants. Although the berry is edible, it will never keep you awake at night or replace that cup of joe in the morning.

# 2

# FRANCONIA NOTCH

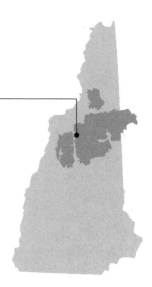

## LAY OF THE LAND

The Franconia Notch region is the westernmost part of the White Mountains. It includes the Kinsman Range, Franconia Notch, and the Franconia Range. The latter, with its beautiful cone-shaped peaks, rises to greater than 5,000 feet, making it the second highest range in the White Mountains. The hiking opportunities described here are easily accessible from I-93. There are numerous waterfalls, unique geological formations, and terrific scenery. The Franconia region is a popular tourist destination and includes such well-known sites as the Flume, Echo Lake, and Cannon Mountain.

For fishing enthusiasts with a valid New Hampshire license, Profile Lake is stocked with trout. Nonmotorized boats are permitted. The Pemigewasset River is also a popular fishing spot.

## SUPPLIES AND LOGISTICS

The village of Franconia is at the north end of Franconia Notch, off I-93, and Lincoln and North Woodstock are a few miles to the south. These have grocery stores, pharmacies, gas stations, restaurants, motels, and country inns. Those traveling to the notch from the north on US 3 may find it more convenient to stop for supplies in Twin Mountain, about 12 miles away.

The Flume Gorge and Lost River have visitor centers with tourist information, snack bars, rest rooms, and gift shops. The Flume Gorge Visitor Center also has a restaurant. At Profile Lake there are rest rooms, a small interpretive nature center, and a snack bar that serves ice cream and other treats. Echo Lake has a small snack bar and rest rooms, and there are rest rooms at the Basin.

## NEARBY CAMPING

Lafayette Place Campground in Franconia Notch State Park has more than 200 sites as well as picnic tables for day use, rest rooms, water, a small camp store with limited groceries, information on trails, and ranger naturalist programs. A number of national forest campgrounds are within a 30-minute drive. The Zealand and Sugarloaf campgrounds (the latter providing limited facilities for people with disabilities) are near Twin Mountain. The Big Rock and Hancock campgrounds are at the western end of the Kancamagus Highway. The Wildwood Campground is on NH 112 west of Lincoln. There are also a number of private campgrounds in the North Woodstock Lincoln area.

## TRIP 9
## PEMI TRAIL

**RATING:** Easy
**DISTANCE:** 4.0 miles one-way
**ELEVATION CHANGE:** 500-foot elevation gain
**ESTIMATED TIME:** 2–3 hours
**MAPS:** AMC's *White Mountain National Forest Map and Guide*, H4
AMC's *White Mountain Guide*, 27th ed., Map 2: Franconia–Pemigewasset, H4
**WMNF PARKING FEE:** None
**WINTER NOTES:** Cross-country skiing (moderately difficult)
**OTHER ACTIVITIES:** Fishing

**This trail boasts a combination of flowing water, wildflowers, occasional views, and possible wildlife sightings. Sheltered by a dense "tunnel" of forest most of the time, this is a good trail for a hot summer day (and you can swim at Echo Lake after you finish).**

The Pemi Trail is a relatively level hike that runs along the Pemigewasset River in Franconia Notch from the Flume to Profile Lake, a total distance of 5.6

miles. You can gain access at a number of points along its length, so you have the option of hiking part or the entire trail. The four-mile section between the Basin and Profile Lake is described here.

With two cars you can avoid backtracking and thus be inspired to hike a greater distance along the trail. The elevation change is so gradual that it really does not make much difference which direction you hike. For a shorter hike you could park a second car by the hiker's parking lot at the Lafayette Place Campground, about halfway between the Basin and Profile Lake.

Traffic noise may be evident for much of the walk, particularly from Lafayette Place Campground to Profile Lake. However, the numerous small cascades and wonderful views of the cliffs and talus slope of Cannon Mountain more than make up for this nod to civilization.

For those looking for a longer hike, the 1.6-mile section between the Flume and the Basin is generally similar to the part described below. It does have several stream crossings that could be difficult in high water.

## DIRECTIONS

This description assumes you are hiking from the Basin to Profile Lake. Park at the Basin parking lot on either side of I-93 about 5 miles north of Exit 32 (Lincoln, NH 112) and follow the signs to the Basin. The first sign for the Pemi Trail is a short distance beyond the Basin, near the trailhead to the Basin-Cascade Trail. There are many little trails in the area, but you should have no trouble finding the Pemi Trail.

(To get to the trailhead at the Profile Lake end, leave the Franconia Notch Parkway I-93 at Exit 34B [Cannon Mountain Tramway, Old Man Historic Site] and follow the signs to the viewing area for the Old Man of the Mountain. Find the trailhead by climbing up a set of stairs at a point where the road loops behind the parking lot. The first Pemi Trail sign is at the top of the stairs.)

## TRAIL DESCRIPTION

The trail is marked with blue blazes and parallels the Pemigewasset River, the Franconia Notch Highway, and a bike path through the notch for its entire length. The trail is not too heavily used, so the path tends to be softer on feet than many White Mountain trails. At various points in the first section you walk on the sandy soil of the river's flood plain.

After 2 miles (about an hour) from the Basin you reach Lafayette Place Campground. The exact route of the trail is hard to follow within the campground, but if you walk along the road closest to the river you'll eventually pick up the blue trail blazes again. The campground is a convenient place to

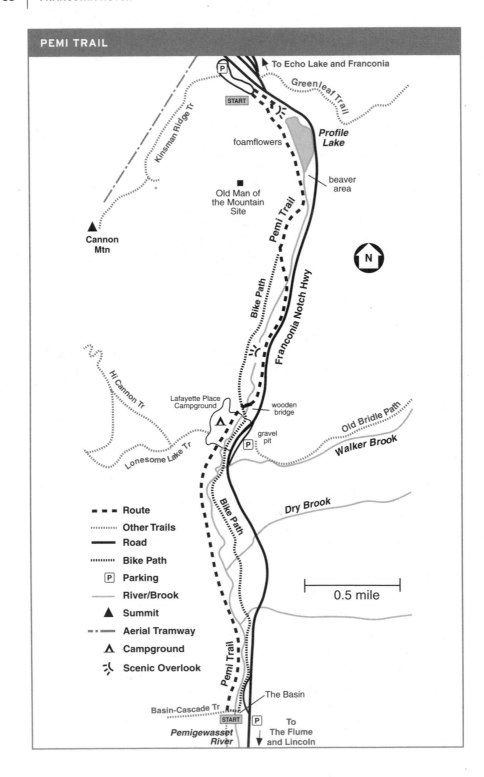

**PEMI TRAIL**

To Echo Lake and Franconia

Greenleaf Trail

START

Profile Lake

foamflowers

beaver area

Old Man of the Mountain Site

Pemi Trail

Kinsman Ridge Tr

Cannon Mtn

N

Bike Path

Franconia Notch Hwy

Hi Cannon Tr

Lafayette Place Campground

wooden bridge

Old Bridle Path

Walker Brook

gravel pit

Lonesome Lake Tr

Dry Brook

- - - Route
......... Other Trails
——— Road
......... Bike Path
P Parking
▲ Summit
-··-·· Aerial Tramway
⛺ Campground
⚡ Scenic Overlook

Bike Path

0.5 mile

Pemi Trail

The Basin

Basin-Cascade Tr

START

P

To The Flume and Lincoln

Pemigewasset River

use rest rooms, have a lunch at the picnic grounds, refill your canteens, or end your walk if you've had enough. Visit the small camp store to pick up soda, snacks, and worms and crawlers for fishing before resuming the second half of the walk.

After departing the Lafayette Place Campground, the trail passes over the bike path and enters a boggy area with lots of sphagnum moss. It traverses the slowly moving water on wooden boards, then crosses to the east side of the Pemigewasset River on a wooden bridge. Soon after, a left fork of the trail takes you to a wonderful vista of the cliffs of Cannon Mountain.

Pass back to the west side of the river on another bridge. The trail joins up with the paved bike path for a short distance, becomes a dirt path again, and passes a series of beaver dams near the south end of Profile Lake. The trail then follows the west shore of Profile Lake with great views of Eagle Cliff and Mount Lafayette. At the north end of the lake, a right turn at a side trail takes you across a marshy area to the viewing area for the former Old Man of the Mountain, or you can continue straight for a more direct route to the parking lot.

## NATURE NOTES

The sand you see in the flood plain between the Basin and the Lafayette Place Campground may seem out of place in the mountains, but it reveals the handiwork of the river. When snow melts and heavy rains fall in spring, rushing water erodes the sides of the mountains, carrying all kinds of soil particles into the river. The smaller particles of silt and clay are carried farther down the river, leaving the heavier sand behind. In spring the river typically overflows its channel, covering the entire flood plain in some very wet years. Evidence of this flooding is the sandy soil beneath your feet on the trail.

Between the campground and Profile Lake the banks of the river are steep sided, with no obvious flood plain. This is an area where the gradient of the river is steeper, and the rushing water is still eroding a channel through newly exposed bedrock.

The trail has a particularly rewarding view of the Cannon Mountain cliff. Unlike the crowded lookouts on the highway, you will likely have this vista all to yourself. The huge pile of broken rock, called talus, at the base of the cliff is formed from rocks plucked from the cliff by the freezing and thawing of water that had seeped into cracks in the cliff.

The forest is northern hardwoods for much of the trail, and the understory is dominated by hobblebush. Look for a stand of large red spruce near the Basin. Hemlock grow along the edge of the river.

If you hike in spring, you'll see a good assortment of White Mountain wildflowers in bloom. This is a particularly good trail to find foamflower, a low plant with three lobed leaves and clusters of small white flowers with feathery stamens that give it a foamy appearance. Foamflower tends to grow in colonies, so if you find one you are likely to see quite a few. This species and another you might see on this trail, the early saxifrage, are both types of saxifrages. "Saxifrage" means rock breaker, which tells you what these plants do to survive on thin soils.

Chipmunks and red squirrels are the most obvious mammals in the area. The beaver that made the dams near the outlet of Profile Lake are hard to see unless you are there at dawn or dusk and get lucky. You will also see a number of trees riddled with woodpecker holes and may even catch a glimpse of a crow-sized pileated woodpecker, a starling-sized downy woodpecker, or other species working on a tree. The holes they drill become home to many animals.

## TRIP 10
## BALD MOUNTAIN AND ARTIST'S BLUFF

**RATING:** Moderate

**DISTANCE:** 1.5 miles on the trail

**ELEVATION CHANGE:** 350-foot elevation gain

**ESTIMATED TIME:** 1–2 hours

**MAPS:** AMC's *White Mountain National Forest Map and Guide*, G4
AMC's *White Mountain Guide*, 27th ed., Map 2: Franconia–
Pemigewasset, G4

**WMNF PARKING FEE:** None

**OTHER ACTIVITIES:** Swimming at Echo Lake

**Bald Mountain and Artist's Bluff command great views of Franconia Notch for relatively little effort. This is an ideal family outing because it is short, has a well-defined goal, and begins and ends near Echo Lake, a picturesque swimming beach.**

The trail to Bald Mountain and Artist's Bluff forms a semicircle with both ends on NH 18 less than a third of a mile apart. The recently blazed Short Circuit connects the semicircle, so you can now do a loop without having to walk on the road.

This has been a popular family destination for decades. Before the age of Vibram soles and Gore-Tex parkas, hikers in long, frilly dresses, starched collars, and neckties walked up Bald Mountain and Artist's Bluff from the Profile House in Franconia Notch and other grand hotels that have long since disappeared. Since that time, ski development and the Franconia Notch Highway have become part of the scenery.

This trail is very close to the scenic attractions in Franconia Notch State Park: Echo and Profile lakes, Cannon Mountain, the Old Man site, the Basin, and Eagle Cliff. Despite the crowds, these natural wonders are worth a stop before or after your hike. Echo Lake has a snack bar, rest rooms, information, and a picnic area.

Although the highest elevation on this trail is only 2,340 feet, it is still a good idea to bring a windbreaker, particularly if you plan to have a picnic at either vista.

## DIRECTIONS

From the south, take the Franconia Notch Highway, the extension of I-93 through Franconia Notch. As you approach the north end of the notch, the cliff of Artist's Bluff looms ahead. Take Exit 34C (NH 18/Echo Lake/Peabody Slope), drive about a half-mile west, and park in the hiker lot (indicated by a sign) on the right (north) side of NH 18 by the Peabody Memorial Slope area of Cannon Mountain. Walk across the skier's parking lot (closed to cars in summer) to where the trail enters the woods.

From the Twin Mountain area, follow US 3 south toward Franconia Notch and pick up NH 18 at the entrance to the notch, where NH 3 and I-93 come together, and then follow the above directions.

## TRAIL DESCRIPTION

The trail, marked with red blazes, is fairly steep initially but relatively wide. After about ten minutes of steep climbing through northern hardwoods, the spur trail that ascends the summit of Bald Mountain enters from the left. The last time we hiked it, someone had apparently pilfered the trail sign at this junction, but it was still obvious where you are supposed to turn. Follow this to the left and continue ascending, now through a forest of red spruce and balsam fir. A short distance farther, the vegetation becomes scrubby, and a little bit of scrambling on rocks is required before you reach the summit of Bald Mountain, 0.4 mile from the trailhead.

After enjoying the view, retrace your steps back to the trail junction. If you have had enough for the day, take the right fork and descend to the parking

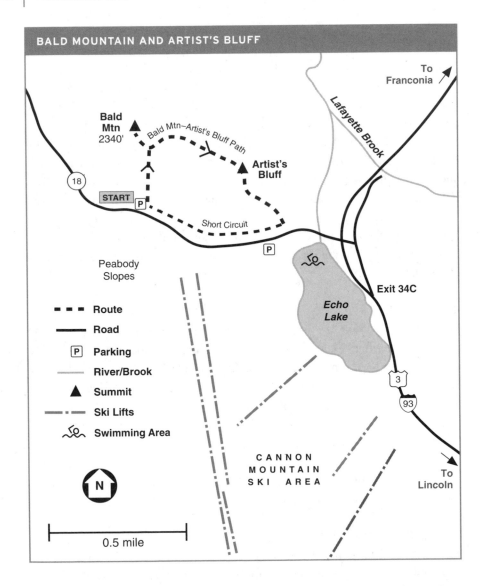

BALD MOUNTAIN AND ARTIST'S BLUFF

To Franconia

Bald Mtn 2340'

Bald Mtn–Artist's Bluff Path

Artist's Bluff

Lafayette Brook

18

START P

Short Circuit

P

Peabody Slopes

Echo Lake

Exit 34C

**Legend:**
- ▪ ▪ ▪ Route
- ▬ Road
- P Parking
- River/Brook
- ▲ Summit
- ▪–▪ Ski Lifts
- Swimming Area

N

3

93

CANNON MOUNTAIN SKI AREA

To Lincoln

0.5 mile

area. For Artist's Bluff, 0.4 mile away, follow the left fork. The trail descends to a gravelly gully, passes a huge boulder, ascends over a wooded hump, and then descends steeply for about five minutes to the junction with the short spur trail that leads left to Artist's Bluff.

From Artist's Bluff the trail descends steeply in a gully, first on some conveniently placed rocky stairs. In about ten minutes it intersects with the Short Circuit to the right, which leads 0.3 mile back to your car, paralleling NH 18 closely. Reward yourself with a swim in Echo Lake.

**The hike to Artist's Bluff provides a quick reward.**

## NATURE NOTES

The views reveal the recent geological history of Franconia Notch. From Bald Mountain, the Peabody Slopes of the Cannon Mountain Ski Area are immediately across from you to the south. Farther to the east (your left) is the glacially carved valley that is Franconia Notch. From Artist's Bluff, Echo Lake is immediately below, and you look directly down the notch.

Try to imagine this area completely covered by ice thousands of feet thick as recently as 12,000 years ago. The glacier acted like a giant piece of sandpaper, grinding and smoothing the walls of the valley as it moved slowly through the region. North–south valleys in the White Mountains were particularly well scoured by the north–south movements of the continental ice sheet and so have characteristically broad bottoms and steep sides.

Mount Lafayette, at 5,260 feet the highest mountain of the Franconia Range, forms the eastern wall of Franconia Notch. You will immediately be struck by how "pointy" the summits of Mount Lafayette and other peaks of the Franconia Range are, compared to the broad, smooth summits of the Presidential Range. This is because the tops of the Presidentials were flattened out by the massive continental glacier while, in contrast, the Franconia Ridge was scoured from the sides by mountain glaciers. The freezing and thawing of the ice literally plucked out chunks of rock from both sides of the Franconia Ridge, leaving behind a narrow ridge.

Another noteworthy feature of Mount Lafayette is the steep ravine carved in the side of the mountain by the rushing water of Lafayette Brook. This was formed in postglacial times. Eagle Cliff is the dramatically rugged shoulder of Mount Lafayette. Legend has it that golden eagles used to nest there, and in recent years peregrine falcons have taken up residence (very hard to see even with binoculars).

Looking east, you will see evidence of clear-cutting on Big Bickford and Scarface mountains. Beyond that is Mount Garfield, a picturesque cone-shaped peak.

The notch is a great north–south divide between two completely different drainage patterns. Below you Echo Lake has an outlet to the northwest that flows into the Gale River, which joins the Connecticut River and flows into Long Island Sound. Profile Lake is just a little south of Echo Lake, on the other side of an almost imperceptible rise in the land. A drop of water falling in Profile Lake flows south through the Pemigewasset River to the Merrimack River and eventually reaches the Atlantic Ocean at Newburyport, Massachusetts.

Watch for the changes in the forest as you hike up. Northern hardwoods, including some good-sized yellow birches, dominate at the beginning of the trail. Past the junction of the spur to Bald Mountain, you enter red spruce–balsam fir forest. The spruce and fir trees grow shorter as you ascend. At the summit the ledges are covered with stunted spruce and fir, and shrubs such as mountain holly, blueberry, and meadowsweet. Note the three-toothed cinquefoil growing in cracks in the rocks where some soil collects. These and bunchberry cover the ledges with white flowers in mid-June. At Artist's Bluff you will also find wild raisin and mountain alder.

You may notice "flag trees," with branches on only one side of the trunk. The reason for this lies in the prevailing winds which in combination with ice, kill buds on that side of the trunk before they even have a chance to sprout. On Bald Mountain most of the flag trees point east, indicating that the wind is usually from the west. Exceptions do occur, perhaps where the winds whip around the side of the mountain.

The understory vegetation is particularly lush between the two overlooks, with abundant ferns, moss, clintonia, club moss, false Solomon's seal, mountain wood sorrel (particularly near the junction with the Bald Mountain spur), red and painted trillium, and pink lady's slippers (both pink- and white-flowered varieties). Striped and red maples are common understory shrubs. Other plants to look for are bristly and wild sarsaparilla, goldenrod, rattlesnake root, wild oats, and Canada mayflower.

If you are lucky you may see one of the White Mountains' largest and most charismatic animals at a distance so safe that you'll need binoculars. In recent years black bears, often a mother bear with cubs, have taken to foraging on berries in the open ski trails high up on Cannon Mountain during daylight. This is about as good a chance as you'll have to see bears in the White Mountains, since they normally are secretive. The bears' presence along the ski trails shows that these trails are not without value to some wildlife.

## TRIP 11
## MOUNT PEMIGEWASSET

**RATING:** Moderate
**DISTANCE:** 3.6 miles round-trip
**ELEVATION CHANGE:** 1,150-foot elevation gain
**ESTIMATED TIME:** 4 hours
**MAPS:** AMC's *White Mountain National Forest Map and Guide*, H4
AMC's *White Mountain Guide*, 27th ed., Map 2: Franconia–Pemigewasset, H4
**WMNF PARKING FEE:** None

**The Mount Pemigewasset Trail climbs to the 2,500-foot summit of Mount Pemigewasset. The climb is a good one for children, since it's never very steep, and the views from the top are excellent.**

Mount Pemigewasset is the location of the famed Indian Head profile, which sits at the southern end of Franconia Notch. This rocky ledge is actually best seen from the valley in the vicinity of the Indian Head Resort. The profile is not obvious from anywhere on the trail on this hike. The formation of the Indian Head is the result of water seeping into cracks in the granite rock, then freezing and expanding, thereby causing pieces of the granite to break off. What remains behind happens to resemble a profile. But like all good things, it is only a temporary feature of the landscape, and over geological time the Indian Head will eventually turn into something less than a face, as happened to the Old Man of the Mountain several miles to the north.

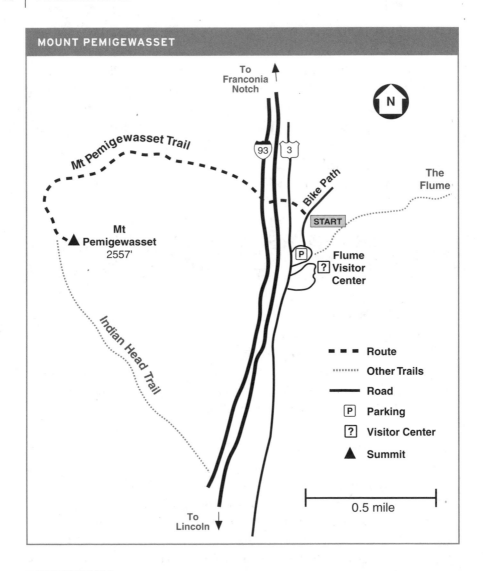

**MOUNT PEMIGEWASSET**

To Franconia Notch

N

93 | 3

Mt Pemigewasset Trail

Bike Path

The Flume

START

▲ Mt Pemigewasset 2557'

P Flume
? Visitor Center

Indian Head Trail

Route
Other Trails
Road
P Parking
? Visitor Center
▲ Summit

0.5 mile

To Lincoln

## DIRECTIONS

The trailhead is reached from the parking lot of the Flume Visitor Center in Franconia Notch State Park. This is at Exit 34A (Flume Gorge, US 3) of the Franconia Notch Highway, the extension of I-93 through Franconia Notch. The exit is about 4 miles north of Exit 32 on I-93, the exit for Lincoln, North Woodstock, NH 112, and the Kancamagus Highway. For this trail it is most convenient to park at the northwest side of the parking lot near the beginning of the bike path that heads north through the notch. The actual trailhead is off the bike path.

## TRAIL DESCRIPTION

The Mount Pemigewasset Trail is marked with blue blazes, but it would be hard to get lost on this well-trod path even if you didn't see them. Start walking north on the bike path for about 150 yards, then follow the trail to the left. The trail goes through three tunnels, the first under old Route 3, which is now a service road for the highway, and the second and third for the northbound and southbound sides of I-93. After about 0.5 mile and several stream crossings on bog bridges, the trail heads uphill at a somewhat steeper angle. Approximately 1.3 miles from the trailhead, the trail makes a bend to the left and passes a huge boulder. At 1.7 miles the Indian Head Trail, marked with yellow blazes, comes in from the right. The open ledges of the summit are reached 0.1 mile farther on the Mount Pemigewasset Trail.

Some of the ledges at the summit end rather abruptly with steep drop-offs. Parents will want to keep a close watch on young children. Another caution: Avoid following yellow blazes you might pick up at the summit ledges. These lead down the mountain by a very steep, unmaintained trail.

On the return downhill, a small white arrow with a handwritten sign on a balsam fir says To The Flume Parking Lot at the trail junction with the Indian Head Trail. Follow this arrow to the right for the Mount Pemigewasset Trail. It is possible to return via the Indian Head Trail, which ends up on a short

Inspecting a mushroom along the Mount Pemigewasset Trail.

gravel road just south of the Indian Head Resort off Route 3. But be warned that the Indian Head Trail is not well marked and would require a 0.75-mile walk along the highway to reach your car, unless you spot a car at its trailhead beforehand.

## NATURE NOTES

For most of the hike you are walking through a northern hardwood forest, where the dominant trees are yellow birch, American beech, and sugar maple. Hobblebush, with some striped maple, form the understory. Woodland wildflowers to look for under the hardwood trees include wild sarsaparilla, partridgeberry, mountain wood sorrel, false Solomon's seal, and white wood aster. Clintonia becomes more frequent the higher up you are. Shield fern, shiny club moss, and a variety of true mosses are also quite common. A variety of mushrooms abound in midsummer through early fall.

The birds you are likely to hear in the forest include black-throated green warbler, black-throated blue warbler, red-eyed vireo, golden-crowned kinglet, and hermit thrush. Red squirrels and chipmunks scamper through the forest.

There is a huge rock, possibly a glacial erratic, about a half-mile from the summit, where the trail makes a distinct turn to the left. This is a nice place to stop for a snack or lunch. Just beyond this rock look for some jelly fungus (also called witch's butter, a bright yellow-orange blob) on a cut log.

At a clearing about 50 yards past the huge rock, note the shallow root structure of an overturned tree in a small clearing. There is not a great depth of soil on these slopes. Wild oats, northern fly honeysuckle, and hobblebush now grow in the clearing, but this may change over time. The death of this tree creates opportunities for some sun-loving plants such as hay-scented fern to take advantage of the light penetrating to the forest floor.

Near the summit you will notice that the hardwood forest is replaced by a spruce-fir forest. You might first become aware of this at the junction with the Indian Head Trail.

The summit has broad, flat rocks that are fun for scrambling and are interspersed with some small trees, many of which have been sculptured by the wind to form "flag" trees. There are some great views of surrounding mountains. Mount Moosilauke is to the west, South Kinsmen to the northwest, and Mounts Flume and Liberty to the east. By walking around the summit a bit, you can get a view north toward Cannon Mountain. The villages of Lincoln and North Woodstock are to the south.

## TRIP 12
## COPPERMINE TRAIL TO BRIDAL VEIL FALLS

**RATING:** Moderate (fairly level but long for families with children)
**DISTANCE:** 5.0 miles round-trip
**ELEVATION CHANGE:** 1,100-foot elevation gain
**ESTIMATED TIME:** 3–4 hours
**MAPS:** AMC's *White Mountain National Forest Map and Guide*, G4
AMC's *White Mountain Guide*, 27th ed., Map 2: Franconia–
Pemigewasset, G4
**WMNF PARKING FEE:** None

**The Coppermine Trail has an aura of mystery and romance about
it. It takes you along Coppermine Brook to Bridal Veil Falls, one of
the most beautiful waterfalls in the White Mountains.**

But the mystery does not come from the waterfall itself. Along the way, you will
find a plaque on a large boulder along the brook with an enigmatic inscription:

> In Memoriam to Arthur Farnsworth
> "The Keeper of Stray Ladies"
> Pecketts 1939
> Presented by a Grateful One.

For the rest of the hike, you can ponder who Arthur Farnsworth was,
whether he met a tragic fate along Coppermine Brook, why the tribute was
placed in such an obscure place, and who was this "grateful one" who chose to
eulogize Mr. Farnsworth in this manner (read on and find out!).
    The Coppermine Trail itself is a pleasant walk on the western side of Can-
non Mountain. Most of it grades gently uphill along Coppermine Brook. The
Coppermine Shelter, located near the falls, is an open-ended lean-to with an
outhouse nearby.

## DIRECTIONS
The Coppermine Trail is off NH 116, about 3.4 miles south of the village
of Franconia. If you are traveling north through Franconia Notch, take the
Franconia exit on I-93 (Exit 38) and then go south on NH 116 for 3.4 miles.
Alternatively, from the North Woodstock and Lincoln exit on I-93 (Exit 30),

travel west on NH 112 for about 8 miles and then north on NH 116 for 7.7 miles. Look for Coppermine Road on the east side of NH 116. Park your car right, where there is ample space on Coppermine Road just after turning off NH 116, and walk along the road to the trailhead. Be careful not to wander off any of the side roads to new developments.

## TRAIL DESCRIPTION

Coppermine Trail departs from the left side of Coppermine Road approximately 0.4 mile from NH 116. It starts out as a smooth dirt road, very easy

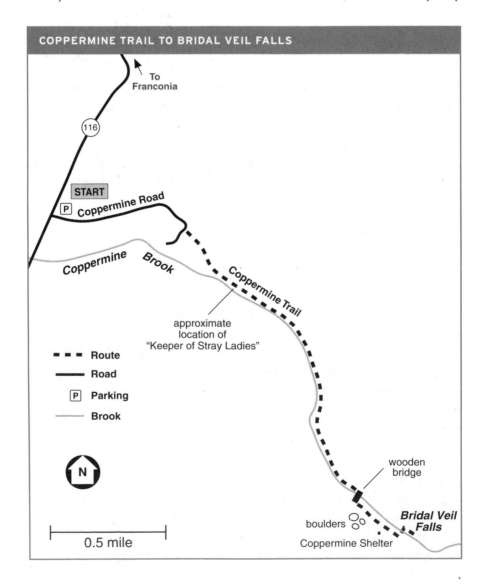

**COPPERMINE TRAIL TO BRIDAL VEIL FALLS**

on the feet, and then becomes a wide path for most of its length. The trail is enclosed in a pleasant woodland setting of northern hardwood trees for its entire length. Coppermine Brook comes in from the right after a short distance and is within sight or earshot of the trail for practically its entire length. After about an hour to an hour and a half (about 2 miles), the trail crosses over the brook on a wooden bridge, passes the Coppermine Shelter, crosses back over the stream on rocks (no problem), climbs moderately, and then ends at Bridal Veil Falls 0.2 mile after the bridge. The more adventurous can walk up to the top of the falls on the right for a different view.

If you decide to cut the walk short, several places where the trail runs right along the brook make for a pleasant short (or long) stop before turning around.

## NATURE NOTES

Bridal Veil Falls is really several connected cascades, some forming "shoots" along sloping rock faces and others tumbling over rocks into pools, like the large one at the bottom. Like most waterfalls in the White Mountains, the best time for viewing is when water levels are relatively high, either early in the season or just after a rainstorm. If you scramble up the side of the waterfall, you will be rewarded with a view of a second, very pretty pool that is not visible from the bottom.

**The mysterious message along the Coppermine Trail.** Photo by Nancy Schalch.

While walking along the dirt road at the beginning of the trail, look for circular clumps of interrupted fern, a large fern whose leafy green pinnae (leaflets) are "interrupted" along the stalk by brownish reproductive pinnae. Unfortunately, not all interrupted ferns will be producing these reproductive structures, so the name may be as much of a mystery as the "keeper of stray ladies." You may also notice the raspberries growing in disturbed areas near the road. These might make a great treat if birds and other hikers haven't gotten there first.

The northern hardwood forest through which the Coppermine Trail runs is dominated by yellow birch, sugar maple, and American beech. Yellow birch is especially abundant along this trail. Conifers, particularly Canadian hemlock but also red spruce and balsam fir, occur along the side of the brook where the microclimate is shadier, damper, and cooler. The most abundant understory shrub is hobblebush. Mountain maples, with their characteristic arching stems, are at the bridge crossing the brook and around the Coppermine Shelter.

Most wildflowers growing along the trail bloom in May and June. These include trout lily, foamflower, rosy twisted stalk, Canada mayflower, clintonia, false Solomon's seal, Indian cucumber-root, jack-in-the-pulpit, starflower, wild sarsaparilla, and shinleaf.

Little caves are created by fern- and moss-covered boulders and overhanging tree roots between the bridge and the waterfall. These look like great dens for animals or for weary elves. The small evergreen ferns that grow right on top of the boulders are appropriately named rock ferns, or Virginia polypody.

And, finally, the mysterious story of the Keeper of Stray Ladies. What follows is a summary of an article by Lyn McIntosh in the Autumn 1987 issue of *Magnetic North*. Arthur Farnsworth was a handsome young Vermonter who was employed at Pecketts, a fashionable, year-round resort in the 1930s on Sugar Hill, just west of Franconia Notch. Guests of Pecketts rode on horseback to land owned by the resort on Coppermine Brook for hiking, fishing, snowshoeing, or simply enjoying the beautiful rushing stream. Farnsworth's job was to make guests feel at home at the lodge. In 1939 the actress Bette Davis came to Pecketts for a period of rest after a particularly exhausting time of movie-making. In brief, Davis fell in love with Pecketts, the whole region, and Farnsworth. The simple life of the North Country and the strong, honest gentleman who did not find her fame particularly intimidating was just the antidote the actress needed from her life as a movie star. Legend has it that Bette Davis strayed from a hiking party at Coppermine Brook, knowing that

Farnsworth would be sent to find her. They were married in 1940 and lived happily in California, occasionally escaping to the White Mountains. Unfortunately, in 1943 tragedy struck. Farnsworth died after he fell down some stairs at their home on Sugar Hill. Davis continued to come back to the White Mountains for a while but sold her home on Sugar Hill in 1961. The plaque mysteriously appeared on Coppermine Brook sometime around then.

The plaque is located about 0.25 mile from the junction of the Coppermine Trail with Coppermine Road (0.75 mile, twenty-minute walk from NH 116). Look for a spot where the trail first comes near the brook and there is a steep slope through conifers down to the brook on the right. Between the trail and the brook is a flat area where people often pitch tents. You need to scramble a bit to reach the stream bed, and then use caution because the rocks are slippery. Look for the plaque on a big boulder that is on the same side of the brook as the trail. The boulder juts out into the stream roughly halfway along the flat area. The plaque itself faces downstream.

For most trails in this book, we have focused on the mysteries of nature. For the Coppermine Trail, the human mystery is just as intriguing.

## TRIP 13
## CLOUDLAND FALLS

**RATING:** Moderate with a few steep sections

**DISTANCE:** 2.6 miles round-trip

**ELEVATION CHANGE:** 1,100-foot elevation gain

**ESTIMATED TIME:** 2 hours

**MAPS:** AMC's *White Mountain National Forest Map and Guide*, H4
AMC's *White Mountain Guide*, 27th ed., Map 2: Franconia–Pemigewasset, H4

**WMNF PARKING FEE:** None

**Hiking the Falling Waters Trail to Cloudland Falls, those names conjure up a vivid image of ascending along a beautiful mountain stream with many cascades and ending up at a waterfall steeped in mist. This hike will satisfy every waterfall lover and everyone who loves the intoxicating sound of falling water within a cool, dense forest.**

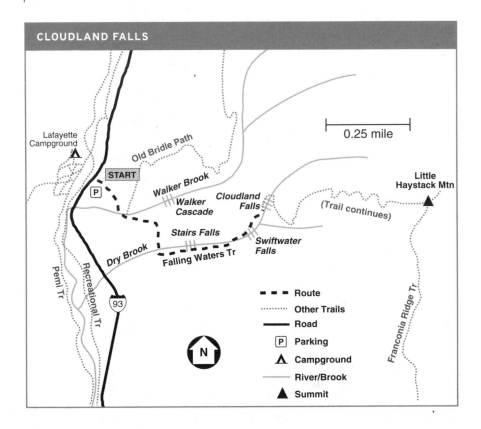

**CLOUDLAND FALLS**

The Falling Waters Trail is the first part of a wonderful, strenuous, long day hike up to Little Haystack Mountain, across the Franconia Ridge to Mount Lafayette, down to Greenleaf Hut on the Greenleaf Trail and then back to the parking area via the Old Bridle Path. That is for hikers in good shape with lots of energy and the proper gear for above treeline hiking. What is described here is the first part of that hike, a great family hike past a number of waterfalls. There are several stream crossings that could be challenging in high water.

If you are considering hiking beyond the waterfalls up to the ridge, you should check with the hiker information booth at the trailhead for weather conditions above treeline.

## DIRECTIONS

The Falling Waters Trail departs from Lafayette Place parking area in Franconia Notch State Park off the Franconia Notch Parkway (I-93) at milepost 108. This is about 1.5 miles north of the Basin and 1.5 miles south of the former Old Man in the Mountain parking area. Northbound, the sign says "Trailhead Parking." Southbound, it is also the exit for the Lafayette Place Campground.

**Swiftwater Falls.**

The parking area for this trail is on both sides of the highway, and which side you end up in depends on whether you are coming from the north or the south. The trail leaves from the east side of the parkway, which is where you park if you have been traveling north through Lincoln and Woodstock. If you are traveling south on the parkway, park on the west side of the highway and reach the trailhead through a tunnel underneath the highway.

## TRAIL DESCRIPTION

Leaving the parking area, the trail passes the hiker information kiosk and then runs together with the Old Bridle Path for the first 0.2 mile. The Falling Waters Trail then makes a sharp right turn and crosses Walker Brook on a bridge. At 0.7 mile, the trail crosses Dry Brook on rocks (use care during high water), and then ascends the south bank to Stairs Falls. Continuing above Stairs Falls, the trail passes by some overhanging rocks (Sawtooth Ledges) and then crosses back to the north side of the brook (another potential challenge in high water) just below Swiftwater Falls, a beautiful 60-foot cascade. The trail then crosses a smooth rock slab and ascends past some boulders along the waterfall. Beyond Swiftwater Falls, the trail continues on some switchbacks and along an old, gravelly logging road to the bottom of Cloudland Falls. Take a moment to enjoy the view looking up from the bottom of this 80-foot cascade, then follow the trail along the north side of the falls to its top, where there are views across Franconia Notch to Mount Moosilauke. At this point, note the two small waterfalls at almost right angles to each other. This is a good turnaround spot.

## NATURE NOTES

The waterfalls and the rushing water are the obvious highlights of this walk. There are a number of places, particularly around Stairs Falls, that beckon you to sit on a rocky ledge and enjoy the sounds of falling waters and the smells of the forest.

At the top of Cloudland Falls, the two small streams that come together in small waterfalls represent two different "sub" watersheds. The one to the north drains the upper sections of Mount Lincoln, whereas the other drains Little Haystack. Their flows join together to form Dry Brook, which then descends Cloudland Falls, reaches to the Pemigewassett River in Franconia Notch, and eventually meets the Merrimack River.

Jumbles of boulders that tumbled down the mountain in landslides form interesting caves that will appeal particularly to younger hikers.

Ferns can be difficult to tell apart, but the mountain wood fern, found along the lower section of this trail, has some distinctive features for those willing to take a close look. A fern frond is equivalent to a leaf, and the mountain wood fern's frond is divided first into pinnae and then each pinna into pinnules. The second pinnules on the lowest pinnae are very uneven in size, such that the lower one hangs down quite a bit. Another feature of this and its close relatives is that its stipe (stem) is covered with rusty scales.

The forest along the Falling Waters Trail starts out as northern hardwoods, with lots of yellow birch, but it very quickly changes to red spruce, balsam fir, and Canadian hemlock. Spruce and fir go together in the forests of the White Mountains above 2000 feet, and hemlock is a frequent denizen of cooler river valleys. The most common understory shrub is hobblebush. Clintonia, bunchberry, and mountain wood sorrel comprise much of the herb layer.

# 3

# OFF THE KANCAMAGUS HIGHWAY

## LAY OF THE LAND

The Kancamagus Highway (NH 112) is a scenic highway running east–west for about 40 miles between the towns of Conway and Lincoln. It provides access to many trails. The highway follows the Swift River in its eastern section and the East Branch of the Pemigewasset closer to Lincoln, so it never is far from rushing water. The area is heavily wooded and particularly beautiful—and crowded—during fall color season. Here you can enjoy waterfalls, mountain ponds, and several small mountains that have excellent views for relatively little effort. The White Mountain National Forest maintains a number of picnic areas, campgrounds, and recreation areas along the highway.

The highway is named for a Native American who became chief of the Penacooks in 1685. Kancamagus (pronounced *kank-a-maw-gus*) was the grandson of Passaconaway and the nephew of Wonalancet, two other Penacook chiefs who also had mountains named after them. Angered by the continued intrusion of white settlers, Kancamagus led the last uprising of the Penacooks. Eventually he and the remnants of his tribe emigrated north to Canada.

## LOGISTICS AND SUPPLIES

The Saco Ranger Station of the White Mountain National Forest is on the Kancamagus Highway at its eastern terminus at NH 16. The Lincoln Woods

Ranger Station is on the highway about 4 miles east of Lincoln. Stop in for trail information and to pick up descriptive pamphlets for guided nature hikes along the highway. The ranger stations also have water, rest rooms, and displays of the local natural history. Trail information and rest rooms can also be found at the Passaconaway Historical Site, about 3 miles east of Sabbaday Falls. There are rest rooms at the Rocky Gorge and Lower Falls scenic areas.

There are no stores or gas stations along the Kancamagus Highway, so make sure you are well supplied with lunch, snacks, and gas before heading out. If you are coming from the east, Conway and North Conway have stores, gas stations, restaurants, motels, hot tubs, crafts, factory outlets, and other amenities. Along NH 16, south of Conway, there is a small general store in Chocorua and a few others between Chocorua and the Kancamagus Highway.

If you approach from the west, there is a shopping center with a supermarket on NH 112 right in Lincoln. Those coming from Crawford Notch will want to stop in Bartlett before traveling south on Bear Notch Road to the highway.

## NEARBY CAMPING

The Kancamagus Highway has six campgrounds (more than 250 sites) and six picnic facilities spread conveniently along the entire length of the highway. White Ledge Campground, also run by the national forest, is off NH 16, a few miles south of the highway. The campgrounds fill up on popular weekends, so check at the information board on NH 112 just off I-93 in Lincoln (west end), or at the Saco Ranger Station (east end), on availability before you start your drive on the highway.

## TRIP 14
# ROCKY GORGE AND THE LOVEQUIST LOOP AROUND FALLS POND

**RATING:** Easy
**DISTANCE:** 0.9-mile loop
**ELEVATION CHANGE:** Minimal elevation gain
**ESTIMATED TIME:** 0.5–1 hour
**MAPS:** AMC's *White Mountain National Forest Map and Guide*, I9
AMC's *White Mountain Guide*, 27th ed., Map 3: Crawford Notch–
Sandwich Range, I9
**WMNF PARKING FEE:** Yes
**WINTER NOTES:** Although this trail is not a cross-country ski trail, the
same trailhead gives you access to miles of cross-country ski trails
along the Swift River.
**OTHER ACTIVITIES:** Swimming 2 miles east at Lower Falls, fishing

**The Rocky Gorge Scenic Area is a popular destination where families can have picnics on the abundant flat rocks by the river's edge, perhaps throw a fishing line in the water, or just hang out. Falls Pond is a quiet pond hidden by a dense forest of conifers.**

This is a short, easy hike right off the Kancamagus Highway. It includes a walk on a bridge over a small gorge on the Swift River and a peaceful walk around a small pond. The Lovequist Loop is named in honor of a dedicated White Mountain National Forest ranger.

## DIRECTIONS

Rocky Gorge Scenic Area is about 9.5 miles west of the intersection of the Kancamagus Highway (NH 112) and NH 16 in Conway. The well-marked turnoff is about 2 miles west of the turnoff for Lower Falls, another scenic area. You'll find rest rooms right at the parking area.

If you are coming from the Crawford Notch area, take US 302 to Bartlett, turn right on Bear Notch Road and then left (east) when you reach the Kancamagus Highway. (Bear Notch Road is closed in winter.) The parking area for Rocky Gorge Scenic Area is on the left in about 3.5 miles.

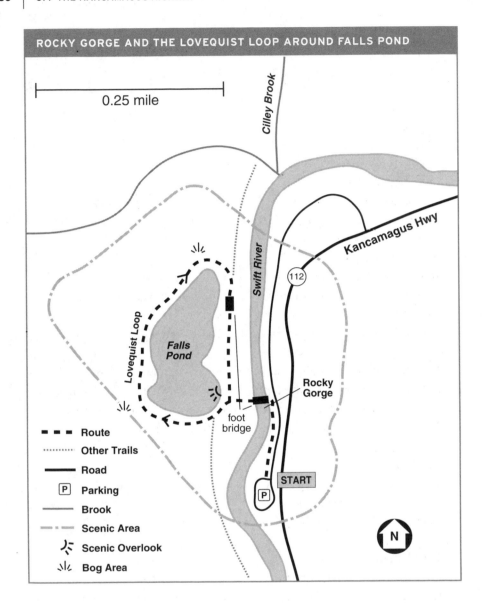

ROCKY GORGE AND THE LOVEQUIST LOOP AROUND FALLS POND

0.25 mile

Cilley Brook

Kancamagus Hwy

Swift River

112

Lovequist Loop

Falls Pond

Rocky Gorge

foot bridge

- - - Route
......... Other Trails
—— Road
P Parking
—— Brook
-·-·- Scenic Area
⅄ Scenic Overlook
Ψ Bog Area

START

P

N

## TRAIL DESCRIPTION

From the parking area walk northeast on the paved path along the river until you see the footbridge over Rocky Gorge. Cross the river, then stroll up wooden steps through hemlock to get to the junction with the loop trail. Go straight across to the shore of the pond for a nice view before beginning the Lovequist Loop.

The Lovequist Loop is a short, wide path, essentially free of rocks. Return to the junction and head clockwise around the pond. Go up a small hill, then turn right at the next junction (straight ahead is the Nanamocomuck Ski Trail). This next section of the Lovequist Loop is particularly pleasant. You are high above the pond, but it's visible through tall spruces with little understory.

At another fork, veer slightly left and start heading downhill. A Caution sign reveals that the Lovequist Loop is part of the cross-country ski trail system maintained by the Forest Service. Turn sharply right at a boggy area at the bottom of this hill.

The trail goes through a small section of hardwoods roughly halfway around the loop, then the spruce returns. Two short spur trails give you access to the pond shore. Take either or both for a vista from this side of the pond and for exploring its shore life.

The trail crosses over a stream surrounded by a wetland with lots of sphagnum. Soon after, follow an arrow directing you back to Rocky Gorge. A solid wooden bridge crosses the outlet from the pond. At the end of the loop, turn left to return to Rocky Gorge and your car.

## NATURE NOTES

When you stand on the bridge over the narrow gorge, note that the walls of the canyon are fairly rectangular, at least in part because granite fractures along definite joints. It's a surprise when natural things are organized into such familiar geometric shapes. Notice too that the granite rocks are crisscrossed with white pegmatite dikes.

Signs make it very clear that you should not attempt to swim at Rocky Gorge. The strong currents in the gorge make it dangerous. Check out Lower Falls, 2 miles east, for swimming.

Falls Pond feels remote, despite its proximity to the Kancamagus Highway. For most of the hike the dominant trees are red spruce and white pine. Some of the spruce are massive, particularly along the south shore of the pond. Many young spruce are also in the understory, indicating that this area is likely to remain heavily endowed with spruce for a long time.

Spruce is easily recognized by looking at its needles—they are individually attached on twigs (in contrast to pine, in which the needles are in bunches of two to five) and feel decidedly prickly when you grab them. Spruce needles are square in cross section, so that you can twirl them between your fingers, unlike the flat, untwirlable needles of hemlock and balsam fir. One way to remember all this is that to "spruce up" is to look sharp, just like spruce needles.

Red spruce is presently most abundant at mid-elevations (roughly 2,000 to 4,000 feet) in the White Mountains. The elevation of Falls Pond is only 1,100 feet, so you might wonder why it is so common here. Before the advent of wide-

**Red spruce dominates the forest around Falls Pond.**

spread logging in the White Mountains, red spruce was a dominant part of the forest, even at lower elevations. Unfortunately for the spruce, they were preferred by many loggers, and the forests that replaced them often grew up in northern hardwoods rather than spruce. So appreciate this great stand of spruce and the fact that it is apparently sustaining itself well.

An interesting thing to try is spruce gum. Find some exuded resin, pick out as much dirt as possible, and start chewing. The taste is pleasant and piney, and after a while it will become the texture of chewing gum.

The boggy wetland at the southwest corner of the pond exists because the topography does not allow water to drain. A number of plants historically important to people grow there. Sphagnum moss soaks up water like a sponge and creates acidic conditions in the bog by secreting hydrogen ions. Because sphagnum absorbs water so well, it has been used as a natural diaper. Its acidity has also led to its use as a sterile compress. And, of course, it is the peat moss that we use to condition the soil in our gardens.

In August you will be greeted by joe-pye weed, a tall plant with large purple or pink, flat-topped flower clusters comprised of many small individual florets. Joe Pye, or Jopi, was a Native American who reportedly used the plant to cure typhus and other fevers in colonial times.

The trees growing in the boggy area are red maples, famous for their brilliant, red fall foliage.

## TRIP 15
## LINCOLN WOODS TRAIL TO BLACK POND
## AND/OR FRANCONIA FALLS

**RATING:** Moderate (easy trail but relatively long)
**DISTANCE:** 6.8 miles round-trip to Black Pond, 6.6 miles to Franconia Falls, 8.0 to both
**ELEVATION CHANGE:** 500-foot elevation gain to Black Pond
**ESTIMATED TIME:** 3–5 hours depending on route
**MAPS:** AMC's *White Mountain National Forest Map and Guide*, H/I5
AMC's *White Mountain Guide*, 27th ed., Map 3: Franconia–Pemigewasset Range, H/I5
**WMNF PARKING FEE:** Yes
**WINTER NOTES:** The Lincoln Woods Trail is great for novice cross-country skiers. You can warm yourself at the visitor center before and after your outing.
**OTHER ACTIVITIES:** Fishing, swimming

**The Lincoln Woods Trail provides easy access to the Pemigewassett Wilderness, a vast protected area in the heart of the White Mountains, along the bed of an old logging railroad. Explore Black Pond, a quiet and peaceful pond framed by mountains, and Franconia Falls, an intensely exciting rush of water over flat rocks.**

The Lincoln Woods Trail is a great trail for anyone who does not like walking uphill or on rocks, but still wants to go for a long walk in the forest. It follows the west bank of the East Branch of the Pemigewasset River, so flowing water is never far away. It is very straight and wide, and you can often see what seems like at least a half a mile ahead. The elevation gain is imperceptible. The railroad bed along which this trail was built once brought loggers and devastation to the region—sparks from a train engine ignited a devastating forest fire here (see more history in Nature Notes). The seemingly pristine forests and mountains are a tribute to the regenerative powers of nature.

The trail is heavily used, both by day hikers and backpackers. To alleviate chronic problem congestion and habitat degradation, the Forest Service requires people who want to visit Franconia Falls to get a permit before setting out. Permits are available from the visitor center at the trailhead.

The Pemi East Side Trail, also called the East Branch Truck Road, departs from the same trailhead and follows along the east bank of the river. You might be tempted to do a loop hike, but keep in mind that there is no bridge for crossing back to the Lincoln Woods Trail at its terminus in the wilderness area. Fording the river at that point is at best a nuisance and at worst dangerous if water levels are high.

## DIRECTIONS
The Lincoln Woods Trail is off the Kancamagus Highway (NH 112) 5 miles east of the Exit 32 (NH 112, Lincoln) on I-93 just beyond the Hancock Campground. The U.S. Forest Service operates a visitor center at the trailhead, so you can stop in to talk with the rangers about trail conditions and pick up brochures on this and other trails.

## TRAIL DESCRIPTION
From the visitor center, take the stairs down to the river, walk over the suspension bridge, and then turn right. For the next 2.6 miles you walk on a wide, straight, flat, old logging railroad bed still studded with old but well-preserved railroad ties made from local hemlock. Sometimes iron rails and spikes are present and there are places where you can see old stone bridge abutments. (Please do not disturb any artifacts.) The Lincoln Woods Trail never strays far from the river, which will be your constant companion on your right. At 1.4 miles, the Osseo Trail diverges to the left for Mount Flume and the Franconia Ridge at a point where a stream also comes in from the left. Just beyond this junction, a small old field on the west side of the trail provides a little diversion. This was the site of an old logging camp. It is a good place to look for butterflies fluttering around goldenrods on a sunny summer day. At 1.7 miles, the Lincoln Woods Trail approaches the bank of the river. Stop here to admire the river and the view of Mount Bond. Shortly after that, the trail crosses Birch Island Brook, a tributary of the East Branch. The Black Pond Trail departs to the left at 2.6 miles. The Lincoln Woods Trail then passes through the old Franconia Brook Campground, which has now been relocated to the East Pemi Trail on the other side of the river. The Lincoln Woods Trail officially ends at a stone wall at 2.9 miles and becomes the Wilderness Trail. The spur trail to Franconia Falls departs to the left. Straight ahead, the Wilderness Trail heads across Franconia Brook on a foot bridge and continues through the Pemigewasset Wilderness, providing access to a host of backcountry trails and camping opportunities.

For Black Pond: The first part of the trail to Black Pond, which goes past the ice pond used by the logging camps, is part of a spur from the old railroad.

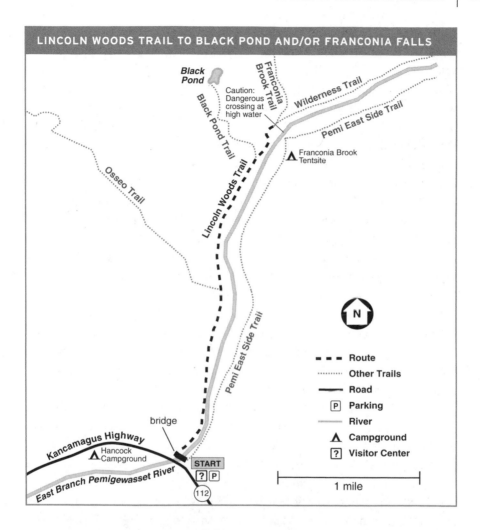

The pond is rapidly becoming a marsh, and you need to be careful to follow the yellow blazes where the flooding has forced the trail to be relocated. The trail then follows the northeast bank above Birch Island Brook for about 0.2 mile. It then crosses several small streams and passes the outlet to Black Pond where there is a nice view of Owl's Head. It reaches Black Pond 0.7 mile from the Lincoln Woods Trail at a great sitting rock. Any further exploration of the shoreline involves some bushwhacking.

**For Franconia Falls:** Follow the trail leading to the left at the stone wall marking the end of the Lincoln Woods Trail. It is a short, mostly level walk to Franconia Falls (0.4 mile). There are plenty of flat sitting rocks spread out over about 50 yards along the brook, so you can enjoy a number of perspectives of the falls.

## NATURE NOTES

The most compelling natural theme of this walk is logging history. This is well summarized in C. Francis Belcher's *Logging Railroads of the White Mountains* (AMC Books, 1980). The area that is now called the Pemigewasset Wilderness was still an undisturbed wilderness known only to hunters, trappers, and a few hikers when logging baron J. E. Henry purchased the logging rights in 1892. Henry's logging company had been busily laying waste to the Zealand Valley since 1880 (see Trip 48), and this purchase was an expansion of his empire. He built the East Branch and Lincoln Railroad, which started in Lincoln, followed the present course of the Kancamagus Highway, and then turned north to follow the East Branch of the Pemigewasset River. One logging camp was built near the present site of the White Mountain National Forest's visitor center on the Kancamagus Highway, another near the junction of the Lincoln Woods Trail and the spur trail to Black Pond. At the present site where the Lincoln Woods Trail ends, the railroad split into two branches, one continuing north along Franconia Brook and the other heading east along the East Branch of the Pemigewasset River. The former is now the Franconia Brook Trail and the latter the Wilderness Trail. These two rail lines were further divided like branches of a tree as J. E. Henry's company expanded deeper into the wilderness. Along with the rail lines came more logging camps.

On weekends, the railroads carried tourists into the mountains to sightsee, visit the logging camps, and pick blueberries. Hikers, hunters, and fishermen also used the railroad to reach the backcountry.

Eventually the logging operations laid waste to the area, and it came to be known as the "so called Pemigewasset Wilderness." In 1917 Henry sold his land to Parker-Young, another logging company. Parker-Young sold the land to the U.S. government in the 1930s, but retained logging rights through 1946. The railroad ceased operating in 1948. The Pemigewasset Wilderness, encompassing 45,000 acres, began to recover from the logging and was officially designated by an act of Congress in 1984.

From the forester's perspective, the large numbers of white birch, which thrive in recently logged areas, are evidence that this is second growth. Along the Lincoln Woods Trail, the typical vegetation is a canopy of northern hardwoods, but in many places the understory is dominated with conifer, particularly red spruce. Eventually the spruce will reclaim their dominant place in the region, as they were before the logging.

Black Pond is framed by a dense spruce fir forest and Mount Bond. With a little bushwhacking you explore more of the shoreline and see other mountains, such as Mount Garfield. It is a wonderfully peaceful place, where dragonflies patrol over the water, trout swim, and you might even see a moose. Their tracks were very obvious in a grassy marsh northwest of the "sitting rock." The shoreline vegetation includes red and green sphagnum mosses (see Trip 30), meadowsweet. leatherleaf, and Labrador tea. These plants, along with steeplebush and sedges, also occur around the marsh at the fringes of the ice pond.

Franconia Falls is a different kind of experience than Black Pond. Its smooth granite ledges and chutes of water make it a popular spot for swimming and sunning in summer, so you are likely to have lots of company. Along the edge of the brook at the falls, look for speckled alder (rounded toothed leaves, branchlets with speckles, and cone-like fruits), northern wild raisin (a viburnum with opposite leaves), hobblebush, white pine, and red sprucc.

One of the largest trembling aspens you will ever see grows along the spur trail opposite to the largest cascade. Normally this tree is about 30–40 feet tall and has smooth grayish green bark. The specimen growing near Franconia Falls is over 50 feet tall and its bark is also gray but deeply furrowed. When trees are allowed to grow old, they often take on characteristics different from that of younger specimens. Hopefully this process will be a common occurrence in the Pemigewasset Wilderness for years to come.

## TRIP 16
## GREELEY PONDS

**RATING:** Moderate

**DISTANCE:** 3.2 miles round-trip to the upper pond or 4.6 miles to both ponds

**ELEVATION CHANGE:** 350-foot elevation gain

**ESTIMATED TIME:** 2–4 hours

**MAPS:** AMC's *White Mountain National Forest Map and Guide*, I6 AMC's *White Mountain Guide*, 27th ed., Map 3: Crawford Notch–Sandwich Range, I6

**WMNF PARKING FEE:** Yes

**WINTER NOTES:** There is a moderately difficult cross-country ski trail that parallels the hiking trail and crosses it in several places. You can ski to the ponds all the way to or from Waterville Valley.

**OTHER ACTIVITIES:** Swimming, fishing

**Set dramatically near the height of Mad River Notch between Mounts Osceola and Kancamagus, the Greeley Ponds are reached by a relatively easy trail that crosses numerous split-log bridges over muddy sections. This hike can easily provide a full day of swimming, picnicking, and fishing.**

The two Greeley Ponds are classic mountain ponds bordered by rugged slopes that descend abruptly to the shoreline. The Greeley Ponds Trail going south from the Kancamagus Highway is suitable for all ages, with perhaps a little assistance and encouragement from parents. Be prepared for some mud, although the worst sections are bridged. The ponds are a popular destination so do not expect solitude in summer. Beyond the ponds, the trail continues to Waterville Valley (about 3 miles from the lower pond), so with two cars, you could do a longer hike.

## DIRECTIONS

The parking area for the Greeley Ponds Trail is on the south side of the Kancamagus Highway (NH 112) at a hairpin turn in the road about 9 miles east of I-93 in Lincoln. The lot is small, and given the popularity of this trail it may be full. There is also parking about 0.25 mile to the east where the cross-country ski trail begins.

The winter ski trail to Greeley Ponds is also marked with a sign for Greeley Ponds. We ran into several unhappy hikers who had walked the ski trail by mistake and had been slogging knee-deep in mud. You will find the hiking trail muddy enough to satisfy whatever craving for goo you might have. If you park at the ski-trail lot because the hiking trail lot is full, walk along the road to get to the correct trailhead.

If you are heading west on the Kancamagus Highway, the trailhead is about 0.25 mile west of the Hancock Scenic Overlook. The distance from NH 16 in Conway is about 25 miles.

## TRAIL DESCRIPTION

The Greeley Ponds Trail, marked with yellow blazes, is a gradual uphill until it reaches the height-of-land in Mad River Notch. Then it descends gently to the ponds. Particularly at the beginning, it's heavily eroded with lots of exposed tree roots. The cross-country ski trail, marked with blue diamonds, intersects the hiking trail several times.

The trail starts out through a dense forest of balsam fir. You soon cross

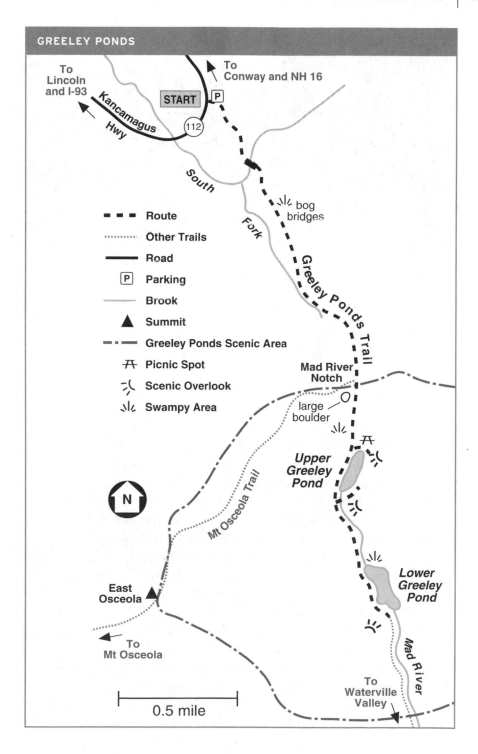

**GREELEY PONDS**

To Lincoln and I-93

To Conway and NH 16

Kancamagus Hwy

START

P

112

South Fork

bog bridges

Greeley Ponds Trail

- - - Route
········· Other Trails
—— Road
P Parking
—— Brook
▲ Summit
—·—·— Greeley Ponds Scenic Area
⅄ Picnic Spot
⸝⸜ Scenic Overlook
⸝⅃⸜ Swampy Area

N

Mad River Notch

large boulder

Upper Greeley Pond

Mt Osceola Trail

East Osceola

To Mt Osceola

Lower Greeley Pond

Mad River

To Waterville Valley

0.5 mile

**It's easy to spend a leisurely day at the Greeley Ponds.**

over two streams and a number of small wetlands on a series of wooden bog bridges.

The trail enters the Greeley Ponds Scenic Area and reaches the height-of-land near where the Mount Osceola Trail comes in from the right 1.3 miles from the trailhead. (The Mount Osceola Trail climbs very steeply and is not an appropriate family walk.) Just beyond this junction you pass a huge boulder that probably tumbled down from the cliffs of East Osceola. Stay right at the next fork (with the ski trail again) and cross over another bog bridge.

At 1.6 miles (1–1.5 hours) a short side path to the left leads to the north end of the upper pond. There is a flat sandy area here, great for a picnic unless the water levels are too high. If there's time, walk around to the open areas on the southeast shore. To get there, continue along the main trail to the south side of the pond and take the short side trail leading left.

It takes ten to twenty minutes along the Greeley Ponds Trail to hike from the south end of the upper pond to the lower pond. There is an interesting open area at the north end, but hike a little farther to a small cove near a stand of paper birch for the best vista.

Retrace your steps for the return trip, but be careful at the various intersections with the ski trail. Just beyond the big rock, make sure you stay right at a fork or else the ski trail might take you to the Osceola Trail. If you find yourself ascending very steeply, turn around and walk back to the junction of the Greeley Pond Trail.

## NATURE NOTES

The Greeley Ponds are named after Nathaniel Greeley, who ran an inn in Waterville Valley in the nineteenth century when the valley was still a quiet, secluded place. He was one of the pioneer trail builders in this part of the White Mountains.

The upper pond is deeper, with steeper shorelines and better swimming than the lower pond. The best vista is from the southeast corner of the upper pond—the craggy East Peak of Mount Osceola is particularly impressive. You can get a sense of how the glacier that swept through this valley plucked rocks from the side of the mountain, creating the cliff you now see.

By August the water temperature may even be tolerable (the loudest screech I ever heard was from someone who boldly dove into Greeley Pond in mid-June). Watch out for snags in the water. You may also discover a few leeches, or they may discover you, but don't let them deter you. They are generally small and won't likely bother you if you keep moving.

The snags that stick out of the water are great perching spots for ebony jewelwings and dragonflies. Ebony jewelwings, also known as black-winged damselflies, are boldly marked with unmistakable electric-green bodies and black wings, striking colors that you might expect more in a tropical jungle than here. Damselflies hold their wings vertically when at rest, unlike dragonflies, which hold their wings horizontally.

The lower Greeley Pond is less than 100 feet lower in elevation than the upper pond. The vistas from its two vantage points are not as dramatic as those of the upper pond, and it is too shallow for swimming but is equally interesting from a natural history perspective. There is much evidence of beaver activity, particularly lots of standing dead trees in the water indicating recent flooding.

At the north end of the lower pond there is a boggy area with lots of peat (sphagnum) moss. Leatherleaf, Labrador tea, tall meadow rue, and sweet gale are the most obvious shrubs and cotton sedge, white turtlehead, marsh Saint John's wort, bog club moss, and twig rush the most common nonwoody plants. Cotton sedge has dense balls of white, cottony hairs that surround its inconspicuous flowers. Its other name is hare's tail.

The sphagnum mats harbor sundews, tiny plants whose rounded leaves are bordered with sticky hairs that trap insects. Bogs are low in nutrients, so the sundew feeds itself in a very unplantlike way—catching and digesting insects. Be careful to avoid trampling the sphagnum when you hunt for sundews.

The forest along the Greeley Ponds Trail contains a rich assortment of woodland wildflowers, particularly in the section between the two ponds. There are lots of clintonia, goldthread, painted trillium, hobblebush, rosy and clasping-leaved twisted stalks, sharp-leaved aster, and rattlesnake root (the last having big, bizarre leaves in three parts and drooping, greenish flowers in late summer). Snowberries, whose tiny rounded leaves smell like wintergreen when crushed, are particularly abundant at the side trail at the south end of the upper pond. In wet swales there are white turtlehead, sedge, peat moss, hobblebush, and (just beyond the big boulder) New England aster. Look for blue-colored algae growing on damp, moldy wood, the bright blue looking more like paint than a living thing.

Except for the red squirrel, birds and other animals are much less predictable than plants. You may see ravens flying overhead. They roost on cliffs, such as those on East Peak of Osceola. And keep your eyes and ears open for the passage of guilds of small birds in the forest (see Trip 19).

## TRIP 17
## CHAMPNEY FALLS

**RATING:** Moderate
**DISTANCE:** 3.5 miles round-trip
**ELEVATION CHANGE:** 600-foot elevation gain
**ESTIMATED TIME:** 3 hours
**MAPS:** AMC's *White Mountain National Forest Map and Guide*, J9
AMC's *White Mountain Guide*, 27th ed., Map 3: Crawford Notch–
Sandwich Range, J9
**WMNF PARKING FEE:** Yes

**The hike to Champney Falls is an ideal family walk. At the end you will be rewarded with two waterfalls that are particularly impressive just after a heavy rain.**

The trail runs along the brook for much of the walk, passing by some weirdly shaped trees on rocks and a good assortment of White Mountain wildflowers. At the top of the falls, you have a view of nearby mountains.

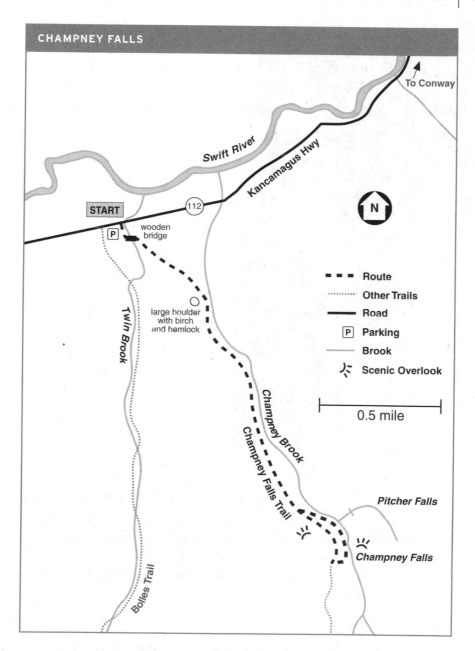

CHAMPNEY FALLS

START

wooden bridge

large boulder with birch and hemlock

Swift River

Kancamagus Hwy

To Conway

112

N

Twin Brook

Champney Brook

Champney Falls Trail

Bolles Trail

Pitcher Falls

Champney Falls

- - - Route
········· Other Trails
——— Road
P Parking
——— Brook
Scenic Overlook

0.5 mile

## DIRECTIONS

The parking lot for the Champney Falls Trail is on the south side of the Kancamagus Highway (NH 112) about 11 miles west of its junction with NH 16 and about 1.5 miles east of Bear Notch Road.

**Pitcher Falls.**

## TRAIL DESCRIPTION

The Champney Falls Trail is marked with yellow blazes. It is heavily used and has a large number of exposed tree roots. It begins by crossing Twin Brook on a wooden bridge with a railing on one side. After about fifteen to twenty minutes, the trail reaches Champney Brook and parallels the west bank of the brook for the rest of the hike.

Take a left at the junction to the loop trail to Champney and Pitcher falls at 1.4 miles (1–1.25 hours). In about ten minutes you pass a small waterfall—more like a shoot—that empties into a pool. Soon after, you reach Champney Falls. After admiring Champney Falls, make sure to walk about 100 yards east between two narrow ledges to the base of Pitcher Falls. Pitcher Falls is more likely to have significant water flowing over it all year.

Continue on the loop trail and ascend the west side of Champney Falls to the top of the falls, where there is a restricted view. Be cautious when scrambling around the rocks, because the shade tends to keep them damp and slippery.

Follow the trail away from the falls to the upper junction of the loop trail with the Champney Falls Trail (2–2.25 hours). Turn right and begin the gradual 1.7-mile descent back to your car.

## NATURE NOTES

Champney Falls is named for Benjamin Champney, a White Mountain artist of the nineteenth century. Here, water plunges (or, in dry weather, trickles) over a series of stairlike ledges. There is a large rectangular boulder in the streambed at the base of the falls. Pitcher Falls is a beautiful, thin cascade of water that looks like it somehow got lost and changed its course. It is in a narrow gorge bounded by two almost vertical sidewalls. Instead of being at the far end of the gorge as you might expect, it plunges over one of the sides. The stream above Pitcher Falls likely changed its course at some point, since erosion by water created the gorge in the first place.

The top of the falls is another communal stop on this hike. You will likely find other people there, perched out on rocks admiring the brook and the view of nearby mountains. The view is refreshing, particularly after the long walk through a dense forest. There is another good overlook on the section of the Champney Falls Trail between the upper and lower junctions with the loop trail.

You pass a small cascade that empties into a pool surrounded by moss-covered rocks just before the falls. The pool is deep enough for wading, but the shadiness keeps the temperature of the water at penguin level for most of the year. Look for water striders in the pools.

The falls aren't the only thing of note on this trail. On the way look for natural bridges and dams created by tree falls. Each will exist for a few years, then will disappear during late spring floods as the trees decompose. Nevertheless, they can trap debris and small stones, and create pools that last as long as the trees stay in place.

At the point where the trail first reaches Champney Brook, there is a marvelous duo of a yellow birch and hemlock on top of a large boulder. Both trees look like they are growing right out of a rock, and their roots have intertwined as they reach for a foothold in the ground beneath the boulder.

The forest is of northern hardwoods with lots of hemlock early in the trail, particularly along water. Hobblebush and striped maple form the understory. There are a number of particularly "stripy" striped maples on the Champney Falls Trail between the upper and lower junctions of the loop trail.

The Champney Falls Trail has a good variety of wildflowers and other small plants, particularly near the trailhead. Indian cucumber root, partridgeberry, and shiny club moss are common. Also, look for painted trillium, shinleaf, rosy twisted stalk, jack-in-the-pulpit, and a few pink lady's slippers. Bunchberry, wintergreen, and hobblebush border the brook right at the ledge above the falls.

With the falls and the flowers, you will have a very satisfying half-day outing.

## TRIP 18
## BOULDER LOOP TRAIL

**RATING:** Moderate

**DISTANCE:** 3.1-mile loop

**ELEVATION CHANGE:** 950-foot elevation gain

**ESTIMATED TIME:** 2–4 hours

**MAPS:** AMC's *White Mountain National Forest Map and Guide*, I10
AMC's *White Mountain Guide*, 27th ed., Map 3: Crawford Notch–
Sandwich Range, I10

**WMNF PARKING FEE:** Yes

**OTHER ACTIVITIES:** Wading in Swift River nearby

**Most self-guided nature trails are simple, short, and flat, usually on
a well-manicured path. The Boulder Loop Trail has more ambition.
It takes you up about 1,000 feet to rocky ledges on a shoulder of the
Moat Range, where there are fine views across the Swift River valley
to a number of 4,000-footers south of the Kancamagus Highway.**

The trail lives up to its name by passing jumbles of huge boulders deposited
by landslides. The loop is appropriate for younger hikers who have some experience on trails or for nonhikers who can be easily carried in a backpack.
Along the way you pass eighteen numbered stations at sites of particular geological or ecological interest. An informational leaflet, available at the Saco
Ranger Station, provides a narrative at each station. On a clear day you can
see Mounts Chocorua, Passaconaway, and Middle Sister and the Tripyramids
from the ledges. Immediately below is the valley of the Swift River. This river is
a tributary of the Saco River, which flows into the Atlantic Ocean in southern
Maine.

### DIRECTIONS

The Boulder Loop Trail is 6 miles west of the intersection of the Kancamagus
Highway (NH 112) and NH 16. Turn right at the sign to the Covered Bridge
Campground on Passaconaway (formerly Dugway) Road and drive through
the Albany Covered Bridge (constructed in 1858, renovated in 1970). Park
in the first parking area beyond the bridge and find the trailhead at the north
side of the road. In winter the bridge is closed to cars, so you'll need to park
before the bridge.

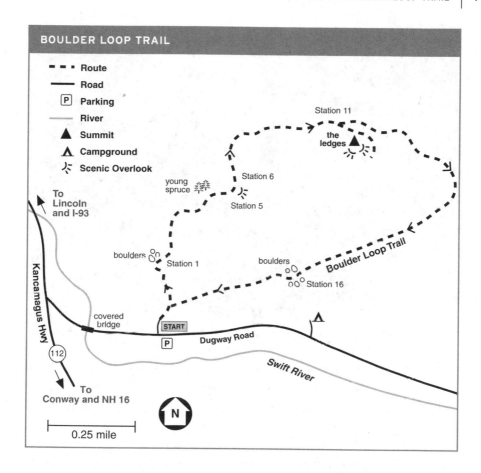

If you are coming from the Crawford Notch area, take US 302 to Bartlett, turn right on Bear Notch Road, and then turn left (east) when you reach the Kancamagus Highway. (Bear Notch Road is closed in winter.) Passaconaway (Dugway) Road is about 6 miles east.

## TRAIL DESCRIPTION

The Boulder Loop Trail is marked by yellow blazes. The loop begins 0.2 mile (five minutes) from the parking area. Turn left to follow the sequence with the numbers of the nature trail. Right away you pass ledges, a huge boulder where the trail bends to the right and then a few more impressive boulders. The trail ascends and after about 40 minutes passes an opening (around Station 5 of the nature trail) that provides the first vista out over the valley and across to ledges. At 1.3 miles (another twenty minutes), you reach a sign that reads To the View, 0.2 mile (Station 11). Follow the short side trail up the stone steps that takes you to the ledges.

**Albany Covered Bridge at the trailhead to Boulder Loop Trail.** Photo by Nancy Schalch.

The side trail extends in the open for about a third mile. The views are all great, but don't get too close to the edge, particularly if it's rainy, because the drop-off is steep. At 1,965 feet, these ledges are the highest elevation on the trail. A large, yellow spot marks the spot where you turn around.

After backtracking to the main trail, turn right for the one-hour descent. Just below the ledges, you pass a huge rock that is at least as large as ten blue whales. The trail continues downhill, crosses a small stream (Station 16), and enters another area of huge boulders strewn by a landslide 2.3 miles from the trailhead (Station 17). You will also observe caves created by the jumble of rocks. Beyond this, the trail flattens out and traverses a few small streams. At the loop junction, go straight to return to the parking area.

## NATURE NOTES

The leaflet for the self-guided nature trail provides you with a wealth of information on forest dynamics and geological processes of this area. The two most striking aspects are the giant boulders and the ledges. Although more subtle, the forest dynamics are also quite interesting.

Two particularly impressive jumbles of large boulders are located at Station 1, right at the beginning of the hike, and at Station 17 near the end. Major landslides formed these boulder fields. Station 1 has two especially huge boulders, one with a crack in it that forms a cave and another covered with rock-tripe lichen. The most notable formation at Station 17 is an overhanging rock that is a good place to get out of the rain and still be able to sit on a flat rock.

Forest dynamics are easy to follow along the Boulder Loop Trail. The trail begins in a northern hardwood forest with an understory of hobblebush and striped maple. By Station 2, increasing numbers of red spruce indicate a transition to the boreal forest. Note the area of young spruce trees (around Station 4) growing in a former clearing. At the clearings on the ascent, such as around Stations 6 and 7, red spruce are largely replaced by red oak and white pine. Oak and white pine survive better than spruce in drier, sunnier, warmer areas such as these open ledges.

Other things to note about the forest are large holes made by pileated woodpeckers (in one of the white pines at Station 6) and white ash (Station 7). White ash is a broad-leafed tree whose leaves are composed of many leaflets and arranged in pairs along the twigs. Its wood is used for baseball bats. Common woodland wildflowers include Canada mayflower, clintonia, pink lady's slipper, false Solomon's seal, spikenard, wild sarsaparilla, silverrod, various goldenrods, shinleaf, and sharp-leaved aster. The descent is particularly rich in hobblebush (colorful berries in late summer) and spinulose wood fern.

The ecology at the ledges differs from the lower forest, partly because the thin soil supports only a few trees. Like the clearings described earlier, this area receives more sunlight and is drier, so red oak and white pine are mixed in with some red spruce. Note how the white pines have relatively short needles, possibly an adaptation to reduce water loss in this wind-exposed location.

Mountain ash, a small tree of the boreal forest with distinct compound leaves, is common on the ledges. Mountain ash is really not an ash at all but a relative of apple and pear. In June it displays showy white flowers, and in late summer, its red berries, borne in flat-topped clusters, are relished by birds. Their twigs are a favorite food of moose.

Low shrubs at the ledges include lowbush blueberries, shadbush, and dwarf juniper. Wildflowers include goldenrod and cowwheat. Look for bristly sarsaparilla, a thorny relative of the more common wild sarsaparilla, near the yellow spot marking the end of the spur trail. Reindeer lichen, a pale green lichen, forms an ornate border around trees and shrubs, giving the feel of a rock garden.

## TRIP 19
## HEDGEHOG MOUNTAIN

**RATING:** Moderate with some challenging sections
**DISTANCE:** 4.8-mile loop
**ELEVATION CHANGE:** 1,300-foot elevation gain
**ESTIMATED TIME:** 3.5–5 hours
**MAPS:** AMC's *White Mountain National Forest Map and Guide*, J8
AMC's *White Mountain Guide*, 27th ed., Map 3: Crawford Notch–
Sandwich Range, J8
**WMNF PARKING FEE:** Yes

**This loop off the Kancamagus Highway takes you to the summit of 2,532-foot Hedgehog Mountain, a small mountain with rocky ledges that provide great vistas of nearby peaks. It is surrounded by 4,000-footers, so you have the sense of being in the mountains rather than on top of them.**

The elevation gain is mostly gradual, with a few short steep sections. The trail takes you past three outlooks: the east ledges, the summit, and Allen's Ledge. If you are short on time, just hike to Allen's Ledge, which is a little over a mile from the parking area. On a clear day you can see as far as the Presidential Range.

The UNH Trail should be hiked only when the weather is good, for two reasons: First, the ledges around the summit could be hazardous in wet weather; and second, you don't want to miss the views.

You can combine this hike with a visit to the Russell Colbath House, a restored 1830s house that shows how some of the first settlers in the area lived. It is about a mile east of the trailhead along the Kancamagus Highway.

### DIRECTIONS
The trailhead for the UNH Trail is on the south side of the Kancamagus Highway, about 15 miles west of its intersection with NH 16. It is also the trailhead for the Downes Brook and Mount Potash trails. Turn left (south) on a gravel road opposite the Passaconaway Campground to find the trailhead. For those coming from Crawford Notch or Lincoln, the trailhead is about 1 mile west of the intersection of the Kancamagus Highway and Bear Notch Road.

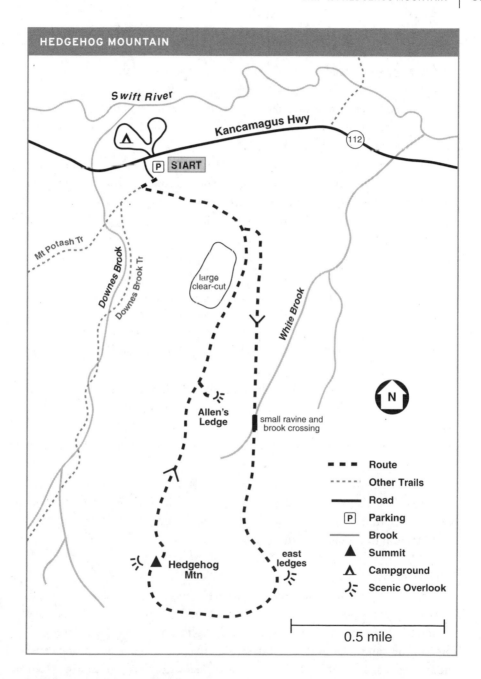

## TRAIL DESCRIPTION

The UNH Trail is named for the University of New Hampshire, whose forestry program uses the buildings you pass early in your hike. The trail runs with the Downes Brook Trail for about 60 yards in an open field, then turns left and enters the forest. The trail is marked with blue blazes, but there are some yellow blazes too.

After a few minutes (0.2 mile) on an old railroad bed, you reach the junction of the loop. We recommend hiking the loop clockwise by taking the left fork. This provides a more gradual ascent while allowing you to enjoy the view from open ledges on the descent. However, if you only have time for Allen's Ledge, take the right fork of the loop.

For the complete loop, the left (east) fork continues straight ahead for another 0.2 mile, then turns right and ascends gradually up an old logging road. It leaves the logging road and continues ascending through a nice stand of hemlock. At 1.6 miles, the trail descends into a small ravine and crosses a brook. It then ascends more steeply through a red spruce forest and comes out on the east ledges (2.0 miles, about 1.5 hours). Stop for a while to enjoy the view.

The trail levels, then climbs steeply to reach the summit of Hedgehog Mountain, about 0.9 mile (40 minutes) from the east ledges and 2.9 miles from the trailhead. Be careful here, because some of the ledges could be slick in wet weather. The best view is not at the summit itself but at ledges a little beyond. Turn left at the trail sign to reach that area.

The UNH Trail descends from the summit of Hedgehog Mountain through open ledges with great views north. In about twenty minutes (0.8 mile from the summit) watch for the turnoff to Allen's Ledge, marked by a sign. Take the side trail back uphill and follow the base of a massive rock to the left and up to the vista.

Returning to the main trail, it is 1.1 miles (about 30 minutes) to the parking area. The trail descends steeply, passing a very large clear-cut. Just before the loop junction, a cross-country ski trail enters from the left. Turn left at the loop junction to get back to your car.

## NATURE NOTES

Two mountains south of the Kancamagus Highway are named after hedgehogs, presumably because the spires of spruce and fir that cover their rounded summits reminded those in charge of naming things of the spines of a porcupine. You can make a game of this by looking at the map and finding other mountains that share the same name. Owl's Head, Sugarloaf, Black Mountain, and Blueberry Mountain come immediately to mind.

The three different vistas on this hike are all distinctive. The view from the east ledges is the most intimate, looking down over a secluded valley bounded by Mount Passaconaway and Mount Paugus. Chocorua is in the background.

Inspecting the view from the east ledges of Hedgehog Mountain.
Photo by Edward Sullivan.

Former clear-cuts, now covered with new growth, testify to logging in years past.

The ledges near the summit offer spectacular views of peaks to the north and south. Carrigain Notch, bordered by Mounts Carrigain, Anderson, and Nancy, is a wonderful example of a glacially carved U-shaped valley. Mount Hancock to the west of Carrigain is a long ridge. To the west, Mount Passaconaway is particularly massive. Potash Mountain, with a number of clear-cuts, is nearby and roughly the same height as Hedgehog. Behind Potash are the three summits of Mount Tripyramid. The Swift River valley separates this assemblage of mountains from Carrigain and Hancock.

Allen's Ledge was named for Jack Allen, a White Mountain guide. From here Mount Washington is visible on a clear day. In front of Mount Carrigain, Green's Cliff is prominent. You also see Bear Mountain, Mount Chocorua, and Mount Paugus.

This is a good trail to see the passage of a guild of forest birds containing a variety of species. Guilds are "teams" of birds of different species that forage together in the forest. The term "guild" comes from the old Dutch craftsmen's associations. You may have noticed on this and other hikes that you usually go a long time without seeing or hearing any birds; then all of a sudden, you are surrounded by chickadees, nuthatches, golden-crowned kinglets, warblers, woodpeckers, and others. They will busily make their way together across your trail and eventually move on.

If you have binoculars, notice that the different species have different ways of feeding. Chickadees and kinglets are acrobats, often hanging upside down as they inspect small twigs for insects or buds. Nuthatches probe the bark of the main trunk and large branches, while woodpeckers poke holes in branches and trunks to catch the insects deeper within the tree. Warblers and flycatchers sally for flying insects, while juncos and thrushes forage among the leaf litter on the ground. By using different feeding methods, these birds reduce competing with each other, although there is undoubtedly some overlap in their menus. The advantage to feeding in guilds is that large numbers of birds are probably more efficient at flushing insects than an individual would be. Also, there are more eyes to watch out for predators like Cooper's hawks, and to mob a predator if one should appear.

If a bird guild should appear while you are walking through the boreal (spruce and fir) forest, keep your eyes open for boreal chickadees. These birds resemble black-capped chickadees, those familiar epicures of sunflower seeds at backyard bird feeders, but they are slightly smaller and have a brown, rather than black, bib. Boreal chickadees inhabit the spruce-fir forests in the White Mountains. At the elevation of Hedgehog Mountain, 2,500 feet, you might very well see both species of chickadees, perhaps even together.

The forest you walk through starts out as northern hardwoods and eventually becomes boreal as you near the ledges. Some understory plants to look for are heart-leaved aster, Indian cucumber-root, Solomon's seal, Indian pipe, and shiny club moss. At the summit of Hedgehog Mountain, red spruce, sheep laurel, mountain holly, and bracken fern grow.

# 4

# CRAWFORD NOTCH AND ZEALAND NOTCH

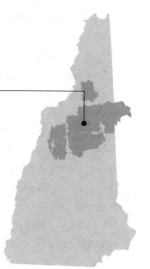

## LAY OF THE LAND

The Crawford Notch/Zealand region lies in the heart of the White Mountains. The area includes two stunning U-shaped valleys and a number of mountains that rise above 4,000 feet. Just getting to this area is a real treat because the drive up US 302 through Crawford Notch and up to the Zealand area is one of the most spectacular in the eastern United States, surpassed only by the drive down US 302 through the same area. An early explorer, quoted by the Reverend Benjamin G. Willey in his 1856 book, *Incidents in White Mountain History*, described it eloquently:

> The sublime and awful grandeur of the Notch baffles all description. Geometry may settle the heights of the mountains, and numerical figures may record the measure; but no words can tell the emotions of the soul as it looks upward and views the almost perpendicular precipices which line the narrow space between them. . . .

The hiking trails selected here take you to hidden ponds, breathtaking overlooks, good wildlife viewing, and some of the highest waterfalls in the White Mountains. In the secluded Zealand Valley many trails follow old logging railroads with gentle grades perfect for young hikers.

## LOGISTICS AND SUPPLIES

A number of places provide information to hikers as well as an introduction to the rich history of the "Great Notch of the White Mountains." The Mac-Comber Family Information Center at Crawford Depot is located in the old historic train station built in 1891 where guests used to disembark for the Crawford House Hotel. The depot is located just north of the point where US 302 passes through the Gateway of the Notch, the highest and narrowest part of Crawford Notch. The Information Center is run by the AMC. It offers displays on the natural and human history of Crawford Notch, rest rooms, water for your canteens, and a store that sells some hiking supplies and souvenirs. The depot also serves as a stop on the Conway Scenic Railroad. Crawford Notch State Park's visitor center is at the Willey House Historic Site off US 302 and has a snack bar, rest rooms, and information. A small kiosk sells snacks and some last-minute hiking supplies at the trailhead to Arethusa Falls Trail.

The original hotel at the "Gateway to the Notch" was built by Abel and Ethan Allen Crawford (father and son) in 1828 and run by Thomas Crawford, brother of Ethan Allen. It evolved into the Crawford House Hotel, which hosted presidents and other dignitaries until it closed in 1975. The building burned down a few years later.

## THE AMC HIGHLAND CENTER AT CRAWFORD NOTCH

This AMC destination is centrally located for day hikes around Crawford Notch and Zealand. It is a few hundred yards from Crawford Depot and is near the site of the Crawford House Hotel. At this new, green building facility you can find lodging, meals, daily programs on the White Mountains, guided hikes, and a wealth of information for hikers. A store within the center sells hiking supplies, guidebooks, and field guides. The Highland Lodge has private rooms with baths for families and provides breakfast and dinner. The Shapleigh Bunk House, an historic building that was the home to artist Frank H. Shapleigh, has two bunk rooms and offers breakfast and limited facilities for heating up your own food. Reservations are needed for both facilities.

This is an area of small towns and small stores, but there are no grocery stores in the immediate vicinity of the center. For picnic and other supplies, plan on stopping at one of the stores you pass on US 302 in Glen, Bartlett, Notchland (in the heart of Crawford Notch), Bretton Woods, or Twin Mountain. The towns of Twin Mountain, Bretton Woods, and Bartlett have a number of restaurants, gas stations, motels, hotels, and tourist cabins.

## NEARBY CAMPING

The Dry River Campground on US 302 is the only public campground in Crawford Notch itself. It is about 1.5 miles south of the turnoff to Ripley Falls and 5.5 miles south of Crawford Depot. The Zealand and Sugarloaf campgrounds of the White Mountain National Forest are in the Zealand area. The Zealand Campground, with eleven sites, is right at the junction of US 302 and Zealand Road. The two Sugarloaf campgrounds are 0.5 mile south on Zealand Road. They have a total of 62 sites and have facilities for people with disabilities. There are private campgrounds near Bartlett and Twin Mountain.

## TRIP 20
## SACO LAKE AND ELEPHANT HEAD

**RATING:** Easy
**DISTANCE:** 1.2 miles round-trip
**ELEVATION CHANGE:** 100-foot elevation gain
**ESTIMATED TIME:** 1 hour
**MAPS:** AMC's *White Mountain National Forest Map and Guide*, G8
AMC's *White Mountain Guide*, 27th ed., Map 3: Crawford Notch–Sandwich Range, G8
**WMNF PARKING FEE:** None
**OTHER ACTIVITIES:** Fishing

**The short trail around Saco Lake is perfect for all ages—it follows the shoreline of the lake and crosses several streams and some large boulders. The short climb to Elephant's Head provides impressive views of the dramatic notch.**

Saco Lake, a small, unassuming pond off US 302, is the headwater for the Saco River, which flows through Crawford Notch and all the way to the Atlantic Ocean. Elephant Head is a large, rocky outcropping that overlooks Crawford Notch at the east side of the gateway. It actually looks like the head of an elephant when viewed from the highway near the depot.

This short walk combines two even shorter walks near the Macomber Family Information Center at Crawford Depot and the AMC's Highland Center at the Gateway of the Notch. You are rarely out of sight of the road. Elephant

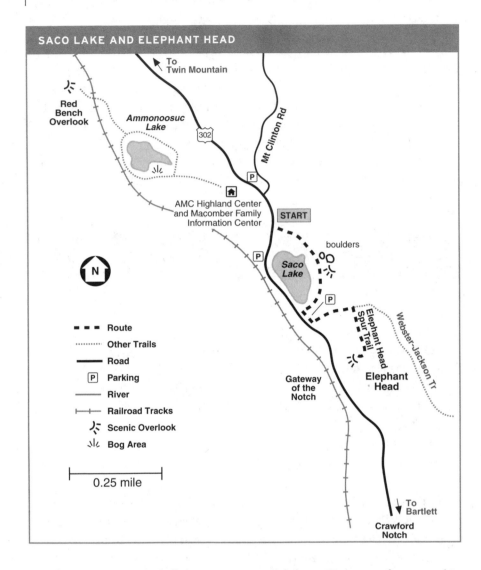

Head requires some uphill (not very taxing) hiking. You can, of course, skip Elephant Head and return to your car after walking around the lake, or skip Saco Lake and hike directly to the Elephant Head.

## DIRECTIONS

From the Jackson–North Conway area, follow US 302 west at Glen where it splits from NH 16. US 302 passes through Bartlett then heads north through Crawford Notch. At the top of the notch, roughly 20 miles from the junction of NH 16 and US 302, the road goes through the narrow pass between two cliffs. Saco Lake is on the right as you face north and the Crawford Depot Information Center on the left just beyond the pass. The AMC's Highland Center is a short distance beyond. The trailhead for the Saco Lake Trail is at the north end of the lake across US 302 from the parking area at the Crawford Depot. There is a white sign at the trailhead that says Saco Lake, Idlewild. If you want to skip the walk around the lake and hike only to the Elephant Head, park near the south end of the lake and follow the signs to the Webster-Jackson Trail.

From Franconia Notch and Twin Mountain, the Highland Center is about 8 miles south of the junction of US 3 and US 302 in Twin Mountain.

## TRAIL DESCRIPTION

The Saco Lake Trail enters the woods and soon crosses a small stream on rocks. In about five minutes you reach the shoreline of the lake. A plank bridge aids in traversing a rocky area with twenty-foot boulders. The Idlewild Outlook, reached by a short, steep spur trail, is on top of these rocks. After the overlook, the trail continues along the shore, eventually crossing over the inlet to the lake on another plank bridge and returning to the highway at the south end.

From this point you can end your hike and walk back to your car along the road or continue on to Elephant Head, a round-trip of 30 minutes. To get to Elephant Head, continue toward the notch (south) along the highway to the trailhead for the Webster-Jackson Trail, just past a small field on the left. Take the Webster-Jackson Trail for a few minutes (less than 0.2 mile) to where the Elephant Head Spur diverges right, marked with a sign that says Great View of the Notch. You pass through a damp area on wooden planks, ascend for a while, then descend slightly to the open ledge, 0.2 mile from the Webster-Jackson Trail. After admiring the view and the rocky ledge, retrace your steps back to the road and return to the Crawford Depot area and your car.

## NATURE NOTES

The walk around Saco Lake is much more interesting than it might appear from the road. The wooden bridges, the chance to toss stones in the water, and the huge rocks all combine to make a great walk for small children.

The huge rock formations around the Idlewild Overlook are covered with rock tripe, a lichen that looks like a piece of boot leather. The rocks are topped with trees that somehow manage to cling precariously to life with very little soil. A beaver house is tucked in among the rocks, as if designed by a landscape architect.

From the lakeshore at this rocky area there is a good view across the lake to Mount Tom (4,051 feet), named for Thomas Crawford. The view from the Idlewild Overlook is now partly overgrown.

**Saco Lake and Old Crawford Depot with Mount Webster in the distance.**

The Saco Lake Trail is a good place to study granite. At the bridge, inspect the coarse texture of the granite for crystals of translucent quartz (grayish) mixed in with feldspar (white) and some biotite mica flakes (black or brownish). Also note that the vertical side of one of the huge boulders you pass is very flat, indicating that this rock broke off from an even larger rock along a flat joint. Another rock overhangs the trail.

In summer, you are likely to see tree swallows and barn swallows flying over the lake. These small birds are very fast and adept flyers. They fly erratically with aerial pirouettes as they catch insects that fly above or emerge from the water. See Trip 31 for more on these swallows. Note the dead wildlife trees riddled with woodpecker holes that provide homes for many birds and mammals.

At the inlet to the lake, poke around among the small stones for salamanders. The lake is stocked with trout, so fishing is a possibility with the proper New Hampshire license.

You can spot the Elephant Head from the highway between Saco Lake and the Webster-Jackson trailhead. White lines and spots of white quartz within the grayish granite give the ledge its distinctive profile. You will get a close-up view of the quartz and granite when you actually reach the Elephant Head. From the top of Elephant Head, there are nice views both up and down the notch. From this perch you can watch for wildlife. Beaver, ducks, and other animals reside in the wetland across US 302. One time we saw an osprey flying over the wetland and then through the Gateway of the Notch, struggling against the ever-present wind the whole way.

At Elephant Head, you can observe the drainage patterns of the land. Water in Saco Lake flows south through Crawford Notch and forms the Saco River, ultimately reaching the coast of Maine. Just north of the lake and the Highland Center, water flows north to the Ammonoosuc River and eventually to Long Island Sound via the Connecticut River.

Note the black-eyed susan, oxeye daisy, and goldenrod in the small field near the trailhead to the Webster-Jackson Trail. These sun-loving plants are completely out of place in the forest. In the shade of the forest you will find mountain wood sorrel, spinulose wood fern, goldthread, clintonia, painted trillium, shiny club moss, and Dutchman's breeches. Northern white violet and sedge grow in the wet part of the trail that is traversed by the planks. Along the lake shore, there are speckled alder, meadowsweet, water lobelia, pipewort, flat-topped aster, goldenrod, and white turtlehead. These four different plant habitats illustrate the wide variety of nature you can enjoy on this short walk.

## TRIP 21
## AMMONOOSUC LAKE

**RATING:** Easy
**DISTANCE:** 1.0- or 2.0-mile loop
**ELEVATION CHANGE:** Minimal elevation change
**ESTIMATED TIME:** 1–2 hours
**MAPS:** AMC's *White Mountain National Forest Map and Guide*, G7
AMC's *White Mountain Guide*, 27th ed., Map 3: Crawford Notch–Sandwich Range, G7
**WMNF PARKING FEE:** Yes (Mount Clinton Road Lot), none at Depot
**OTHER ACTIVITIES:** Swimming, fishing

**A surprising gem, Ammonoosuc Lake feels remote, yet it is only a fifteen-minute walk from the AMC's Highland Center and US 302. It's a great place to spot moose, beaver, or wood duck and a good assortment of forest and wetland wildflowers, or to take a quick dip in the cool waters.**

The Around-the-Lake Trail loops around the shore of Ammonoosuc Lake through a shady forest of evergreen. A side trail directs you to the Red Bench, a strategically placed seat in a clearing with a great view of Mount Washington and the Presidential Range.

It should take you no longer than an hour to hike the one-mile loop, but allow extra time for the Red Bench overlook. Make sure you have insect repellent handy, particularly if you are hiking at dawn or dusk. In damp weather or early spring, expect the trail to have muddy spots.

## DIRECTIONS

Park for Ammonoosuc Lake at the Crawford Depot Visitor Information Center near the AMC Highland Center at the head of Crawford Notch off US 302. See Trip 20 for directions. You can also park at the hikers parking lot 0.2 mile up Mount Clinton Road from US 302. Walk north behind the Highland Center and pick up the Around-the-Lake Trail to your left. An alternative way to access the trail is via the AMC's Stewardship Trail. This is to the right behind the Highland Center and runs for 0.2 mile with twelve numbered stations before intersecting the Around-the-Lake Trail. You can pick up an audio guide to the Stewardship Trail at the Highland Center.

## TRAIL DESCRIPTION

The Around-the-Lake Trail, marked with yellow blazes, heads down toward the lake and in a few minutes reaches the start of the loop. We suggest following it to the left in a clockwise direction. The trail crosses over Crawford Brook on a bridge, passes a spring, and reaches the west shore of the lake.

In about fifteen to twenty minutes, the turnoff to the Red Bench overlook heads left. This side trail to an attractive vista takes fifteen to twenty minutes in each direction. Follow the side trail through the woods away from the lake. It jogs right at the old railroad tracks, crosses over another wooden bridge by a small gorge, and then reaches a clearing in the forest with a red bench conveniently placed for admiring the view. Retrace your steps to return to the lake.

When you get back to the Around-the-Lake Trail, turn left. In about ten minutes, you cross the outlet of the lake, which flows through a culvert in a small dam. The concrete dam has been "improved" by beaver, which probably don't trust their human counterparts to make a structure that will last. The best swimming is by the dam, but beware of leeches. Beyond the dam there is a small meadow on your right and the trail turns away from the lake on an overgrown dirt road. The Around-the-Lake Trail turns right off this road,

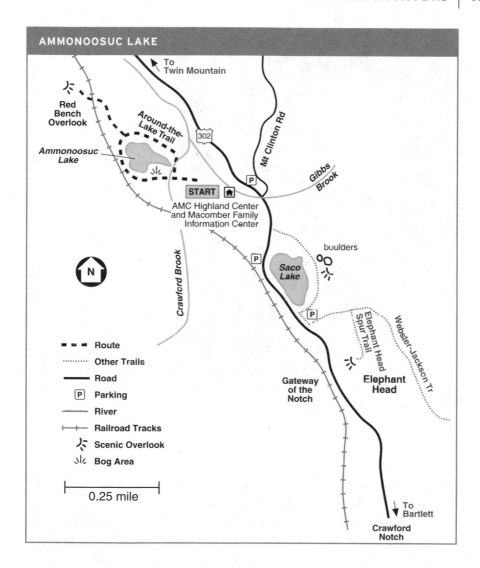

## AMMONOOSUC LAKE

To Twin Mountain

Red Bench Overlook

Around-the-Lake Trail

Mt Clinton Rd

302

Ammonoosuc Lake

Gibbs Brook

**START** 🏠
AMC Highland Center and Macomber Family Information Center

Crawford Brook

N

boulders

Saco Lake

Elephant Head Spur Trail

Webster-Jackson Tr

**Route**
**Other Trails**
**Road**
P **Parking**
**River**
**Railroad Tracks**
**Scenic Overlook**
**Bog Area**

0.25 mile

Gateway of the Notch

Elephant Head

To Bartlett

Crawford Notch

crosses Crawford Brook again, and reaches the end of the loop. Turn left to get back to your car.

## NATURE NOTES

At the start or end of your hike, take a moment to admire the view of Mount Tom (4,051 feet) and examine the field across from the Highland Center. Mount Tom in the Willey Range was named for Thomas Crawford, who managed the original Crawford House. The field provides a sunny contrast to the shaded forest. In midsummer, small, deep crimson flowers with five petals and a black

**Labrador tea grows along the shore of Ammonoosuc Lake.**

ring at the center are bound to catch your eye. These are maiden pinks, a nonnative inhabitant of roadsides and fields. Other nonnative eye-catchers are garden lupines, whose multicolored spikes of pea-like flowers put on a gorgeous display. Garden lupines have "escaped" from gardens and now grow along roadsides in the area. Chipping and field sparrows flitter across the field.

The forest near the lake is mostly red spruce, balsam fir, and paper birch. In wet areas and at the pond's edge the understory has red-berried elder, sheep laurel, northern wild raisin, leatherleaf, and Labrador tea. Much of the path around the lake is lined with snowberry, a small plant with tiny, rounded leaves attached to wiry stems that hug the ground. The leaves have a pleasant wintergreen smell when crushed. It is usually hard to find any of the snow-white berries that give this plant its name, but try your luck. Mountain wood sorrel, Canada mayflower, and clintonia grow abundantly around the lake, and you may find trillium and trailing arbutus there too.

At the turnoff to the Red Bench, look for a good patch of goldthread as well as hobblebush. Along the Red Bench Trail note how the spruce and fir give way to deciduous trees—beech, sugar maple, and yellow birch—probably because the soil is drier.

The view from the Red Bench of Mounts Washington (including the cog railway), Clay, Jefferson, and Eisenhower is worth the extra time. And it's special because you generally have it all to yourself in a small clearing in the forest.

Another plus is that the open clearing usually provides you with some relief from the blackflies and mosquitoes that can be a problem on this walk.

The best swimming is at the south end of the lake by the dam. Guests from the Crawford House would come down to Ammonoosuc Lake to swim and use a bathhouse that was located where the meadow on the shoreline presently is.

In this meadow you may find fireweed. This is a tall (generally three to six feet) wildflower with a very leafy stem and large, showy pink flowers with four petals. It is called fireweed because it is one of the first plants to colonize an area after a forest fire. Fireweed is not limited to burned-over areas—any new clearing will do, such as roadsides, ski trails, and burned and logged areas. Fireweed only lasts a few years in any site before it disappears, replaced by shrubs, trees, and other plants with longer staying power (unless the area is kept open).

The wetter parts of the meadow near the shore of the lake harbor yellow loosestrife, whose bright yellow flowers in spires one to three feet off the ground in mid- to late summer give rise to its other name, swamp candles. If you explore around the wet meadow, be careful where you step, since it's easy to trample this kind of vegetation.

When you complete this hike, stop in at the Highland Center for a snack, to use their library to look up any critters or unusual plants, or to plan your next hike.

## TRIP 22
## RIPLEY FALLS

**RATING:** Easy
**DISTANCE:** 1.0 mile round-trip
**ELEVATION CHANGE:** 300-foot elevation gain
**ESTIMATED TIME:** 1 hour
**MAPS:** AMC's *White Mountain National Forest Map and Guide*, G8/H8
AMC's *White Mountain Guide*, 27th ed., Map 3: Crawford Notch–Sandwich Range, G8–H8
**WMNF PARKING FEE:** None
**OTHER ACTIVITIES:** Wading

**Ripley Falls is one of the most impressive cascades in the White Mountains, particularly when water levels are high.**

The hike to Ripley Falls is a good one, even for younger children. There is a short steep section right at the beginning of the Ethan Pond Trail, but, when you turn off for Ripley Falls, the hike levels out and is a pleasant woodland walk. This is an easier, shorter hike than the one to Arethusa Falls. The Arethusa-Ripley Trail continues past Ripley Falls to Frankenstein Cliff and Arethusa Falls, a 3.8-mile hike with ups and downs. See Trip 27 for more details. The hike to Ripley Falls shares the same trailhead with the Ethan Pond Trail (Trip 30) and can be combined with that hike for a longer outing.

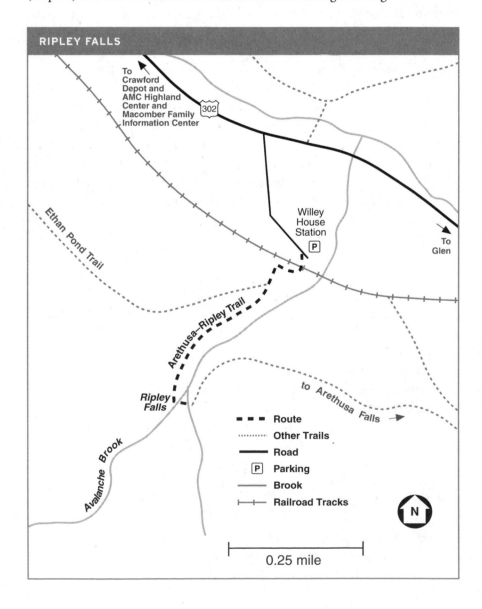

**RIPLEY FALLS**

To Crawford Depot and AMC Highland Center and Macomber Family Information Center

302

Ethan Pond Trail

Willey House Station

P

To Glen

Arethusa-Ripley Trail

Ripley Falls

to Arethusa Falls

Avalanche Brook

- - - Route
·········· Other Trails
—— Road
P Parking
—— Brook
├─┼─ Railroad Tracks

N

0.25 mile

## DIRECTIONS

The trailhead for Ripley Falls is at the site of the old Willey House Station off US 302 in Crawford Notch State Park, about 1 mile south of the Willey House Historic Site. There is a sign for Ripley Falls at the turnoff, which leads up a paved road 0.3 mile to a parking area. The turnoff is about 4 miles south of Crawford Depot and the AMC's Highland Center and 12 miles southeast of the junction of US 302 and US 3 in Twin Mountain. If you are coming up through Jackson or North Conway, the turnoff is about 16 miles northwest of the intersection of US 302 and NH 16 in Glen.

## TRAIL DESCRIPTION

The hike begins with a steep climb on the Ethan Pond Trail, a part of the Appalachian Trail and thus marked with white blazes. Cross over the Conway Scenic Railroad tracks near a trestle. Avoid the temptation to walk along

**Ripley Falls.**

the railroad tracks and on the trestle, since you never can tell when a train might be coming. After 0.2 mile the Arethusa-Ripley Trail, well marked with a sign, diverges left. You'll appreciate the turnoff, since the Ethan Pond Trail continues on steeply whereas the Arethusa-Ripley Trail is quite level.

The Arethusa-Ripley Trail was marked with both yellow and blue blazes at the time of this writing. The trail proceeds high above Avalanche Brook, perched on the side of a steep slope for much of the 0.3 mile between the Ethan Pond Trail and the falls.

When you reach the falls be careful of the slippery rocks just underneath. The ledges at the top of the falls can also be slippery.

## NATURE NOTES

Ripley Falls is 100 feet high and flows gracefully down a slab of granite. The falls are named after Henry Wheelock Ripley, who reported their existence in the 1850s. Like other waterfalls in the area, they began flowing after the continental glacier departed from the area about 12,000 years ago. The glaciers that covered New England deepened the large north–south valleys such as Crawford Notch. Valleys of tributary streams that ran east or west, such as Avalanche Brook, were not similarly gouged and so were left high above the valley floor. These are called hanging valleys by geologists. Water that had once flowed gently into the Saco River now plunged steeply to reach the river in the notch. The picturesque waterfalls that now flow into Crawford Notch from both sides are the result of these hanging valleys.

The forest you walk through is northern hardwoods. Many young sugar maples and birches are growing up along the trail. When you approach the falls, note how the cool water and shady gorge make you feel like you just walked into a refrigerator. This feeling is particularly pronounced (and welcome) on a hot day.

If you have time, climb up the left side of the waterfall and explore above the falls (but not too close to the brink). You'll get away from the crowds and also find a few pretty pools in which you can swim.

## TRIP 23
## TRESTLE TRAIL

**RATING:** Easy
**DISTANCE:** 1.0-mile loop
**ELEVATION CHANGE:** Minimal elevation change
**ESTIMATED TIME:** 45 minutes–1 hour
**MAPS:** AMC's *White Mountain National Forest Map and Guide*, F6
AMC's *White Mountain Guide*, 27th ed., Map 2: Franconia–
Pemigewasset, F6
**WMNF PARKING FEE:** Yes
**OTHER ACTIVITIES:** Wading

**An pleasant, easy hike through a spruce forest and northern hardwoods; along rushing, boulder-strewn waters of the river; and past a very large glacial erratic boulder.**

This loop trail is named for a footbridge that crosses the Zealand River at the site of a trestle of the old Zealand Valley Railroad. Along the way, you can

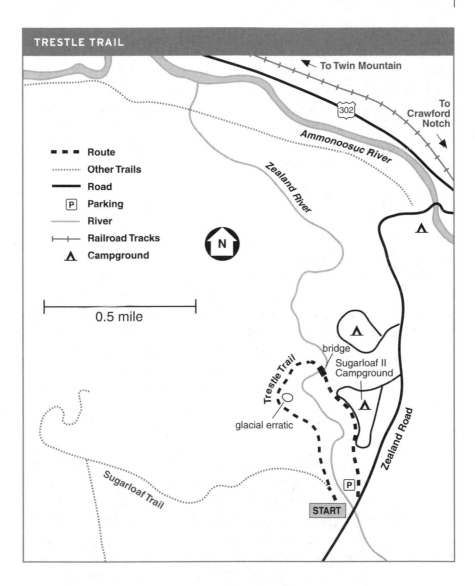

## TRESTLE TRAIL

To Twin Mountain

To Crawford Notch

Ammonoosuc River

Zealand River

**Route** ▪ ▪ ▪
**Other Trails** ⋯⋯⋯
**Road** ━━━
**P** **Parking**
**River** ───
**Railroad Tracks** ├─┼─
**⛰** **Campground**

N

0.5 mile

Trestle Trail

bridge
Sugarloaf II
Campground

glacial erratic

Zealand Road

Sugarloaf Trail

P

START

search for evidence of the old logging railroad that used to haul logs from Zealand Valley to a mill at the now extinct hamlet of Zealand.

You could easily spend a good part of the day at this pleasant spot, having a picnic lunch and wading along the river. Combine this with the Sugarloaf Trail (Trip 25) for a longer, more rigorous outing.

A trail brochure for the Trestle Trail is available from the U.S. Forest Service. You can pick it up at the Ammonoosuc Ranger Station off US 3 between Franconia and Twin Mountain. The last part of the Trestle Trail follows a road in Sugarloaf Campground with ready access to rest rooms.

## DIRECTIONS

The trailhead for the Trestle Trail is the same as that for the Sugarloaf Trail, on Zealand Road about a mile south of its junction with US 302. Pick up Zealand Road about two miles east of Twin Mountain on US 302 and about six miles west (north) of the AMC's Highland Center at the head of Crawford Notch.

Follow Zealand Road for one mile from US 302. The parking area is just before the bridge over the Zealand River. The trailhead is just after the bridge on the west (right) side of the road.

## TRAIL DESCRIPTION

The first 0.2 mile of the Trestle Trail coincides with the Sugarloaf Trail. Keep going straight along the west bank of the Zealand River when the Sugarloaf Trail turns left. After passing through a red spruce forest, the trail ascends to an attractive section where you look down through the trees at the river far below. The trail then descends, crosses over a snowmobile trail, and passes the large glacial erratic, roughly the halfway point of the trail. The trail turns right and follows the snowmobile trail, making another sharp right before reaching the bridge at the site of the old trestle (0.6 mile). Shortly after you cross over the bridge, the trail comes out at Campsite 10 of Sugarloaf II Campground. The trail continues along the campground road for 0.1 mile, then reenters the woods and comes out at Zealand Road by the parking area.

## NATURE NOTES

The Trestle Trail takes you along a very pleasant stretch of the Zealand River. The kids will particularly enjoy the area around the bridge, where they can scramble on some flat rocks along the shoreline, go wading (or swimming if they're short enough), have a picnic, and poke along the shoreline for salamanders and other aquatic life. When we were there, we ran into a family that had taken a long detour downstream along the riverbed itself.

The bridge is at the exact location of the old train trestle from the Zealand Valley Railroad. As with the other trails in the Zealand Valley area, you can usually follow the old railroad bed as it extends into the forest. See Trip 48 for more on logging railroads in this area.

At the river you will find alder, a broad-leafed shrub with rounded leaves that have toothed edges. This wetland plant has small, pineconelike structures on branches that contain the seeds. In sunny spots along the shoreline you will find bluets, little sky-blue or even whitish, four-petaled flowers with thin, straight leaves.

The immense boulder at the halfway point of the trail will certainly catch everyone's attention. This is a glacial erratic, carried from its place of origin to this spot by the glacier of the last Ice Age, about 12,000 years ago. Notice the dead birch tree hooked around the boulder, looking like it originally grew around the contours of this giant rock.

Between the turnoff to the Sugarloaf Trail and the large boulder, the forest is largely red spruce, particularly on the slopes down to the river. Red spruce is now a dominant tree at higher elevations (roughly over 2,000 feet) in the White Mountains, and its presence here at 1,600 feet may mean that it escaped the loggers who decimated much of the lower-elevation red spruce in this area. One particular giant spared the ax is on the slope just before the boulder.

Common wildflowers in the forest include wild sarsaparilla, bunchberry, and clintonia. Shrubs include blueberry, bush honeysuckle, and northern wild raisin. Look for two types of club mosses: ground pine, which looks like a miniature spreading-spruce tree; and shiny club moss, which has individual, erect stalks of small, tightly bunched, dark green sprucelike leaves. Both these club mosses form colonies that are connected by underground stems, so if you tried to pick up one you'd damage them all.

There are numerous small balsam fir trees coming up along the Trestle Trail, so the forest along the Trestle Trail may look substantially different in the future than it does today. Things never stop changing, even without the loggers.

## TRIP 24
## MOUNT WILLARD

**RATING:** Moderate

**DISTANCE:** 3.2 miles round-trip

**ELEVATION CHANGE:** 900-foot elevation gain

**ESTIMATED TIME:** 3–4 hours

**MAPS:** AMC's *White Mountain National Forest Map and Guide*, G8
AMC's *White Mountain Guide*, 27th ed., Map 2: Franconia–Pemigewasset, G8

**WMNF PARKING FEE:** None

**WINTER NOTES:** The Mount Willard Trail is an advanced (most difficult) cross-country ski trail.

**The AMC's *White Mountain Guide* reflects: "probably no other spot in the White Mountains affords so grand a view as Mount Willard for so little effort."**

The hike up this 2,815-foot spur of the Willey Range is fairly steep, and you really don't see much along the way because you are closed in by trees. But at the top of Mount Willard, looking at the incredible panorama of Crawford Notch, you may declare, as my nephew did after grumbling the whole way up, "Oh, this was really worth it!"

Take a windbreaker for the summit. On certain days the wind gets funneled through the notch and really blasts away at the open ledges. The dense cover of conifers provides some shelter near the top, but proper attire will enable you to enjoy the view in more comfort.

Attempts have been made in recent years to reintroduce peregrine falcons to the cliffs beneath the summit. Depending on the progress of nesting, the trail may be closed in late spring and early summer.

## DIRECTIONS

The trailhead for the Mount Willard Trail is located at the Gateway of Crawford Notch behind the Crawford Depot Information Center off US 302. From the Jackson–North Conway area, follow US 302 west at Glen where it splits from NH 16. US 302 passes through Bartlett, then heads north through Crawford Notch. At the top of the notch, roughly 20 miles from the junction of NH 16 and US 302, the road goes through the narrow pass between two cliffs. The parking area for Crawford Depot is a few hundred yards up the road on the left. The AMC's Highland Center is about 100 yards north of the trailhead.

From Twin Mountain, take US 302 east. Crawford Depot is on the right just beyond the turnoff for the AMC's Highland Center, about eight miles south of the junction of US 3 and US 302.

## TRAIL DESCRIPTION

The Mount Willard Trail starts out with the Avalon Trail across the railroad tracks of the old Maine Central line. (It is unsafe and illegal to walk along the tracks, since it is used by the Conway Scenic Railroad.) In 0.1 mile at a display board, the Mount Willard Trail heads left, while the Avalon Trail continues straight ahead. The Mount Willard Trail is marked with blue blazes. It goes uphill at a steady pace, nowhere terribly steep or rocky but nonetheless relentless. Where it follows the old carriage path, the Mount Willard Trail is wide enough for parents and children to walk two abreast.

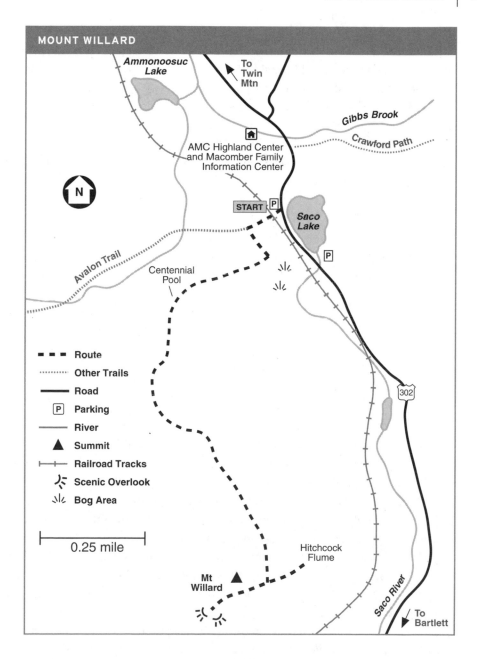

The trail crosses several streams soon after leaving the Avalon Trail. The first is on a log bridge. After 0.5 mile (fifteen to twenty minutes), Centennial Pool will be to the right. This is a small flume with a pretty "mini waterfall" about 10 to 15 feet high. There are nice lunch or snack rocks there if you want a breather. At 0.7 mile, the trail turns right and follows the old carriage path the rest of the way.

Not far from the top (1.5 miles), the spur trail to Hitchcock Flume, an impressive chasm in the side of Mount Willard, departs to the left. This is a rough, 0.2-mile detour steeply downhill with lots of roots, so avoid it if there are wet conditions, if you are not up for the extra time and effort, if you suffer vertigo, or if you have younger hikers. Allow yourself 20 to 30 minutes for this detour.

The open ledges near the summit of Mount Willard are 0.1 mile past the side trail to Hitchcock Flume. The return to Crawford Depot is a pleasant 40- to 60-minute descent.

## NATURE NOTES

The view from the ledges of Mount Willard is one of the most famous in the White Mountains. Before you is a breathtaking panorama of a deep, broad notch bounded by steep-sided mountains. Crawford Notch is one of the best examples of a glacially carved U-shaped valley anywhere in the world. Because Crawford Notch runs north and south, it was a perfect channel for the continental ice sheet that covered this area as recently as 12,000 years ago. The glacier advanced along the course of a river, scouring the sides of the mountains and gouging out rocks. What had formerly been a V-shaped valley with a river at the bottom was transformed into a U.

In preglacial times Silver and Flume cascades, which you pass on US 302 just below the Gateway of the Notch, flowed gently into the river at the bottom of Crawford Notch. By steepening the sides of the Crawford Notch, the glacier left the original valleys of the two streams hanging high above the floor of the notch. The two cascades now plunge steeply down the glacially scoured side of the notch, and their courses are aptly termed hanging valleys.

Another prominent feature of the view from Mount Willard is the impressive evidence of rock slides on Mount Webster and Mount Willey. Many landslides and avalanches have occurred in Crawford Notch. The most famous occurred in August 1826, when several days of heavy rains caused a huge slide onto the homestead of the unfortunate Willey family. The entire family was killed. Moving accounts of the tragedy are in Lucy Crawford's *History of the White Mountains* (AMC Books) and in the Reverend Benjamin G. Willey's *Incidents in the History of the White Mountains* (both available in some libraries).

The rocky ledges at Mount Willard support an interesting array of plants that can tolerate the exposure and thin soil. Three-toothed cinquefoil and moss grow very neatly in cracks in the rocks where small amounts of soil accumulate. There are also patches of meadowsweet, raspberry, bluejoint grass, sedge, and hay-scented fern.

**The view of Crawford Notch from Mount Willard.**

The view from the end of the Hitchcock Flume Spur Trail, though not as sweeping as from the ledges at the summit, is still breathtaking. Charles Hitchcock was the New Hampshire state geologist in the latter part of the nineteenth century and carried out a geological survey that did much to publicize the White Mountains and inspire hikers and vacationers to come. Hitchcock Flume is a very narrow, deep fissure in a rock. There is a sheer cliff at the bottom of this flume with a view across the notch. Since there are no railings to lean against, avoid this spot if you are uncomfortable with heights.

Near the top of the spur trail to Hitchcock Flume, you pass scattered boulders that form caves. Some of the moss-covered rocks are topped with trees.

The forest along the Mount Willard Trail changes as you ascend. You begin in northern hardwoods and paper birch with an understory of wood fern, shiny club moss, ground pine, goldthread, hobblebush, shinleaf, and mountain wood sorrel. Around the point where the trail rejoins the old carriage path, watch for a transitional forest with more and more spruce and fir. The understory includes sharp-leaved aster, large-leaved goldenrod, and Canada mayflower. Near the summit you walk through a boreal forest dominated by balsam fir, with an understory comprised largely of sphagnum, haircap, and juniper mosses.

Peregrine falcons occasionally nest in the area. These falcons catch other birds by flying high up in the sky above their target, then diving through the sky at speeds as fast as 180 miles per hour, knocking the unfortunate victim to the ground. Peregrines were wiped out in the eastern United States, largely because of DDT. This pesticide was picked up by the falcons in their food and caused the birds to lay eggs with thin, easily broken shells. Since DDT has been banned, biologists have successfully reintroduced peregrine falcons into a number of their former eastern haunts. Peregrines nest on inaccessible cliffs, such as those on Mount Willard, and will even use artificial cliffs (skyscrapers) in cities. Don't be disappointed if you find out that the trail is closed because the peregrines are nesting. Instead, feel good about this small victory for a spectacular but still threatened species and make a point of coming back to Mount Willard some other time.

## TRIP 25
## SUGARLOAF TRAIL

**RATING:** Moderate

**DISTANCE:** 3.4 miles round-trip to both peaks

**ELEVATION CHANGE:** 700-foot elevation gain to North Sugarloaf and 900-foot elevation gain to Middle Sugarloaf

**ESTIMATED TIME:** 3–4 hours

**MAPS:** AMC's *White Mountain National Forest Map and Guide*, F6 AMC's *White Mountain Guide*, 27th ed., Map 2: Franconia–Pemigewasset, F6

**WMNF PARKING FEE:** Yes

**OTHER ACTIVITIES:** Rock collecting

**You get great views from the summits of the Sugarloaves for relatively modest effort. Along the way you pass huge glacial erratic boulders, and on North Sugarloaf there is an abandoned quarry where smoky quartz used to be mined. Amateurs are still allowed to collect specimens.**

The Sugarloaf Trail ascends both North and Middle Sugarloaf (2,310 and 2,539 feet, respectively) from Zealand Road near Twin Mountain. If you only have time for one of these small mountains, the hike to North Sugarloaf takes one to one and a half hours, and the hike to Middle Sugarloaf is slightly longer.

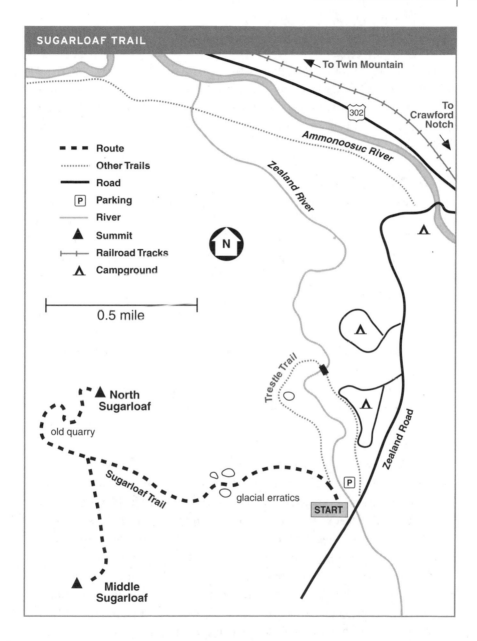

**SUGARLOAF TRAIL**

To Twin Mountain

To Crawford Notch

302

Ammonoosuc River

Zealand River

**Route**
**Other Trails**
**Road**
P **Parking**
**River**
▲ **Summit**
├┼┤ **Railroad Tracks**
⋏ **Campground**

N

0.5 mile

Trestle Trail

▲ North Sugarloaf

old quarry

Sugarloaf Trail

Zealand Road

P

glacial erratics

START

▲ Middle Sugarloaf

The U.S. Forest Service has produced a brochure that describes the Sugarloaf Trail and has a sketch that identifies the mountains visible from Middle Sugarloaf. It is available at the trailhead or at the Ammonoosuc Ranger Station (off US 3 between Franconia and Twin Mountain).

The Trestle Trail (Trip 23), an easy walk, can be a nice extension to the trip.

## DIRECTIONS

The trailhead is on Zealand Road, which branches off south from US 302 at the Zealand Campground, about 2 miles east of Twin Mountain and about 6 miles northwest of the AMC's Highland Center at the head of Crawford Notch.

Follow Zealand Road for 1 mile from US 302. Park just before the bridge over the Zealand River and look for the trailhead just past the bridge on the right.

## TRAIL DESCRIPTION

The Sugarloaf Trail coincides with the Trestle Trail for its first 0.2 mile, following the west shore of the Zealand River. It then branches to the left, while the Trestle Trail continues along the river.

The trail continues moderately steeply through a balsam fir forest and then through an area dominated by yellow and white birch. At about 0.5 mile, it passes by some large glacial erratics and at 0.9 mile reaches a T junction in the col (saddle) between North and Middle Sugarloaf. Turn left for Middle Sugarloaf (0.5 mile) or right for North Sugarloaf (0.3 mile). If you have enough time, climb both peaks and admire the different vistas. The walk from one peak to the other takes 30 to 45 minutes. Make sure in scaling North Sugarloaf that you follow the trail to the very end, since there is an open area with a vista that you could mistake for the summit just before the actual summit.

## NATURE NOTES

The first highlight is the huge boulders in the forest. These "glacial erratics" were picked up and carried southward for miles by the advancing glacier. When the ice from the glacier melted, the rocks were left behind. They are termed erratics because they are originally from somewhere else and were dumped here "erratically" by the glacier. As you wind your way around these immense boulders, even adults will feel like tiny ants.

Note the lush covering of moss, rock fern, and lichen on the boulders. One of the common lichens, rock tripe, forms flat, leathery lobes with dimples. When damp, this lichen turns greenish and even begins to resemble a living organism. It is supposedly edible, but bring along plenty of mayonnaise or mustard. Rock fern (also called Virginia polypody) is a small evergreen fern that thrives on shady cliffs and boulders. If you get a chance, examine the round dots on the underside of its fronds with a hand lens. These are reproductive structures.

The summit of Middle Sugarloaf provides a fine view of Mount Hale, North Twin Mountain, the Presidential Range (including a good view of Mount

**Looking for smoky quartz on North Sugarloaf.**

Washington), and smaller peaks nearby. Look for evidence of logging on the Rosebrook Range and North Sugarloaf. If you have binoculars, try spotting a moose in a small pond and wetland in a logged area off Zealand Road.

The granite rock under your feet is speckled with black and white minerals. The white is a feldspar and quartz and the black is hornblende and biotite mica. Because granite solidifies slowly when first formed, individual minerals such as feldspar and hornblende have time to form distinct crystals.

On the trail between the two Sugarloaves you pass a number of downed trees with their shallow root systems exposed to view. The soil is thin, since much of the trail here is on bare rock, so the trees are very susceptible to being tossed over by high winds. There are some rich areas of wildflowers, particularly on the way to Middle Sugarloaf. These include mountain wood sorrel, clintonia, red and painted trilliums, goldthread, red-berried elder, wild sarsaparilla, Solomon's seal, sharp-leaved aster, and goldenrod.

The abandoned quarry on North Sugarloaf is on your right and slightly up the slope about 0.2 mile from the T junction as you ascend. It looks like an unimpressive jumble of rocks, but kids especially will enjoy a moment to scramble up and poke around. Look for smoky quartz, a dusky-colored version of the familiar translucent rock. Beyond the quarry, you pass through a pleasant red spruce forest and an interesting rock outcropping before reaching the summit.

The summit of North Sugarloaf is about 200 feet lower than Middle Sugarloaf. The views are also fine, particularly those of the Zealand Valley, the Presidentials, and Middle Sugarloaf. Reindeer lichen abounds on this summit. This is a pale green lichen with a delicate branching structure. Lichens thrive on rocky summits with little or no soil because they have the amazing ability to revive even when completely dried out.

## TRIP 26
## SAWYER POND

**RATING:** Moderate

**DISTANCE:** 3.0 miles round-trip

**ELEVATION CHANGE:** 350-foot elevation gain

**ESTIMATED TIME:** 1.5–2 hours, but you could linger at the pond all day

**MAPS:** AMC's *White Mountain National Forest Map and Guide*, I8
AMC's *White Mountain Guide*, 27th ed., Map 3: Crawford Notch–Sandwich Range, I8

**WMNF PARKING FEE:** Yes

**WINTER NOTES:** The Sawyer Pond Trail is moderately difficult for cross-country skiing. Sawyer River Road is not plowed in winter so you need to ski in from its junction with US 302, an additional 3.8 miles.

**OTHER ACTIVITIES:** Swimming, birding, fishing, overnight camping

**Sawyer Pond is a beautiful mountain pond that is the centerpiece of the Sawyer Pond Scenic Area. The elevation gain is gradual in this well-graded trail, making it an ideal family outing replete with picnicking, swimming, and birding.**

Access is via the Sawyer Pond Trail, which runs from Sawyer River Road off Route 302 near Bartlett to the pond. Camping is possible at a shelter on the pond shore or at several tent platforms. Once there you can have a picnic, swim in the cool waters, hike through the forest to Little Sawyer Pond, stare at the impressive cliffs on Mount Tremont and Owl's Cliff, look for loons and other water birds, or simply enjoy the peaceful and remote feeling of the area.

If you are interested in a longer hike, the Sawyer Pond Trail continues

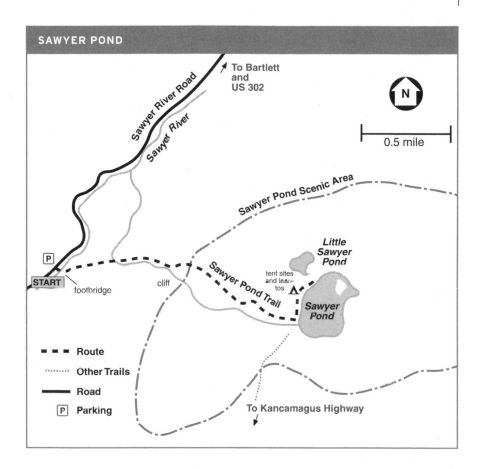

**SAWYER POND**

To Bartlett
and
US 302

Sawyer River Road

Sawyer River

N

0.5 mile

Sawyer Pond Scenic Area

Little
Sawyer
Pond

P

START

footbridge

cliff

Sawyer Pond Trail

tent sites
and lean-
tos

Sawyer
Pond

▬ ▬ ▬  Route

·········  Other Trails

▬▬▬  Road

P  Parking

To Kancamagus Highway

beyond the pond and terminates at the Kancamagus Highway, a distance of about 6 miles. This requires spotting a car at each trailhead.

## DIRECTIONS

Sawyer River Road is a well-packed dirt road that heads southwest from US 302 about 4 miles west of the intersection of US 302 and Bear Notch Road in Bartlett. The parking area for the trail is 3.8 miles down the road from US 302, just before a gate marking the end of vehicular access. Walk around the gate and pick up the trail signs.

## TRAIL DESCRIPTION

About 100 yards from the gate, the Sawyer Pond Trail heads left across a narrow footbridge over the Sawyer River, then turns left again. After several crossings of small streams on bridges, the trail joins the wide path of an old logging road and follows it to the pond. For a while the unnamed outlet brook to Sawyer

Pond runs adjacent to the trail. Near the pond, a sign indicates that you have entered the Sawyer Pond Scenic Area. When you pass a sign indicating the direction to one of the toilets at the campsite, you are almost there. Continue to the pond's outlet and then turn left, leaving the Sawyer Pond Trail. Follow the pond shore, enjoying the vistas and wildlife of the pond and perhaps selecting a spot for a picnic or swim. This trail passes tent platforms and the shelter; the latter a particularly good place to have a picnic or snack. The trail continues a short distance beyond the shelter, providing more perspectives on the pond, its surrounding mountains, and the island before it becomes totally overgrown.

For a view of Little Sawyer Pond, head uphill at the shelter, pass the toilets, and then head right along an unmarked path. The pond will soon be visible through the trees on your left. Keep going until you reach a cleared area with a more open view of the pond.

## NATURE NOTES

Sawyer and Little Sawyer Ponds are named for Benjamin Sawyer, one of the early settlers of Crawford Notch. He and Timothy Nash brought a horse through Crawford Notch in 1772, thereby establishing Crawford Notch as a route from south to north through the mountains.

Sawyer Pond is 47 acres in area, with a maximum depth of 100 feet, according to Steven Smith's *Ponds and Lakes of the White Mountains* (Backcountry Press). This is an impressive depth for a White Mountain pond, the result of

**Mount Tremont and Owl's Cliff from Sawyer Pond.**

glacial scouring. Owl's Cliff and the ledges of Mount Tremont form a striking backdrop to the east side of the pond. From a vantage point past the shelter on the northeast shore, another imposing feature, Green's Cliff, will appear to the southwest. The same point allows you to see the most unique feature of Sawyer Pond, the island off its northeast shore. Steep-sided mountain ponds in the Whites rarely have islands. When you first reach the pond shore at the outlet brook, the knoll across the way looks like part of the shoreline, but as you continue past the shelter it becomes more and more apparent that the land mass is a separate entity.

Loons may be nesting on the island, so enjoy them from a suitable distance. You may also see double-crested cormorants and black ducks. Yellow-rumped and other warblers, black-capped chickadee, and golden-crowned kinglet inhabit the dense canopy of red spruce and balsam fir in the forest surrounding the pond. Look for dragonflies along the pond shore.

Make sure the rather tame and saucy red squirrels do not make off with your snack. As permanent inhabitants of the place, they clearly believe they are entitled to a share of whatever food you are toting.

Angling for brook trout is a popular activity, and the hiking distance is sufficiently close that it is possible to carry in an inflatable raft to help in that endeavor. It is a good swimming pond too, with a sandy, gravely shoreline around a number of access points. Much of the shoreline is bordered with shrubs such as meadowsweet, sweet gale, wild raisin, leatherleaf, and mountain holly.

Little Sawyer Pond is 11 acres in area and is more secluded than Sawyer Pond. A dense layer of shrubs limits the view of the pond except at one or two locations, but it is definitely worth seeing. Trout and waterfowl also occur here.

Because of the relatively short distance from the trailhead to the pond, Sawyer Pond makes a good first-overnight, backpack destination for beginning hikers. The tent platforms and shelter are first-come, first-served, so you may want to go midweek to avoid crowds and ensure a more mellow experience.

The trail to the pond has a number of nice features. The bridges and flowing waters of the outlet brook nearby on the first half of the trail will get everyone off to a very good start. The forest is a transition between northern hardwoods and spruce-fir, so sugar maple, American beech, yellow birch, Canadian hemlock, red spruce, and balsam fir are all to be found. It is a rich forest, something that C. Francis Belcher in *Logging Railroads of the White Mountains* (AMC Books) attributes to the enlightened lumbering practices of the Saunders family who owned this region before it became part of the national forest. Unlike most loggers around the turn of the century, the Saunders did not practice clear-cutting; instead, they did selective logging. They left their legacy in the beautiful, dense forest as well as the painted trillium, Indian cucumber-root, and other wildflowers, and the verdant patches of shiny club moss.

Be sure to appreciate the incredible root formations in this boulder-strewn terrain. Look especially for one large glacial erratic on the part of the trail where it parallels the brook. Two yellow birches and a small balsam fir are perched on top, with roots that somehow snake all the way down the side of the boulder and into the ground. Nearby, some yellow birch trees appear to be on stilts, much like the mangroves in the tropics. Probably the trees first sprouted on top of a fallen "nurse" log. As the little tree matured, its roots grew around the log and down into the ground. Eventually the nurse log completely decomposed, leaving the bottom of the stem that had formerly rested on the dead log hanging in the air and connected to the ground by roots. It is a great natural history lesson of death and regeneration of the forest.

## TRIP 27
## ARETHUSA FALLS AND
## FRANKENSTEIN CLIFF

**HIKE TO ARETHUSA FALLS ONLY:**
**RATING:** Moderate
**DISTANCE:** 2.6 miles round-trip
**ELEVATION CHANGE:** 750-foot elevation gain
**ESTIMATED TIME:** 2 hours

**LOOP TO ARETHUSA FALLS AND FRANKENSTEIN CLIFF:**
**RATING:** Moderate with some steep sections
**DISTANCE:** 4.7 miles
**ELEVATION CHANGE:** 1,300-foot elevation gain
**ESTIMATED TIME:** 4–5 hours

**MAPS:** AMC's *White Mountain National Forest Map and Guide*, H8
AMC's *White Mountain Guide*, 27th ed., Map 3: Crawford Notch–
Sandwich Range, H8
**WMNF PARKING FEE:** None
**WINTER NOTES:** The section of this trail from US 302 to Arethusa Falls is appropriate for cross-country skiing. The Frankenstein Cliff section is not.

**Arethusa Falls is aptly named for a water goddess in Greek mythology. This is the tallest waterfall in New Hampshire, more than 200 feet high. The falls are an especially stunning sight early in the season, when water levels are still high, or right after a rainstorm.**

The Arethusa Falls Trail is a pleasant walk along Bemis Brook, and with only a little additional effort, several smaller waterfalls can also be visited. It is a popular family destination, so expect lots of company, but the view of the falls and the natural history of the area make it more than worth the effort.

You can make a very scenic loop by taking the Arethusa-Ripley Trail from the falls to the Frankenstein Cliff Trail. This takes you past Frankenstein Cliff, from which there are great views of Crawford Notch, and back down to the starting point. There are some steep ups and downs around Frankenstein Cliffs. In spring and early summer the trail may be closed due to nesting peregrine falcons.

Another option is to take the Arethusa-Ripley Trail from Arethusa Falls to Ripley Falls and then continue out to US 302 to the Ethan Pond Trail. This is actually a shorter distance than the loop described above but would require spotting a second car at the Ethan Pond trailhead on US 302. Hiking from this trailhead to Ripley Falls is described in Trip 22.

## DIRECTIONS
From the south take US 302 north about 8.5 miles from its intersection with Bear Notch Road in Bartlett. The turnoff on a short road to the left is well marked with a sign. From the north the turnoff for Arethusa Falls is a right turn 6 miles south of the Crawford Depot at the head of the notch off US 302. Try parking in the upper parking lot, which is closer to the trailhead. If that is filled, there is ample space at the lower lot just off US 302. A small concession stand at the trailhead, part of Crawford Notch State Park, sells refreshments and some basic hiking supplies.

## TRAIL DESCRIPTION
The Arethusa Falls Trail is marked with blue blazes and is easy to follow throughout its length. Cross the railroad tracks of the scenic railroad and head into the forest. The trail initially follows an old logging road and almost immediately passes a wildlife tree full of holes right in the middle of the trail. In 0.1 mile, the Bemis Brook Trail heads left to follow the bank of Bemis Brook closely for 0.4 mile before rejoining the Arethusa Falls Trail. This side trail takes you past two beautiful small waterfalls, Coliseum Falls and Bemis Brook

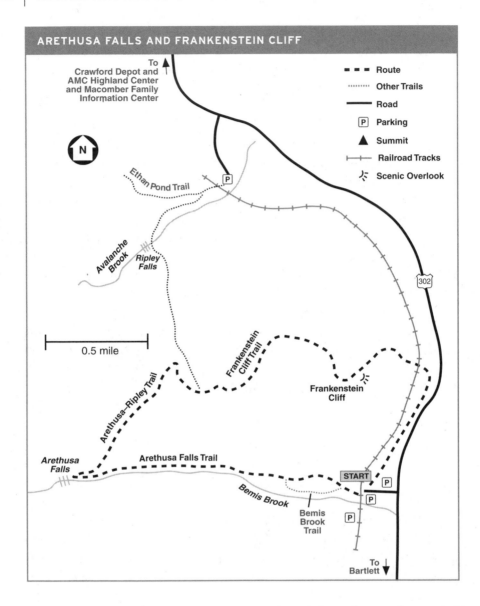

ARETHUSA FALLS AND FRANKENSTEIN CLIFF

To Crawford Depot and AMC Highland Center and Macomber Family Information Center

Route
Other Trails
Road
Parking
Summit
Railroad Tracks
Scenic Overlook

Ethan Pond Trail

Avalanche Brook

Ripley Falls

302

0.5 mile

Frankenstein Cliff Trail

Frankenstein Cliff

Arethusa-Ripley Trail

Arethusa Falls

Arethusa Falls Trail

START

Bemis Brook

Bemis Brook Trail

To Bartlett

Falls, but it is rougher and climbs very steeply with lots of exposed roots and rocks just before it rejoins the main trail. If you have the time, you should take it. In fact, families with very young hikers could end their hike at one of the small waterfalls, spend some time lounging on the flat rocks of the stream bed, and still have a very satisfying outing.

The Arethusa Falls Trail continues on the side of the valley on an old logging road high above Bemis Brook. This section of the trail has recently been relocated with the help of AmeriCorps volunteers because of concern about the safety of hikers on the slippery rocks near the falls and about erosion and trampling of vegetation. At 1.1 miles the trail intersects the Arethusa-Ripley Trail, which comes in from the right. For Arethusa Falls, continue to the left and take the spur trail for another 0.2 mile until it ends at the viewpoint near the falls.

Depending on the time of day, your energy level, and hiking inclinations, you could retrace your steps back to the parking area (1.3 miles back) or hike the loop past Frankenstein Cliff (an additional 3.4 miles). It is one hour or less back to the parking lot by the Arethusa Falls Trail and two to four-plus hours via the Frankenstein Cliff. Due to the elevation changes and switchbacks on the loop, it will take you substantially longer than a casual glance at a map might indicate.

If you opt for the loop, return to the junction of the Arethusa Falls and Arethusa-Ripley trails and follow the

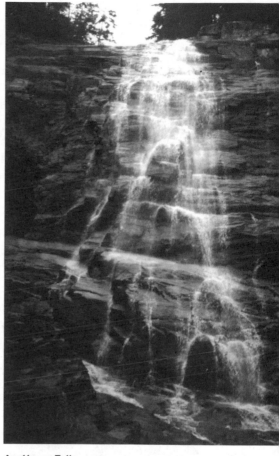

**Arethusa Falls.**

latter. The Arethusa-Ripley Trail, marked with blue blazes, heads gradually up the side of the valley. After a stream crossing, it climbs steeply for a short period, levels off along the side of a slope, with occasional nice views through the trees, and reaches the junction with the Frankenstein Cliff Trail 1.3 miles from the falls.

The Frankenstein Cliff Trail, marked with yellow blazes, ascends slightly to the height-of-land. On a clear day Mount Washington is visible in the distance from a vista just off the trail. The trail then descends through a spruce forest and reaches the outlook ledge on top of the cliffs, 2.1 miles from the falls. The drop-off is dramatic, so keep an eye on kids. From here, it is a steep descent, with steps built into the path. The trail passes a pile of boulders and an impressive cliff before leveling out. It passes under the Frankenstein Trestle of the scenic railroad and heads south through a nice stand of northern hardwoods back to the parking area. Just before reaching the upper parking lot, a short spur heads off left to the lower lot. Before you drive away, look back up to admire the cliffs and your hiking accomplishment.

## NATURE NOTES

The brook just below the falls is strewn with boulders, which preclude any kind of swimming right there. There are a number of small pools and flat rocks for picnicking and wading along the trail before you reach the falls.

Arethusa Falls, like nearby Ripley Falls and the waterfalls visible from the roadside in Crawford Notch, is the result of the last continental glacier deepening Crawford Notch and creating a hanging valley on Bemis Brook. The formation of hanging valleys is described in Trip 22. If you make it to the Frankenstein Cliff and look across the valley to the falls, try to imagine the power of the glacier that carved out the valley, leaving Bemis Brook perched high above the valley floor.

Take time to note the plants that live along the trails and near the falls. Near the trailhead, at around 1,200 feet, most of the trees are northern hardwoods (sugar maple, yellow birch, and American beech). A diversity of wildflowers and shrubs can be seen, including pink lady's slipper, painted trillium, clintonia, hobblebush, snowberry, and lowbush blueberry. At the falls, which are 750 feet higher in elevation than the trailhead, the forest includes a relatively even distribution of trees typically found in higher elevations (the boreal forest: balsam fir and red spruce) and lower elevations (the northern hardwoods).

The misty atmosphere around the falls supports many plants, including long beech and oak fern, northern bush honeysuckle, mountain ash, sharp-leaved and rough asters, mountain twisted stalk, and mountain avens. The last has broad, kidney-shaped leaves with toothed edges and yellow flowers. It is a normally an alpine species but occasionally inhabits lower elevations in the cooler atmosphere along streams (see also Trip 48). Mountain avens also occurs on the wet rocks alongside Bemis Brook Falls earlier in this hike.

Look for evidence of a landslide along the Arethusa Falls Trail about two-thirds of the way to the falls. A number of paper birch fell over as the ground along the slope of the valley slipped downward. Other birches were toppled by the ice storm of January 1998.

For those continuing on to Frankenstein Cliff: Look for a large number of pink lady's slippers on the first part of the Arethusa-Ripley Trail. A walk in late May or early June is a real treat. Other common inhabitants of the forest floor along this trail include wild sarsaparilla, partridgeberry, mountain wood sorrel, sharp-leaved aster, shiny club moss, and hay-scented fern.

As you ascend toward Frankenstein Cliff, the trees become shorter and a large number of blowdowns expose the shallow root systems of the trees. Beech and yellow birch saplings are coming up to fill the voids. There are nice views over Crawford Notch through a thin canopy of trees following the steep ascent after the second stream crossing. This part of the Arethusa-Ripley Trail is really enjoyable—not being in a tunnel of trees so typical at this elevation, but instead being visually connected to the surrounding landscape, even within a forest.

Frankenstein Cliff provides a great view of the southern part of Crawford Notch. The U-shaped valley was carved out as the last continental glacier moved south through the notch about 20,000 years ago. This is a great spot to get out the compass and a map of the region so you can identify the different peaks. From left to right are Stairs Mountain; Mount Crawford (with a distinct ledge at its summit); Mounts Hope and Chocorua; Bear Mountain; and Mounts Bartlett, Haystack, Tremont, and Bemis. Arethusa Falls is visible below the long ridge of Mount Bemis. The Saco River threads its way south in the notch, paralleling NH 302 and the railroad. On the ledge where you sit, there are some sad-looking red pines twisted by the wind and barely hanging on to life.

Take advantage of the wide vista to look for birds of prey and other wildlife. The cliff has been home to nesting peregrine falcons in recent years. These spectacular birds may linger for a time in the area after they nest.

There are a number of interesting things to see on the trail between Frankenstein Cliff and the parking lot. First is an area of jumbled boulders with small caves. Not far beyond that is an open, damp cliff face that harbors a variety of interesting plants, including joe-pye weed, several species of asters, harebell, spreading dogbane, white snakeroot, flowering raspberries (nice to look at, but the fruits are not edible), and northern-bush honeysuckle. But the extra-special botanical treat at this cliff is round-leafed sundews, growing right in water dripping down the cliff face. These small, carnivorous plants are more typically found in bogs or wet sandy areas. When you reach the bottom of the valley, Frankenstein Trestle, the highest railroad trestle in the White Mountains, appears out of nowhere.

## TRIP 28
## MOUNT CRAWFORD

**RATING:** Moderate with some challenging sections

**DISTANCE:** 5.0 miles round-trip

**ELEVATION CHANGE:** 2,100-foot elevation gain

**ESTIMATED TIME:** 5 hours

**MAPS:** AMC's *White Mountain National Forest Map and Guide*, H8
AMC's *White Mountain Guide*, 27th ed., Map 3: Crawford Notch–
Sandwich Range, H8

**WMNF PARKING FEE:** None

**OTHER ACTIVITIES:** Birding (boreal forest birds)

**The 3,119-foot summit of Mount Crawford provides one of the
most stunning vistas in the White Mountains, like being up in a
balloon enjoying an aerial view of the Presidentials, Frankenstein
Cliff, Willey Range, and Mounts Carrigain and Tripyramid.**

Mount Crawford is reached by the Davis Path, one of the oldest hiking trails
in the White Mountains. The trail was completed by Nathaniel Davis in 1845
as a bridle path to the summit of Mount Washington. Davis was a son-in-law
of Abel Crawford, the "Old Patriarch" of the Crawford family, who brought his
family to the area in the 1790s. Abel built the Mount Crawford House near the
current trailhead. Davis, who managed the Mount Crawford House, was married to Hannah, the sister of Ethan Allen Crawford. The trail fell into disuse in
the 1850s and was brought back as a footpath in 1910 by the AMC.

This is definitely a hike to save for a clear day. For much of its distance, it
is a relentless ascent within a tunnel of trees, so you want to be sure that you
see something at the top. The ledges near the summit could be slippery in wet
weather.

### DIRECTIONS

The trailhead for the Davis Path is off US 302, 6.3 miles north of where US 302
crosses Bear Notch Road in Bartlett and 5.6 miles south of the Willey House
Historical Site in Crawford Notch. There is ample parking.

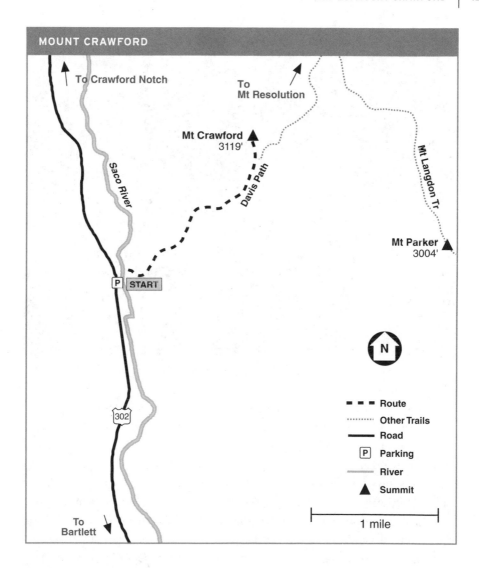

## TRAIL DESCRIPTION

Leaving the parking area, the trail follows a dirt road along the west bank of the Saco River for a few hundred yards. It turns right to cross the river on an interesting footbridge, the Bemis Bridge. Samuel Bemis was a dentist from Boston who summered in the White Mountains from 1827 through 1840, eventually retiring here. The home he built, Notchland, is now an inn and is near the trailhead.

Beyond the bridge, the trail passes through an overgrown field (private property), turns left to follow a powerline right of way for a short distance and

**Bemis Bridge over the Saco River. Mount Crawford in the back.**

then crosses a streambed that is likely to be dry by late summer. It enters the White Mountain National Forest and follows a small brook, which you may not notice since it may be dry. At about 0.5 mile, you pass a sign indicating that you are entering the Presidential Dry River Wilderness (groups limited to ten or less, no bikes, no motorized vehicles). Soon after, a side trail leads right through red pine to a back country tent site. The grade becomes moderately steep as you hook up with Davis's original path. While you are chugging up the mountain, take a moment to marvel at how Davis used a series of well-placed switchbacks to traverse this steep slope so that guests from his inn could be brought up on horseback. On numerous occasions, you think you see the top of the ridge through the trees and that your climb must imminently be over, but the trail then makes another sharp turn and somehow finds more mountain to ascend. At 1.9 miles, the trail levels off, passes through an interesting forest of 10–12 foot spruce and fir, and reaches the first vista at a ledge. At 2.2 miles, the spur trail to the summit of Mount Crawford departs to the left at the base of an open ledge. Take care to follow the blazes up the ledge, and go an additional 0.3 mile to the summit. Use caution in wet weather. Retrace your steps, being careful to follow the blazes back to the Davis Path, and back down to the parking area.

## NATURE NOTES

The summit of Mount Crawford provides a wonderful 360-degree view. This is a great place to get out your compass and trail map and identify mountains and valleys. Mount Hope is immediately to the south, and you can see the route of your ascent between this peak and Mount Crawford. Beyond that in the same direction are Bear Mountain, Attitash Mountain, Mount Tremont, and the valley of the Sawyer River. The small clear-cuts you see near Bear Mountain are in the Bartlett Experimental Forest and are being studied by the University of New Hampshire. Farther in the distance to the south is Mount Tripyramid. To the east, the most prominent features are Mount Resolution and the steps of Stairs Mountain. To the north, the southern Presidentials and Mount Washington frame the horizon. Crawford Notch and the Willey Range are to the northeast. Frankenstein Cliff is a prominent feature in that direction. Finally, Mount Carrigain looms large to the west.

The handiwork of the last glacier is evident in this wonderful scenery. It smoothed out the tops of all these peaks, so that many of them are rounded, most notably Mount Eisenhower. Glaciers also scooped out deep valleys, such as Crawford Notch below. The ledges around the summit of Mount Crawford bear parallel scratches that were etched by small stones squeezed between the moving glacier and the bedrock.

"Flag" (or "banner") trees provide evidence of the power of the wind on this exposed summit. Many of the spruce and fir on the summit have branches only on one side, the side away from the prevailing wind. Other plants adapted to growing on this exposed summit include a large number of heaths: Labrador tea, bog bilberry, black huckleberry, lowbush blueberry, mountain cranberry, leatherleaf, sheep laurel, and rhodora. Three-toothed cinquefoil, black crowberry, reindeer lichen, and poverty grass also like this location.

One special wildflower to look for on your way up is twinflower. Twinflower is a small plant that trails along the ground. Pairs of rounded leaves with slightly scalloped edges come off the wiry stem at regular intervals. In July, you can find its flowers, two small, pink tubular flowers produced on a single upright stalk, hence its name. Twinflower was a favorite flower of Carolus Linnaeus, the Swedish scientist responsible for developing the system of binomial nomenclature used by all scientists now. In Linnaeus's system, all living things have a genus and species names in Latin. Linnaeus is often pictured holding a twinflower. Look for twinflower particularly in the area where you pass the sign informing you that you are entering the Presidential Dry River Wilderness.

The level section of the trail after you attain the ridge has a spruce-fir forest that is a good spot to look for boreal forest birds. You will likely hear their calls and with a little patience you might see golden-crowned kinglet, red-breasted nuthatch, and boreal chickadee. If you are truly lucky, a spruce grouse could surprise you. This is a chickenlike bird, with dark bluish grey coloring and streaks. It can be surprisingly tame and unafraid of people (or seemingly lacking in intelligence, depending on your perspective).

## TRIP 29
## MOUNT AVALON

**RATING:** Moderate with one steep section
**DISTANCE:** 3.7 miles round-trip
**ELEVATION CHANGE:** 1,550-foot elevation gain
**ESTIMATED TIME:** 3–4 hours
**MAPS:** AMC's *White Mountain National Forest Map and Guide*, G7
AMC's *White Mountain Guide*, 27th ed., Map 3: Crawford Notch–Sandwich Range, G7
**WMNF PARKING FEE:** None

**The narrow summit of Mount Avalon provides excellent views, not only of Crawford Notch, but also of the Willey Range and the southern Presidentials, including Mount Washington. For much of its length it follows Crawford Brook, with some particularly attractive cascades.**

Two trails lead from Crawford Depot up the Willey Range to breathtaking, sweeping views of the glacially carved valley of Crawford Notch. The Mount Willard Trail (Trip 24) is the better traveled and gets you up to a vista in just over an hour; however there is little to see along the way. The Avalon Trail is longer with a greater elevation gain, but the trail is more interesting.

For a longer trip, you can make a loop by taking the Avalon Trail to the A–Z Trail, then to the Willey Range Trail and back down the Avalon Trail. This loop, a substantially longer hike then the one described below, takes you over the 4,340-foot summit of Mount Field.

### DIRECTIONS
The trailhead for the Avalon Trail is across the railroad tracks from Crawford Depot on US 302 at the head of Crawford Notch. It is the same trailhead as

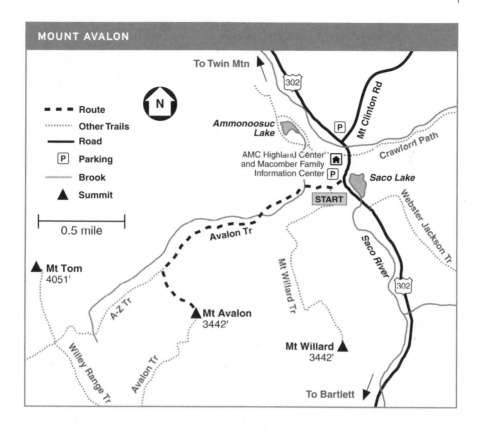

the Mount Willard Trail so check Trip 24 for driving directions. The AMC's Highland Center is about 100 yards north of the trailhead.

## TRAIL DESCRIPTION

The Avalon Trail runs together with the Mount Willard Trail for the first 0.1 mile. Continue straight where the Mount Willard Trail leaves to the left. At about 0.3 mile, the trail crosses Crawford Brook (no problem except if water levels are very high). Beyond the stream crossing, a side trail leads left along the streamside and takes you past Beecher and Pearl cascades before rejoining the main trail. The latter provides better sitting rocks for lunch or a snack. The Avalon Trail continues at an easy grade always within earshot of flowing water. The trail recrosses the brook at 0.8 mile. At 1.3 mile, the A–Z Trail comes in from the west. Follow the Avalon Trail to the left at this junction. The trail then ascends steeply over rocks for the next 0.5 mile with views through trees over a valley toward Mount Tom. The trail then levels and a spur path leads left about 100 yards to the summit of Mount Avalon. Retrace your steps to return to the trailhead. If you have time, when you rejoin the Avalon Trail after visiting the summit, continue west along the Avalon Trail for several hundred yards beyond the spur trail to an interesting flat ledge with views of Mount Avalon in one direction and the summit of Mounts Tom and Field in the other.

## NATURE NOTES

The two special features of this hike are the cascades and the view from the summit of Mount Avalon. According to John Mudge (*White Mountains: Names, Places, and Legends*, Durand Press) Beecher Cascade is named for the famous abolitionist, Henry Ward Beecher, who spent many summers in the White Mountains in the latter part of the nineteenth century, along with his sister Harriet Beecher Stowe, author of *Uncle Tom's Cabin*. Pearl Cascade is undoubtedly named for its frothy, white water. In summer, both falls are particularly attractive after a rainstorm. At the base of Pearl Cascade, note the small tributary that flows through a mossy gorge with abundant peat moss, Indian cucumber-root, and hobblebush just before it joins Crawford Brook. Mudge also states that Mount Avalon was named by Moses Sweetser because it reminded him of the Avalon Hills of Newfoundland.

Mount Avalon is at the boundary of two different watersheds. Crawford Brook drains the valley between Mounts Tom and Field and then flows north to join the Ammonoosuc River streaming down Mount Washington and eventually the Connecticut River. A drop of water flowing over Beecher and Pearl cascades enters the Atlantic Ocean at Long Island Sound. On the south side of Mount Avalon, the drainage is to the Saco River, which flows into the ocean off southern Maine. Saco Lake, visible from the Mount Avalon summit is part of the Saco drainage, and the AMC's Highland Center, across the road from that lake, sits on the height of land that separates the two watersheds.

The summit of Mount Avalon provides a wonderful view of the U-shaped glacially carved valley of Crawford Notch. This was formed by the north to south movement of the last continental glacier that advanced into the area about 100,000 years ago and melted away about 12,000 years ago. For a more detailed discussion, see Trip 24. The view also includes Mount Webster with its impressive cliffs, and all the southern Presidentials through Mount Washington. Looking west, you can see the wooded summits of the Willey Range.

The open area at the Mount Avalon summit is small, which simplifies the botany. The trees found in this limited area include balsam fir, red spruce, larch, pin cherry, and heart-leaved white birch. Shrubs include bog bilberry, lowbush blueberry, mountain ash, and mountain holly. Flowers and low "sub-shrubs" include bunchberry, mountain cranberry, clintonia, painted trillium, and snowberry. While searching for these plants, we were accompanied by

**Crawford Notch from Mount Avalon.**

golden-crowned kinglet and yellow-rumped warbler, but the birds you might run into are always hard to predict.

The flat, ledgy area along the Avalon Trail just west of the spur trail to the summit is an excellent place to see reindeer lichen. This bushy, light green lichen thrives in sunny, dry locations with little soil. Mountain cranberry, with leaves that are small, dark green, glossy, and smooth edged, is interspersed with the lichen. Mountain holly, a shrub noted for its red berries and leaves with a small point on the tip, is also common. Look for a dike where quartz intrudes into the granite along the trail there.

A recurring theme in White Mountain trails that ascend mountains is that they begin in a northern hardwood forest and end up in a boreal forest. On the Avalon Trail, this transition occurs gradually and is complete after you pass the junction with the A–Z Trail. Sugar maple, American beech, and yellow birch dominate the canopy at the beginning of the walk with hobblebush and striped maple in the shrub layer. Common plants of the forest floor include wild sarsaparilla, clintonia, snowberry, sharp-leaved aster, New York fern, cinnamon fern, and intermediate wood fern. The large number of paper birch throughout this hike suggest that the area was disturbed, perhaps by fire or logging in the early part of the twentieth century.

## TRIP 30
## ETHAN POND

**RATING:** Moderate with one steep section
**DISTANCE:** 5.4 miles round-trip
**ELEVATION CHANGE:** 1,550-foot elevation gain
**ESTIMATED TIME:** 4 hours
**MAPS:** AMC's *White Mountain National Forest Map and Guide*, H7/8
AMC's *White Mountain Guide*, 27th ed., Map 3: Crawford Notch–
Sandwich Range, G/H8
**WMNF PARKING FEE:** None

**Hike to remote Ethan Pond bordered on one side by steep cliffs of Mount Willey and on the other by a vista across to the Twin Range.**

The pond is named for Ethan Allen Crawford, who camped there during one of his hunting trips in fall 1829. As recounted in Lucy Crawford's *History of the White Mountains*, Crawford states, "For beauty and grandeur it is nowhere surpassed by any spot to me known about these mountains." The hike has a short steep section at the beginning, but after that is a moderate, pleasant walk.

The hike to Ethan Pond can easily be combined with the hike to Ripley Falls (Trip 22) if you have more time. This would make for a great pond-waterfall combination.

### DIRECTIONS
The trailhead for the Ethan Pond Trail is the same as that for Ripley Falls (Trip 22). It is at the site of the old Willey House Station off US 302 in Crawford Notch State Park, about 1 mile south of the Willey House. There is a sign for Ripley Falls and the Appalachian Trail at the turnoff, which leads up a paved

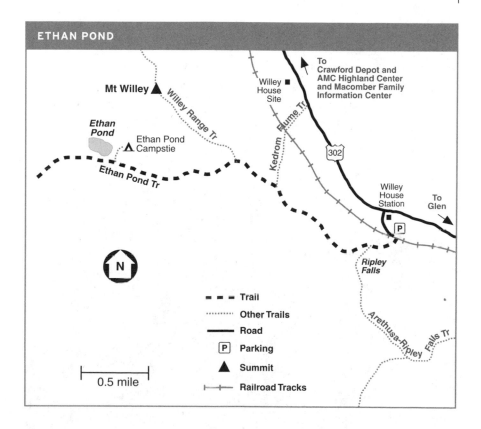

road 0.3 mile to a parking area. If that lot is filled, you need to park off US 302. The turnoff is about 4 miles south of Crawford Depot and the AMC's Highland Center and 12 miles southeast of the junction of US 302 and US 3 in Twin Mountain. If you are coming up through Jackson or North Conway, the turnoff is about 16 miles northwest of the intersection of US 302 and NH 16 in Glen.

## TRAIL DESCRIPTION

The Ethan Pond Trail is part of the Appalachian Trail and is marked with white blazes. It almost immediately crosses the tracks of the Conway Scenic Railroad and ascends steeply uphill. In 0.2 mile, the Ripley Falls Trail leads left and the Ethan Pond Trail continues steeply ahead. In about 0.5 mile, the trail levels off and becomes a very pleasant walk, varying between a gradual ascent and level. The Kedron Flume Trail enters from the right at 1.3 miles. This trail leads past the Kedron Flume (Natural Attractions and Nature Walks 3) to the Willey House Historic Site, but the section between the Ethan Pond Trail and the flume is steep and rough. At 1.6 mile (about 1 hour), the Willey Range Trail intersects at a point where the Ethan Pond Trail turns left. The Ethan Pond Trail climbs gradually for about 0.3 mile beyond that and then passes through a beautiful, level area of boreal forest with lots of small streams, wetlands, and bog bridges. You occasionally get views of Mount Willey through the trees. The trail crosses the height of land (ca. 2,900 feet) that represents the boundary be-

**The outlet of Ethan Pond with Mount Willey.**

tween the Saco River and Pemigewassett/Merrimack River watersheds. At 2.6 miles, the short spur trail that leads in 0.1 mile to Ethan Pond and the Ethan Pond Campsite comes in from the right. This crosses the inlet where you get the best view of the pond and the cliff of Mount Willey. The shelter at the campsite is a good place to have lunch or a snack, but it does not have a view of the pond. Retrace your steps to return.

## NATURE NOTES

When you arrive at the pond, take some time to sit on one of the rocks by the inlet and contemplate the surroundings. You can see why this 4-acre pond was so favored by the legendary woodsman, guide, and innkeeper, Ethan Allen Crawford. He appreciated its beauty and its abundance of fish and wildlife. In Lucy Crawford's *History of the White Mountains*, Crawford reports one fishing trip in which the party he guided caught about 70 "salmon trout" (native brook trout) in a very short time and broiled them over a fire on the banks of the pond. He saw ample signs of moose that fed on the waterlilies. Another story, cited in John Mudge's *The White Mountains: Names, Places, and Legends*, describes a hunting trip where Crawford's group shot two moose at the pond and feasted on moose and trout. They eventually went to sleep within the skins of the moose, paying no attention to the howling of wolves nearby.

On the opposite shore of the pond, the outlet drains into the East Branch of the Pemigewassett River. This flows through one of the largest wilderness areas in the White Mountains. In the same direction on a clear day, you can see North and South Twin mountains. Behind you the cliffs of Mount Willey loom above the campsite, and you may hear the hoarse cawing and croaking of ravens, which roost and possibly nest on the cliff. Peregrines periodically take up residence on the cliffs.

The area is covered with vegetation typical of the boreal forest. Immediately along the shoreline, look for larch, Labrador tea, mountain holly, shadbush, alder, and sweet gale. The leaves of the latter give off the pleasant odor of bayberry when crushed. Black spruce grows along the spur trail leading to the pond. This small tree has short, bluish green needles and is characteristic of northern bogs. The upland forest surrounding the pond is characterized by red spruce and balsam fir.

The forest along the trail is particularly beautiful where the trail is level around the height of land within about 0.7 mile of the pond. Look for dense growth of both green and red peat (sphagnum) mosses along the wetter sections traversed by bog bridges. These two colors actually represent separate species. Peat mosses have an amazing ability to absorb and retain water due to large vacuoles (spaces) in their cells. This is why they are so useful in gardens. There are several dense stands of long-haired sedge in these wetlands too. Other plants include clintonia, goldthread, bunchberry, snowberry, sheep laurel, northern wild raisin, and sharp-leaved and purple-stemmed asters.

The deciduous forest at the beginning of the trail features yellow birch, a few larger sugar maples, many sugar maple saplings, and an understory of striped maple and hobblebush. The shade tolerant sugar maple saplings await the opportunity afforded by the creation of a gap in the canopy to eventually take their place in the forest canopy. Gaps are created when canopy trees fall over due to wind, disease, or insects. Note a particularly distinctive uprooted paper birch along the trail about 0.5 mile from the trailhead. Its shallow root system, which led to its demise, illustrates how rocky the soil is on these slopes. The transition between the deciduous and boreal forest is complete after you pass the Willey Range Trail intersection.

# 5

# PINKHAM NOTCH

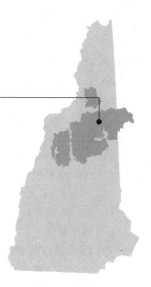

## LAY OF THE LAND

The Pinkham Notch/Gorham region includes the loftiest peaks of the White Mountains. Mount Washington at 6,288 feet is the highest mountain in the Northeast, and five other summits surpass 5,000 feet. In addition to their elevation, the peaks of the Presidential Range are noted for their vast, bowl-shaped ravines. The less-crowded Carter Range, across Pinkham Notch from the Presidentials, rises above 4,500 feet. The entire region is a magnet for hikers attracted by the high elevation, rugged scenery, and broad expanse of alpine terrain with extensive vistas and unique ecological characteristics. A number of trails to ponds, waterfalls, and viewpoints are perfect for day hikers. These are centered around the Appalachian Mountain Club's Pinkham Notch Visitor Center (PNVC) and the town of Gorham. NH 16 passes right through Pinkham Notch between Jackson and Gorham, and provides access to many of the trails described here. Other trails are reached from US 2 west of Gorham.

## PINKHAM NOTCH VISITOR CENTER

The Appalachian Mountain Club's Pinkham Notch Visitor Center is the hub of hiking activities and natural history education in the White Mountains. The Trading Post houses an information center, a store, and a dining room. The Joe Dodge Lodge is a guesthouse with private rooms, bunk rooms, a library, and meeting rooms. Breakfast and dinner are served to overnight guests and are available to others (staff need to know in advance if you want to eat there). In the evenings, and sometimes during the day, you can hear naturalist lectures and participate in other types of programs. PNVC is a great place to get current information on trails and the weather, and to buy hiking guides, nature books, T-shirts, and other supplies. The visitor center also has rest rooms and showers open to the public.

While at the visitor center, do not miss the scale model of the Presidential Range along with displays on mountain geology and ecology. These give a real perspective of the area.

In addition to the hiking trails described below, the Pinkham Notch Visitor Center is also the jump-off point for a network of cross-country ski trails of a variety of skill levels. Check in at the visitor center for a map.

## LOGISTICS AND SUPPLIES

The Wildcat Mountain Ski Area, about 1 mile north, has all the amenities you might expect in a ski resort: a restaurant, snack bar, rest rooms, coffee machines, and gift shop.

If you are coming from the north on NH 16, Gorham has ample restaurants, inns, motels, stores, and gas stations. From the south, Jackson is the nearest town for supplies.

The Androscoggin Ranger Station of the U.S. Forest Service is located on NH 16 just south of US 2 in Gorham. Stop in for information, trail pamphlets, or to use the rest rooms.

## NEARBY CAMPING

The U.S. Forest Service's Dolly Copp Campground is at the junction of NH 16 and Pinkham B Road between Gorham and Pinkham Notch. With its 176 campsites, Dolly Copp is the largest public campground in the White Mountains. Large groups can camp at Barnes Field Group Area adjacent to the Dolly Copp Campground.

## TRIP 31
## LOST POND

**RATING:** Easy

**DISTANCE:** 1.0-mile round-trip to the pond

**ELEVATION CHANGE:** Minimal elevation change

**ESTIMATED TIME:** 1 hour

**MAPS:** AMC's *White Mountain National Forest Map and Guide*, F10

AMC's *White Mountain Guide*, 27th ed., Map 1: Presidential Range, F9

**WMNF PARKING FEE:** None

**WINTER NOTES:** This short trail is suitable for skiing and links to other ski trails.

**This short hike follows the Ellis River through a rich forest and ends up at Lost Pond. Large rocks provide great perches for enjoying the view across to Huntington Ravine and Mount Washington.**

This pond is not far off NH 16 as the crow flies, yet it still feels remote and delightfully lost. A wooden plank bridge over the river at the beginning of the walk, and several others along the way, add to the appeal of this hike. Beyond the pond there is a dramatic area of boulders.

You can combine the hike with a visit to Pinkham Notch Visitor Center (PNVC) or extend the hike to Glen Ellis Falls (Natural Attractions and Nature Walks 2) and then return via the Glen Boulder and Direttissima trails.

You see much evidence of beaver along the way and may even catch a glimpse of them if you are on the trail at dawn or dusk.

## DIRECTIONS

The trailhead for the Lost Pond Trail is across NH 16 from AMC's Pinkham Notch Visitor Center. To get to PNVC from the south, follow NH 16 north through North Conway, Glen, and Jackson. The visitor center is on the left, about 10 miles north of Jackson and 0.7 mile past the turnoff to Glen Ellis Falls. To get to Pinkham Notch from the north, pick up NH 16 in Gorham and go about 10 miles south. The visitor center is on the right, about a mile past the Wildcat Mountain Ski Area. Park at the large parking area for PNVC and walk across NH 16 to the trailhead. This is also the trailhead for the Square Ledge Trail (Trip 34).

**LOST POND**

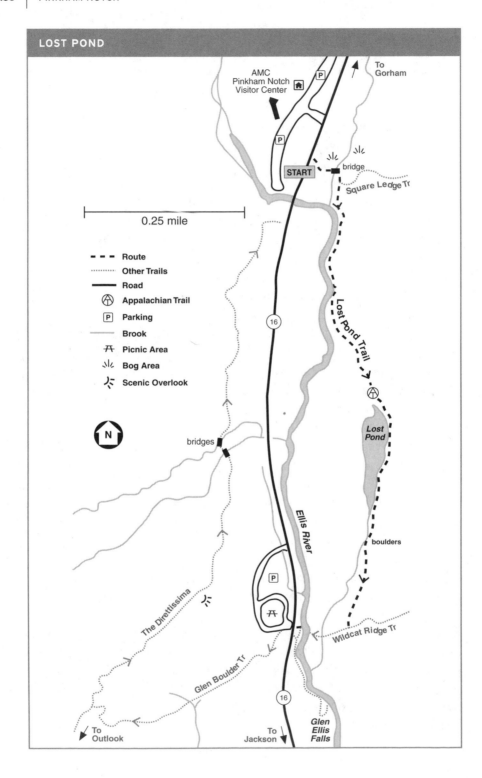

## TRAIL DESCRIPTION

The Lost Pond Trail, together with the Square Ledge Trail, begins in a swampy area across from the PNVC and crosses the Ellis River on a wooden bridge. Both trails turn right after the bridge, but the Square Ledge Trail immediately turns left and starts to ascend. The Lost Pond Trail, which is part of the Appalachian Trail, continues straight ahead, along the east side of the river. The trail to the pond is wide with little ups and downs, and a few rocks, but nothing major. After about 0.3 mile, it angles away from the Ellis River and crosses a tributary over another wooden bridge. At the north end of the pond (0.5 mile), the trail becomes rockier, traversing the east shore of the pond. The section between the south end of the lake and the Wildcat Ridge Trail passes through a riot of boulders. The trail ends at the Wildcat Ridge Trail (0.9 mile).

From here you can retrace your steps or, if you are feeling adventurous, turn right on the Wildcat Ridge Trail and cross over the Ellis River to reach NH 16. Since there is no bridge, it requires careful stepping from rock to rock, a potentially precarious undertaking at high water. If it is passable, you can then walk back to your car along NH 16 or walk over to Glen Ellis Falls and complete the loop mentioned above.

## NATURE NOTES

At the beginning of this trail, there is a swamp at the height of land of Pinkham Notch. Water drains from this swamp both north to the Peabody River and south to the Ellis. You may notice two "speckly" shrubs here. Speckled alder is named for its speckled bark, which looks like it has the chickenpox. The leaves of sweet gale, which grows right next to the wooden bridge, are covered with tiny yellow speckles. Crush a sweet gale leaf in your fingers to get a strong, sweet smell that will remind you of bayberry. White turtlehead flowers bloom in the swamp in August.

**Berries of painted trillium are present through much of the summer.** Photo by Nancy Schalch.

From the first wooden bridge, a beaver dam is obvious to your left. The dam is composed of tree branches stripped of bark and compacted mud. The beaver eat the bark, then use the rest of the branches as lumber for the dam. Beaver build dams to create ponds so they can swim to their supper and have a place for their lodges safe from predators. By flooding the surrounding woodlands, they can enter their lodges underwater and paddle to their major foods, the nutritious inner bark of trees, grasses, and other vegetation.

Small, graceful birds you are likely to see zooming over the swamp are swallows. Barn swallows have distinctive long, forked tails and are bluish black on the back with reddish throats and buff-colored bellies. As the name implies, they sometimes nest in barns and under the eaves of buildings (such as the maintenance building at Pinkham Notch). Tree swallows also have blue-black backs but differ from barn swallows in having notched tails and in being completely white underneath. They sometimes use nest boxes. These aerial acrobats catch insects on the wing.

The Lost Pond Trail follows the Ellis River initially through a forest of balsam fir and birch and eventually through northern hardwoods with a hobblebush understory. The flow of the Ellis is greatly increased by the addition of the Cutler River flowing down from Tuckerman Ravine. Note how clear the water is in a beautiful, deep pool in the river you walk by. If you stand quietly by this pool for a minute or two, you may catch a glimpse of brook trout. Water striders may also be present.

In June, look for blooms of Canada mayflower, clintonia, false Solomon's seal, painted trillium, and pink lady's slipper. In damp spots along the trail, wild white violet and inflated sedge abound. Normally sedges are fairly nondescript, but inflated sedge has amusing, inflated bladders in clusters around each of its seeds.

In midsummer, mountain wood sorrel blooms in profusion here. The three leaves of this small plant will remind you of clover, but it is not related. Other midsummer bloomers are goldenrod and tall meadow rue.

There are several beaver houses at Lost Pond. At dusk you stand a chance of seeing the beaver themselves cavorting about. Look for another dam at the outlet of the pond.

Along the shore of Lost Pond there is one particularly large flat rock that will compel you to sit and quietly enjoy the peaceful scenery, perhaps with a picnic lunch. The view of Mount Washington is impressive—Huntington Ravine stands out, and you can also see Boott Spur, the Lion Head, and the Gulf of Slides from various vantage points.

Look for two different types of water plants: waterlily and bur reed. The leaves of waterlily float right on the surface of the water and provide the underwater parts of the plant with air through a system of gas channels. Bur reed is a great duck food with grassy, straplike leaves. Water striders skim across the surface of the pond, and dragonflies patrol the shoreline, looking for unwary insects.

As you make your way around the pond, you may observe water stains on the rocks and the trunks of trees at the shore. These indicate how high the water levels rose during the past spring. There is also a good display of bunchberry, a small relative of dogwood that produces creamy white dogwood-like flowers in the latter part of June and clusters of red berries during the summer. At one point, you may notice a tree that seemingly grows right out of a rock. Its trunk and roots form a little cave. Note also a wildlife tree laced with woodpecker holes.

If you venture beyond the pond, you will pass through an impressive boulder field. These rocks were deposited by an avalanche off Wildcat Mountain many years ago and make a fitting contrast to the peaceful pond.

## TRIP 32
## WATERFALL LOOP

**RATING:** Easy (Fallsway) or moderate (Brookbank)
**DISTANCE:** 1.5 miles round-trip
**ELEVATION CHANGE:** 400-foot elevation gain
**ESTIMATED TIME:** 1–2 hours
**MAPS:** AMC's *White Mountain National Forest Map and Guide*, E9
AMC's *White Mountain Guide*, 27th ed., Map 1: Presidential Range, E9
**WMNF PARKING FEE:** None
**OTHER ACTIVITIES:** Wading

**Pretty waterfalls and many flat rocks along the trail and brook invite you to have a picnic, get your feet wet, and relax while listening to the sounds of rushing water.**

This loop in the northern Presidentials runs along picturesque Snyder Brook through the deep, cool hemlock forests of the Snyder Brook Scenic Area. The route we recommend should take one to two hours. A shorter, easier loop is possible by returning on the Valley Way, or you can simply retrace your steps after taking in a waterfall or two. A network of connecting trails leads to other waterfalls and vistas for a more extended journey.

## DIRECTIONS

The Fallsway leaves from the Appalachia parking lot off US 2 about 5 miles west of the point where NH 16 splits off to the north from US 2 in Gorham and

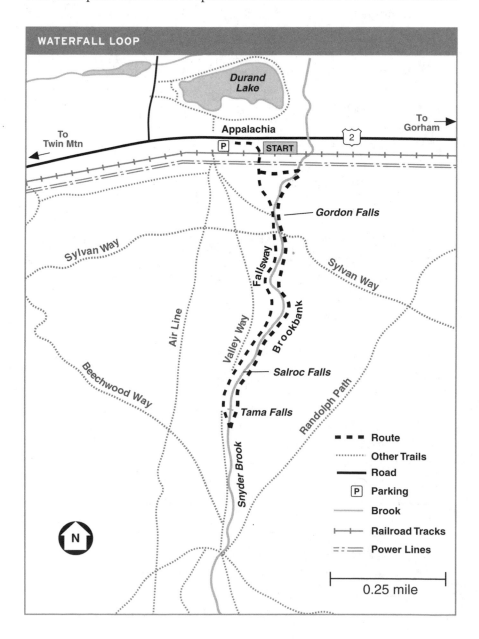

WATERFALL LOOP

Durand Lake

To Twin Mtn

Appalachia

To Gorham

2

START

Gordon Falls

Sylvan Way

Fallsway

Sylvan Way

Air Line

Valley Way

Brookbank

Beechwood Way

Salroc Falls

Tama Falls

Randolph Path

Snyder Brook

| | |
|---|---|
| ▬ ▬ ▬ | Route |
| ·········· | Other Trails |
| ▬▬▬ | Road |
| P | Parking |
| ▬▬ | Brook |
| ⊢⊢⊢ | Railroad Tracks |
| = = = | Power Lines |

N

0.25 mile

about 0.8 mile west of Pinkham B Road (Dolly Copp Road). If you are coming from the west through the Twin Mountain area, the trailhead is about 7 miles east of the junction of US 2 and NH 115. The parking lot is on the south side of US 2.

The parking area is well marked and large, since it is the trailhead for a number of trails into the northern Presidentials. The Fallsway leaves from the east side of the parking lot and is also well marked.

## TRAIL DESCRIPTION
The first part of this loop, the Fallsway, is a wide, easy uphill path through a relatively open woods along running water. It is marked with yellow blazes. The Brookbank is a little rougher and less well traveled, but shouldn't be much of a problem.

The Fallsway starts through a short section of woods before crossing an open area with power lines and an overgrown railroad track. The trail then re-enters the forest of sugar maple and hobblebush, meets up with Snyder Brook, follows the west bank of the brook, then passes by Gordon Falls. This part of the White Mountains is laced with many short trails and trail junctions, but they are all well marked. Just keep following the signs for the Fallsway. After passing Lower and Upper Salroc falls, the Fallsway joins the Valley Way for a short stretch (for a shorter loop, you can return to the parking lot on the Valley Way). At the sign for Fallsway Loop, turn left and walk 0.1 mile to Tama Falls, the final destination of this hike, 0.7 mile from the parking lot.

At Tama Falls, pick up the Brookbank for the rest of the loop (0.8 mile back to the parking lot), cross over Snyder Brook on some flat rocks (no problem except in extremely high water), and start your descent. The Brookbank Trail follows the east bank of Snyder Brook, providing good access to the brook at a number of locations and a different perspective of the same waterfalls you saw on the way up. The trail has one short, rocky section that may be slick in wet weather or high water. Eventually it crosses back over Snyder Brook at the point where the trail reaches the open area (may be difficult at high water). Walk back along the power lines to the Fallsway Trail and then to the parking lot.

## NATURE NOTES
The waterfalls are the major attraction. At Gordon Falls the amazing erosive power of rushing water is apparent in the channels and shoots in solid rock. Mosses and ferns thrive in the mist along the sides of the waterfalls.

Lower and Upper Salroc falls also have interesting geological features. An impressive deep plunge pool has been carved out of the streambed by Lower

**Bunchberry is a common flower along most trails.**

Salroc Falls. This pool will be over the head of even adults, at least early in the season. Dikes of basalt and pegmatite are visible in the streambed. The pegmatite appears as whitish stripes of large crystals within the granite rocks of the area; the basalt dikes are black and finely grained. The dikes were formed when molten lava from deep within the earth flowed up into cracks in the granite and then hardened. If it cooled slowly, then large crystals had time to form and pegmatite was the result. A basalt dike occurred when the lava cooled rapidly, near the surface of the earth. There is also an extensive flat rock, great for a picnic if it is not underwater.

Tama Falls is the largest of the group and arguably the most attractive. A graceful veil of water flows down a natural granite staircase.

Hemlocks dominate along the banks of the stream because they favor the cool, shady, damp atmosphere. Away from the water in drier, warmer habitat, northern hardwoods, particularly sugar maple and yellow birch, thrive. From just about any White Mountain viewpoint, dark lines of hemlock reveal the courses of streams. Along the Fallsway and Brookbank trails, you experience this dynamic more intimately.

Mosses abound in the cool woods along the Brookbank Trail and the damp rocks around the waterfalls. One of the most intriguing is named piggyback moss, because new moss "plantlets" grow right out of the "backs" of older shoots. Look for one nice patch of piggyback moss (also called fern moss) just below Tama Falls on the Brookbank Trail, near where a yellow birch is growing right out of a big boulder. Patches of sphagnum moss also occur.

You may observe the difference in the understory between the well-traveled Fallsway Trail and the less well-trod Brookbank. The Fallsway is largely barren of undergrowth, which has succumbed beneath the feet of too many trampling hikers wandering off the trail for views of the brook. In contrast, the Brookbank is characterized by lush growth of mosses, ferns, and small herbs because far fewer people use it. It is a great illustration of why everyone should stay on trails.

## TRIP 33
## THOMPSON FALLS

**RATING:** Easy

**DISTANCE:** 1.4 miles round-trip

**ELEVATION CHANGE:** 200-foot elevation gain

**ESTIMATED TIME:** 1–2 hours

**MAPS:** AMC's *White Mountain National Forest Map and Guide*, F10

AMC's *White Mountain Guide*, 27th ed., Map 1: Presidential Range, F10

**WMNF PARKING FEE:** None

**OTHER ACTIVITIES:** Wading

**A short, easy hike to a lovely waterfall and cascades near the Wildcat Mountain Ski Area.**

The first part of the trail follows the route of a nature trail, the Way of the Wildcat, along the Peabody River. This is a great place to throw leaves into the water and watch them slowly make their way downstream to the ocean (well, maybe not quite that far). You may enjoy dabbing your toes in the water and picnicking on the large flat rocks in the stream bed when the water is low.

Above the falls Thompson Brook has a fascinating series of cascades, riffles, and pools. There are nice views of Mount Washington framed by the trees along the sides of the brook and lots of wildflowers in spring.

The Wildcat Mountain Visitor Center is open year-round and provides various amenities before or after your walk.

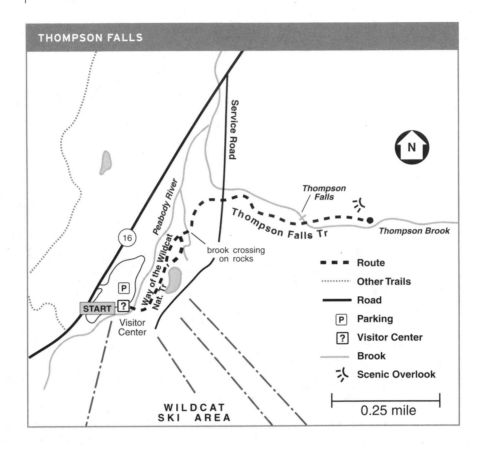

**THOMPSON FALLS**

Service Road

Peabody River

Thompson
Falls

16

Thompson Falls Tr

Thompson Brook

brook crossing
on rocks

Way of the Wildcat Nat. Tr

P

START

?

Visitor
Center

WILDCAT
SKI AREA

N

- - - Route

.......... Other Trails

—— Road

P Parking

? Visitor Center

—— Brook

Scenic Overlook

0.25 mile

## DIRECTIONS

The trail is within the Wildcat Mountain Ski Area roughly halfway between Gorham and Jackson off NH 16. Park in the ski area parking lot on the east side of NH 16, about 1 mile north of the AMC's Pinkham Notch Visitor Center. Walk past the information and ticket booths, cross a bridge, and follow signs pointing left to the Way of the Wildcat Nature Trail. The nature trail leads to the Thompson Falls Trail.

## TRAIL DESCRIPTION

The first part of this hike, where it follows the Way of the Wildcat Nature Trail, is an easy, wide, leisurely stroll with sixteen numbered stops. A free pamphlet describing each of these stops is available in the Wildcat Mountain Visitor Center. After about a ten-minute walk, the Thompson Falls Trail, marked with yellow blazes, leaves the nature trail at the farthest point in the loop. The trail crosses a small stream on stones (may be difficult early in the season due to high water) and then crosses a service road.

The next section is still easy, with only a moderate gradient to Thompson Falls. The distance from the nature trail to the falls is about 0.2 mile. Since the trail steepens after the falls, those with very young children may want to turn around at this point.

After you pass the first waterfall, you need to do some moderate scrambling up rocks and then cross a stream (may be difficult in high water). The trail then levels out and provides views of Mount Washington. It follows the bank of the brook where beautiful cascades continue until the trail dead-ends about 0.2 mile above Thompson Falls.

When returning, take the right fork of the Way of the Wildcat loop to see the Peabody River.

## NATURE NOTES

The main feature of the Thompson Falls Trail is the wonderful series of waterfalls and cascades described above. Thompson Falls are named

**White and pink forms of the pink lady's slipper.**

for Colonel J. M. Thompson, the owner of the first Glen House, which was located at the base of the Mount Washington Auto Road. You will enjoy the graceful stream of water flowing over the falls, but the pool beneath the falls is a little shady for swimming—the smaller potholes and pools above the falls in Thompson Brook are a better bet.

The view of the east side of Mount Washington is especially attractive in fall, when the trees along the brook form a colorful frame.

The walk, particularly above the first waterfall, goes through a good example of a boreal forest. The boreal forest floor receives very limited light because of the dense, year-round canopy of conifers. Nonetheless, one small plant that thrives in the understory and is abundant along the Thompson Falls Trail is goldthread. This relative of the buttercup has three small leaflets that are roundish with scalloped edges. Delicate white flowers, one per stem with five to seven petals, appear in May at lower elevations. A golden underground stem, technically a rhizome, connects different individuals, in the same way that individual strawberry plants are connected by runners. In early days goldthread was used medicinally to combat a variety of ailments, such as toothache.

The pink lady's slipper is another distinctive plant of the forest floor that you'll find along the Thompson Falls Trail. This orchid occurs below 4,000 feet, particularly in deciduous woodlands, but it is nowhere abundant. It flowers in June; hence, visitors to Thompson Falls have a better chance of catching it in bloom than the earlier spring wildflowers such as goldthread.

The pink lady's slipper is one of the showiest wildflowers in the White Mountains and is bound to make even the most driven hiker stop for a minute. A typical pink lady's slipper has a pair of large, smooth, almost round, glossy leaves that hug the ground, and a single flowering stalk. The flower has a distinctive pink veiny pouch that resembles a shoe (more like a heavy clog than a slipper). The flower also contains three thin, greenish sepals. Another name for it is moccasin flower (whoever named it had footwear in mind). Many of the pink lady's slippers (as many as one in four) in the White Mountains are not pink at all but are white. Why this region should be blessed with so many white ones (they do occur elsewhere but much more rarely) is a mystery.

The lady's slipper is a type of orchid, a large family of mostly tropical plants that are much sought after by horticulturists and florists for their beautiful, distinctive flowers. Many orchids, including the pink lady's slipper, have been dug up by collectors or others who selfishly want to savor their beauty for themselves or to sell them to unwary gardeners. This is futile for both the grower and the plant. Pink lady's slippers are very difficult to grow in "captivity," because they have special growing requirements. Their roots, which are easily damaged upon transplanting, require a special partnership with a fungus in order to take up nutrients from the soil. Tissue culture techniques are now being developed to propagate orchids, so no one needs to destroy wild plants to have them around the house. Enjoy pink lady's slippers in the woods and leave them for the next people who pass this way.

## TRIP 34
## SQUARE LEDGE

**RATING:** Moderate with a short, steep section
**DISTANCE:** 1.0 mile round-trip
**ELEVATION CHANGE:** 500-foot ascent
**ESTIMATED TIME:** 1–2 hours
**MAPS:** AMC's *White Mountain National Forest Map and Guide*, F10
AMC's *White Mountain Guide*, 27th ed., Map 1: Presidential Range, F10
**WMNF PARKING FEE:** None

**A short trail to an overlook that has a great open view of Pinkham Notch and Mount Washington. Hangover Rock, which "hangs over" the trail, is interesting enough on its own to be worth the hike.**

This could be a great first experience for youngsters on a steep trail. They'll feel like real hikers when they reach the beautiful view.

## DIRECTIONS
The trail begins right across the road from Pinkham Notch Visitor Center (PNVC), at the same trailhead as the Lost Pond Trail. See Trip 31 for directions.

## TRAIL DESCRIPTION
The trail runs together with the Lost Pond Trail for a short distance from NH 16. After crossing a wooden bridge, the two trails make a sharp right turn, after which the Square Ledge Trail makes an immediate left uphill. The trail is initially wide with a gradual uphill. Stop at Ladies Lookout (short spur trail to the left) at 0.1 mile for a view of Pinkham Notch. After the trail passes Hangover Rock, it becomes steep and has a short section with loose rocks that may make some children (and even adults) a little uncomfortable. At 0.5 mile, it reaches Square Ledge. Use caution on Square Ledge since there is a steep drop-off.

## NATURE NOTES
The breathtaking view of Mount Washington and Pinkham Notch from Square Ledge is the main feature of this trail. The steep headwall of Huntington Ravine is particularly dramatic. This was carved out by a mountain glacier during the last Ice Age. J. S. Huntington was a researcher who was one of the first people to spend a winter on the summit of Mount Washington (1870–1871).

Square Ledge itself is comprised of schist, the same metamorphic rock that underlies much of the Presidential Range. The rock dates back approximately 400 million years and was formed when muds beneath an ancient sea were squeezed together between two colliding continents.

Your hike begins at the Ellis River, which flows into Lost Pond. This interesting section crosses a wetland and beaver habitat on a wooden bridge and is described under the Trip 31.

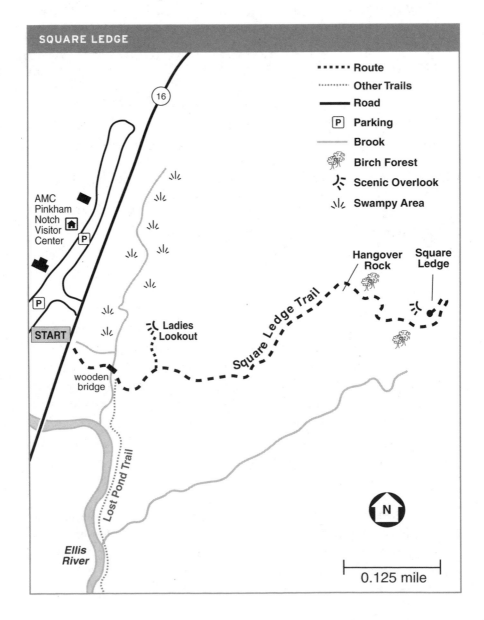

At the turnoff to Ladies Lookout there is a particularly lush growth of striped maple. In the White Mountains this small tree generally remains in the understory. You will appreciate its bright, green-and-white-striped bark on branches and young trunks and its extremely large, three-lobed leaves (the latter giving rise to the name goosefoot maple). Often trees and shrubs growing in its shade must have very large leaves in order to catch the small amount of light that filters down through the canopy. Striped maple is also called moosewood because moose like to eat it.

The name Hangover Rock has nothing to do with being a former watering hole for travelers in Pinkham Notch. Instead it is a large boulder that projects over the trail, making a cozy hangout when it rains.

Slow down after Hangover Rock to enjoy the grove of paper birches. Whoever thought of making a tree with such white bark! Only mature trees have white bark. Young saplings and the branches of adult trees are a rich, reddish brown color that has a more subdued beauty.

In addition to having the honor of being the state tree of New Hampshire, paper birches have a distinct ecological role in the White Mountains. They range from low elevations up to the treeline, thriving in disturbed areas where the former trees have been destroyed by fire, logging, wind, or other disasters. As short-lived, temporary residents during the natural succession of a disturbed area from an open field back to mature

**Inspecting paper birch and bracket fungi.**
Photo by Jerry Shereda.

forest, paper birches are eventually replaced by maples, red spruce, and other more long-lived species. Fortunately for paper birches, and for those who admire their columns of white in a sea of grayish brown and green, natural disturbance to the forest is frequent enough in the White Mountains to ensure a plentiful supply of this species, even in the absence of human activities.

The shagginess of paper birch along with thoughts of the birch-bark canoes of Native Americans might tempt you to peel some of the bark off. Keep in mind, however, that this will leave a permanent ugly scar on the tree, so please resist the temptation.

Shiny club moss is an abundant plant of the forest floor along the Square Ledge Trail. These are low, dark green plants whose upright stems covered with small leaves resemble bottle brushes.

## TRIP 35
## PINE MOUNTAIN

**RATING:** Moderate
**DISTANCE:** 3.5 miles round-trip
**ELEVATION CHANGE:** 750-foot elevation gain
**ESTIMATED TIME:** 2.5–4 hours
**MAPS:** AMC's *White Mountain National Forest Map and Guide*, E10 and Kilkenny inset
AMC's *White Mountain Guide*, 27th ed., Map 1: Presidential Range, E10
**WMNF PARKING FEE:** Yes

**Pine Mountain is the northernmost peak of the Presidential Range. At 2,405 feet, it is quite a bit lower than its more renowned cousins, but it provides excellent views of the Presidential and Carter ranges for only moderate effort.**

The hike up Pine Mountain is a pleasant stroll, mostly along a little-used dirt road through an airy forest dominated by paper birch. It also has prominent samples of scratches carved by the last glaciers and a striking vertical dip of rocks near the summit. A sporty loop can be made with the Ledge Trail.

## DIRECTIONS

Pine Mountain Road departs from Pinkham B (Dolly Copp) Road (unmaintained in winter) in the town of Gorham. If you are coming from Jackson or North Conway, head north on NH 16 past Jackson and Pinkham Notch. Make a left on Pinkham B (Dolly Copp) Road, about 6.5 miles north of the AMC's Pinkham Notch Visitor Center (PNVC). The trail to Pine Mountain is 2.4 miles from NH 16 on the right (northeast) side. There will be signs to the

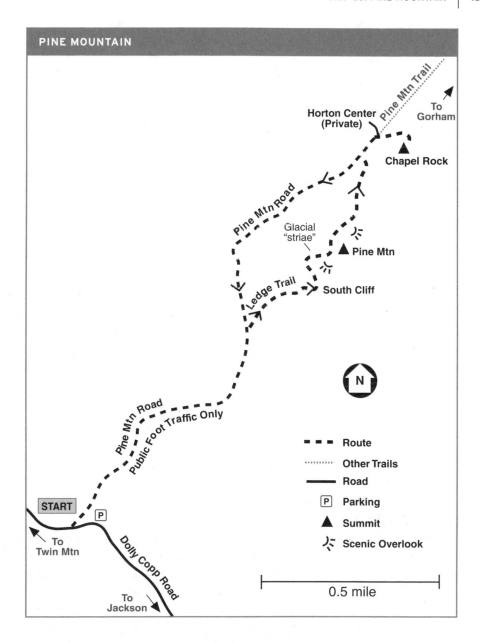

Horton Center (see below) as well as Pine Mountain.

If you are coming from the Twin Mountain or Franconia area, take US 3 to NH 115 in Twin Mountain, then take 115 about 12 miles to US 2. Make a right on US 2 and travel about 8 miles to Pinkham B (Dolly Copp) Road (0.8 mile past the Appalachia parking area) and make another right. The trailhead is about 3 miles on the left.

## TRAIL DESCRIPTION

The trail to Pine Mountain is a private, unpaved road (Pine Mountain Road) that leads to the Douglas Horton Center, a retreat run by the United Church of Christ near the summit of Pine Mountain. The center is not open to the public, but you are welcome to hike the trail and enjoy views from the summit and Chapel Rock at the center.

Pine Mountain Road runs through pleasant, relatively open woods and ascends gradually for much of its length. It is wide enough to walk several abreast, but remember to be watchful for occasional automobiles that use the road to reach the Horton Center. At 1.0 mile, the Ledge Trail departs to the right. Stay to the left and on the road for the more moderate hike. The road ends at the Horton Center (1.6 miles), and the trail turns right and ascends for a short distance to the actual summit (2.0 miles). Side trails lead to views northeast toward the Androscoggin River valley and Mount Moriah. At the summit you will find the foundation of an old fire tower. For the best views of Mount Washington and Carter Notch, walk past the foundation to the open ledges a little beyond.

You can make an interesting loop by hiking a mile (about 20 to 40 minutes) along the road and turning right onto the Ledge Trail. The Ledge Trail offers a shorter, steeper ascent to the summit with excellent views from the south-facing cliff along the way. A little scrambling is required. From the summit you can then descend along the Pine Mountain Trail back to your car. The entire loop is 3.5 miles. The U.S. Forest Service may eventually extend the Ledge Trail to Pinkham B Road, so you may not need to use Pine Mountain Road in the future.

## NATURE NOTES

There are two important geological stories about Pine Mountain. The first has to do with the formation of the rocks. Look behind you when you are sitting on the rock-carved bench at the summit ledges and observe the vertical layers of rock. These rocks were once horizontal beds of sandstones and muds deposited on the bottom of an ancient sea that predated the modern Atlantic. About 400 million years ago, there was a giant collision between North America and an ancient island continent called Avalon. The heat and pressure of the crash metamorphosed the deposits into schists and quartzites, and folded and thrust them up into their present dramatic, vertical position.

Glaciation is the second geological story. On the open ledges just down from the summit on the Ledge Trail, look for the parallel stripes (called striae) embedded in the rock in a northwest–southeast direction. These are scratches made by the gouging action of stones under the continental glacier as it crept along like a frozen river southwest over Pine Mountain. The rocks, stones, and other debris at the bottom of the glacier, squeezed by the tremendous weight of ice, acted like sandpaper, etching and scouring the earth below.

Another indication of glaciation visible from the summit of Pine Mountain on a clear day is the view of Carter Notch. The beautiful U-shaped notch and the rounded summit of Wildcat Mountain are characteristic features of valleys and mountains smoothed by glaciers.

Although geology is center stage on this hike, everyone should still take note of the forest and plants. The forest along Pine Mountain Road is more open and "airy" than most others in the Whites, with beautiful ribbons of dappled sunlight penetrating to the forest floor. Paper birch is abundant, suggesting that this area was probably logged or otherwise disturbed in recent history.

A common shrub along Pine Mountain Road in wet swales is the red-berried elder. This shrub has compound leaves that branch off in pairs along the stems. The branches themselves are covered with corky spots. The numerous flowers, produced around early June, are in showy, white pyramidal clusters. Unfortunately, the dark-red berries found during the summer are often inedible, unlike those of its close relative, the elderberry.

Many spring wildflowers and other small plants grow along the trail, an

**Glacial scratches near the summit of Pine Mountain.**

added feature if you are hiking in May or early June. Common ones include painted trillium, Canada mayflower, clintonia, bunchberry, wild sarsaparilla, wild white violet, and starflower. Interrupted fern and lady fern (a variety with a red stem) thrive along the edge of the road, and you also should be able to find shiny club moss and ground pine. Ground pine will remind you of a tiny Christmas tree. Look for pink lady's slipper in June and sharp-leaved aster in late summer.

The ledges along the Ledge Trail are home to reindeer lichen, rhodora, blueberry, Labrador tea, heart-leaved white birch, and wild currant. Reindeer lichen is a low, delicate lichen with thin, bluish gray, tangled branches. It frequents rocky areas with thin soil in the mountains, often around and under blueberry shrubs. It usually looks so neat and prim that it is hard to believe a landscape gardener didn't deliberately place it there.

Rhodora is a small wild rhododendron with smooth, blue-green leaves. It is common in bogs and lower summits such as Pine Mountain. Around Memorial Day in the White Mountains, its beautiful, large pink flowers put on a dazzling display, as befits a rhododendron.

With its geological and botanical treasures, your outing to Pine Mountain will certainly be satisfying.

## TRIP 36
## LOWS BALD SPOT VIA OLD JACKSON ROAD

**RATING:** Moderate to challenging
**DISTANCE:** 4.2 miles round-trip
**ELEVATION CHANGE:** 850-foot elevation gain
**ESTIMATED TIME:** 3–4 hours
**MAPS:** AMC's *White Mountain National Forest Map and Guide*, F9
AMC's *White Mountain Guide*, 27th ed., Map 1: Presidential Range, F9
**WMNF PARKING FEE:** None
**WINTER NOTES:** Old Jackson Road is an intermediate ski trail.

**Lows Bald Spot is an accessible outlook with a terrific view of the Great Gulf and Mounts Adams and Madison. Along the way you will cross over streams and are likely to see some unusual mushrooms and other fungi.**

As to the identity of Low, according to the *Gorham Mountaineer* of September 14, 1910:

> About a year ago, Mr. J. Herbert Low from Brooklyn, NY, a big man with a thousand friends, discovered the rocky knoll and was so charmed with the delightful view it affords . . . that to share his discovery he marked an easy trail to it from the carriage road.
>
> In the first party to be conducted to the outlook was Mrs. Vera Johnson of New York, who evoked peals of laughter from the party by impulsively crying out, "Oh, Mr. Low! What a beautiful view from your Bald Spot!" . . . This name was one of the unpremeditated kind that sticks, and Low's Bald Spot it has been ever since.

The area has long been called Lowe's Bald Spot. The extra *e* likely was added because it was assumed that the name referred to the Lowe family of Randolph, well-known White Mountain guides and trailbuilders, and not Herbert Low from Brooklyn. In December 2003, however, in response to a proposal by the AMC, the U.S. Board on Geographic Names officially changed the name to Lows Bald Spot (and not "Lowes Bald Spot, Lowe's Bald Spot, [or] Mr. Low's Bald Spot").

Old Jackson Road was the former carriage route from the town of Jackson to the Mount Washington Auto Road, and it goes right past the present site of the AMC's Pinkham Notch Visitor Center (PNVC). It has been incorporated into the White Mountain trail system, meeting the Mount Washington Auto Road at the latter's two-mile marker. From there a short section of the Madison Gulf Trail leads to Lows Bald Spot.

The round trip to Lows Bald Spot from Pinkham Notch takes about three to four hours, depending on how fast you walk and how long you linger at the viewpoint. The trail is generally fairly gradual, with a few steep sections near the end. Younger children, and those who are not particularly enthusiastic hikers, might find it a bit long.

## DIRECTIONS

The trail begins at the AMC's Pinkham Notch Visitor Center off NH 16. (See Trip 31 for directions to PNVC). Walk past the outdoor water fountain and the outdoor scale (for backpackers and kids to figure out their loads). The Old Jackson Road Trail branches off from the Tuckerman Ravine Trail right behind the visitor center.

## LOWS BALD SPOT VIA OLD JACKSON ROAD

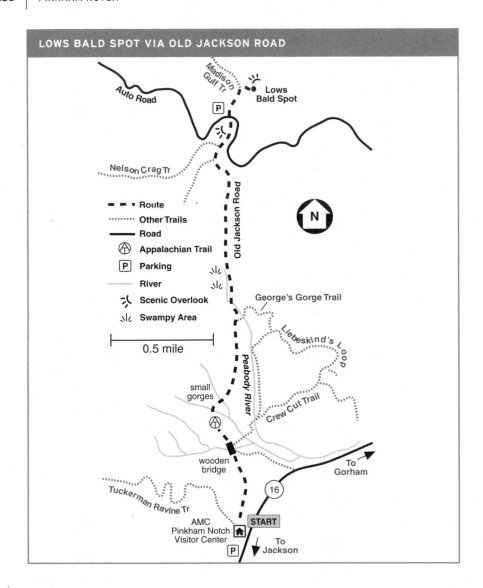

## TRAIL DESCRIPTION

Both Old Jackson Road Trail and the Madison Gulf Trail are part of the Appalachian Trail and are marked with white-paint blazes. This hike begins not on the actual Old Jackson Road itself but on a link that brings you shortly to the old road. Be sure to follow the signs to the Old Jackson Road carefully, since it crosses a maintenance road, a ski trail (indicated by blue diamonds), and other hiking trails.

At 0.4 mile the Old Jackson Road Trail widens out and looks like you'd expect an old road to look. Shortly after, the trail crosses a solid wooden bridge

**The view of Mount Adams from Lows Bald Spot.**

right at the point where the Crew Cut Trail comes in from the right.

The Old Jackson Road then goes uphill moderately steeply and crosses a pleasant, shady gorge with a small waterfall. Take a moment to enjoy the cool, mossy atmosphere and the sound of running water. Soon after, the trail crosses another small gorge (dry in August).

After about 40 minutes (0.9 mile), the trail reaches a junction with the upper end of the George's Gorge Trail and then levels. It crosses a rivulet and passes a swale on the left and then a damp, muddy section traversed by double logs.

In another fifteen minutes, the trail makes a sharp left turn and heads uphill on rock steps at a point where an old section of trail is blocked off. You can hear cars from the Auto Road through the trees, although you still have about 0.5 mile to go before you cross it. The Old Jackson Road continues straight, past the Raymond Path (1.7 miles), crosses a few small rivulets on logs, and then passes the Nelson Crag Trail.

After this the trail ascends and opens up a bit, passing through an old gravel pit with a nice view of Nelson Crag (a shoulder of Mount Washington). The Old Jackson Road ends at a parking area on the Auto Road, 1.9 miles from Pinkham Notch.

To continue on to Lows Bald Spot, walk across the Auto Road and follow the Madison Gulf Trail into the Great Gulf Wilderness. At 0.2 mile beyond the

Auto Road, take the turnoff leading uphill to the right. There is no sign that actually says Lows Bald Spot, but it is easy to find. In another few minutes you reach the summit of Lows Bald Spot.

Return the same way you came. Within 0.4 mile of Pinkham Notch, make sure not to take the left fork where the Link (also Connie's Way and Go Back ski trails) comes in. If you do, you will end up on NH 16 about 0.3 mile north of PNVC.

## NATURE NOTES

The view from Lows Bald Spot is a major highlight of the walk. A vast section of the Great Gulf Wilderness lies before you. Mount Adams, the second-highest peak in the White Mountains, is particularly impressive with its picturesque cone shape. The treeless alpine zone at the upper part of the mountain is very obvious. You can easily see the distinction between the forest dominated by broad-leafed trees at the bottom of the mountain, the boreal forest (spruce and fir) midway up, and the alpine zone.

Between Mount Adams and Mount Madison is Madison Gulf, a tributary ravine of the Great Gulf. Madison Gulf is a cirque—a bowl-shaped ravine on the side of a mountain carved out by a mountain glacier. The section of the Madison Gulf Trail that climbs up this ravine is one of the most difficult hikes in the White Mountains. To the southwest you'll see two shoulders of Mount Washington, Nelson Crag, and Boott Spur. Across Pinkham Notch to the east the prominent peaks are Wildcat Mountain, Carter Dome, and the Imp Face. Endless peaks stretch out to the north.

The view isn't the only thing to see at Lows Bald Spot. You will probably notice a particularly gleaming white piece of quartz and a number of "flag" trees (see Appendix B, Natural History of the White Mountains).

Plants growing at Lows Bald Spot include red spruce, balsam fir, mountain holly, sheep laurel, Labrador tea, crowberry, and a few scrawny blueberry bushes.

The rivulets and swales (low, damp areas) at the level section of the trail about midway to Lows Bald Spot are home to some distinctly shaped flowers. Early in summer look for white bog orchid, 1- to 3-foot-tall plants with slender spikes of small white flowers. Once we spotted one of these orchids among the dense vegetation at the edge of the largest swale and then watched as a tiger swallowtail butterfly found a number of others, flying from orchid to orchid, ignoring all the other plants. If you have a hand lens, take a close look at one of the flowers. From a distance they don't look like anything special, but close up you will see an exotic shape typical of orchids, with a lower lip and a spur.

This walk is a particularly good one for seeing that mysterious group of organisms, the fungi. They are denizens of the forest floor, thriving in rich soils or on decaying wood.

Fungi can be found in a rich assortment of colors and odd shapes. Late summer is an especially good time to look for them in the White Mountains. One of the most eye-catching is the coral fungus, which looks like someone stuck a piece of branching coral from a tropical ocean onto a log. Look for nice patches of coral fungus around the junction of the Old Jackson Road with the Link. Shelf (bracket) fungi growing out of dead trees sometimes reach monstrous sizes. Russulas (robust mushrooms with wide, reddish brown or yellow caps and thick stalks), mycenas (delicate mushrooms with thin stalks and conical caps), amanitas (most species are highly toxic), and many other types cover the forest floor. Admire them, but consider them all inedible and potentially poisonous.

What you actually see of a mushroom or other fungi are their reproductive structures, which are really only a small part of their "bodies." The soil below is laced with myriad thin filaments of numerous species of fungi. Some penetrate plant roots and aid the plants in taking up nutrients. Others such as the coral fungus and the bracket fungus penetrate into dead wood, breaking it down to basic elements. In this way fungi play a critical role in the ecology of the forest.

The Indian pipe looks like a fungus because it is all white. It is actually a flowering plant and produces white flowers. This plant has no green leaves because, unlike most plants, it feeds on dead organic matter in the soil rather than producing its own food. So ecologically it is more like a fungus than a plant.

## TRIP 37
## TUCKERMAN RAVINE

**RATING:** Moderate with challenging sections

**DISTANCE:** 4.8 miles round-trip

**ELEVATION CHANGE:** 1,850-foot elevation gain

**ESTIMATED TIME:** 4.5 hours

**MAPS:** AMC's *White Mountain National Forest Map and Guide*, F9
AMC's *White Mountain Guide*, 27th ed., Map 1: Presidential Range, F9

**WMNF PARKING FEE:** None

**WINTER NOTES:** The John Sherbourne Ski Trail (for advanced skiers) closely parallels the Tuckerman Ravine Trail and leads downhill from Hermit Lake. *Skiers are not to walk up the ski trail.*

**Tuckerman Ravine is one of the most dramatic landscapes in the White Mountains, if not the entire northeast. The ravine is a huge glacially carved bowl set deeply into the northeast flank of Mount Washington. Its 700-foot headwall rises almost vertically from the ravine floor.**

The trip described here takes you to Hermit Lake, a small pond at the base of the ravine from which you can view the headwall and surrounding cliffs. The hike is on an old, heavily eroded tractor road and is moderately steep throughout with virtually no views. Do this hike for the wonderful reward at the end, not for the process of getting there.

Beyond Hermit Lake, the Tuckerman Ravine Trail climbs through the ravine and up the headwall, eventually ascending the summit cone of Mount Washington. This is the most popular route up New England's highest mountain, but you must have the proper gear, have extra time, and be prepared for rough weather if you desire to hike beyond Hermit Lake. Sections of the trail beyond Hermit Lake may be closed to hikers even in June due to heavy snow accumulation.

The AMC and White Mountain National Forest run ten shelters (open on one side, fit eight people each) and three tent platforms at Hermit Lake. If you want to spend more time exploring this exquisite area, consider camping overnight. You must purchase a ticket in person (first come, first served) at the Pinkham Notch Visitors Center before hiking up.

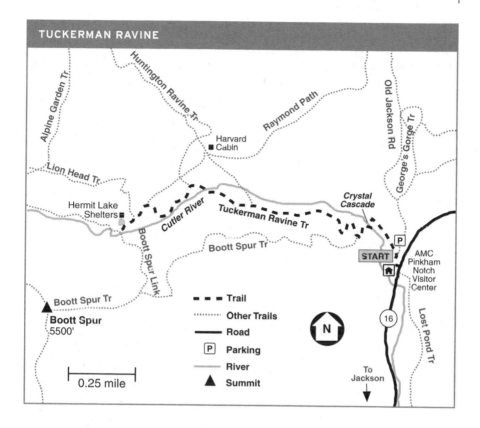

## DIRECTIONS

The trailhead for the Tuckerman Ravine Trail is at the AMC's Pinkham Notch Visitor Center (PNVC) on the west side of NH 16. See Trip 31 for directions. Walk past the Trading Post until you see the large sign for this trail.

## TRAIL DESCRIPTION

The first part of the trail is the most interesting because it follows the Cutler River closely. Be careful not to follow Old Jackson Road, which goes off to the right near the trailhead or the Blanchard Ski Trail, which crosses the trail soon after it starts. At 0.3 mile, the trail makes a sharp left and crosses the river on a solid bridge. After a short steep section, you reach the viewing area for the Crystal Cascade. This is a fine destination in its own right (see Natural Attractions and Nature Walks 1). At the junction with the Boott Spur Trail (0.4 mile), the Tuckerman Ravine Trail turns right and continues climbing relentlessly at a moderately steep rate. Landmarks along this section of the trail are the junction with the Huntington Ravine Trail (1.3 mile), a bridge back over to the north side of the Cutler River (1.6 mile), and the junction with the Raymond

Path (2.1 miles). At 2.3 miles, the Lion Head Trail goes right and at 2.4 one of the grandest vistas in New England opens up before you as you reach the information building at the floor of the ravine. There are benches conveniently placed for having lunch and enjoying the view.

After walking this distance, you owe it to yourself to explore the area further. Follow a trail past one of the shelters to the right to see Hermit Lake. The Cutler River is to the left, crossed by the Boott Spur Link. If you have time, continue along the Tuckerman Ravine Trail, relatively level at this point, over the Little Headwall to the base of the headwall (0.7 mile from the Hermit Lake area). The vegetation will become shorter in stature with some alpine species mixed in as you approach the headwall. *Caution:* A snow arch forms at the base of the headwall in winter and may still be present through early July. Although attractive to look at, it is unstable so do not climb on or under it.

## NATURE NOTES

Tuckerman Ravine is a textbook example of a cirque, a geological term used for a bowl-shaped glacially carved valley on the side of a mountain. The ravine was carved by a small mountain glacier sometime before the area was completely covered by the last continental ice sheet 50,000 years ago. As the climate cooled, glaciers first formed in the mountains. Water freezing and expanding in cracks in the bedrock plucked rocks from the sides of the mountain, leaving the bowl-shaped ravines for which the Presidential Range is noted: Tuckerman, Huntington, King, Great Gulf. These cirques all have flat bottoms that grade into steep headwalls. They formed on the north and eastern sides of mountains where the most snow is deposited by prevailing winds. Lakes that form within the bowl of a cirque, such as Hermit Lake, are called tarns. Eventually the whole area, including the summit of Mount Washington, was covered by the continental ice sheet.

Hermit Lake is tiny (less than 0.5 acre) and shallow (less than a foot deep in most places), but its setting is exquisite. The view from Hermit Lake as you face the ravine includes the Lion Head, a particularly impressive rock face on your right that resembles its namesake when seen from NH 16 below and the long alpine ridge of Boott Spur with its rocky Hanging Cliffs to the left. The headwall of the ravine is straight ahead. The lake itself is surrounded by a dark spruce-fir forest.

Many of the landmarks of the White Mountains are named for botanists and other scientists who were among the earliest explorers of this region. Francis Boott (of Boott Spur) was a botanist who explored the region in the early 1800s. Dr. Edward Tuckerman was a Professor of Botany at Amherst

**Tuckerman Ravine.**

College and a well-known lichenologist (scientist who studies lichens). He initially came to the White Mountains in the 1830s to study the flora and returned many times. (See John Mudge's *The White Mountains, Names, Places, and Legends.*) Tuckerman was one of the first scientists to describe the effects of elevation on plant communities of the White Mountains.

If you are hiking in spring, you are likely to meet up with many skiers willing to trudge up the mountain with skis on their backs in order to experience the thrill and tradition of spring skiing in Tuckerman Ravine. The reason for the deep snow accumulation in the ravine is that snow from the exposed area around the summit of Mount Washington is blown into the ravine by the prevailing northwest winds of winter. The thick snow layer in the ravine, besides being a boon to skiers, also serves to protect plants from bitter winter winds, but it delays their season (see below).

The streamside flora is particularly interesting as you approach the ravine. Look for Indian poke (false hellebore), a large herbaceous plant whose broad, deeply veined leaves look like cabbage. Don't be fooled by appearances; the leaves are highly toxic. Indian poke is related to lilies; its green flowers have the same structure as our showy garden lilies—three petals, three sepals, six stamens, and three stigmas. Such a tall herbaceous plant like Indian poke would not survive in very exposed areas due to wicked winter winds, but in the floor of the ravine, it is protected by the thick blanket of winter snow.

Green alder is a common streamside shrub. It has rounded, toothed leaves and its conelike fruits remain on the plant throughout the summer. Meadowsweet is a type of spiraea with clusters of white, fuzzy flowers at the tips of branches. This small shrub blooms in early summer at lower elevations, but at the elevation of Tuckerman Ravine, meadowsweet flowers can still be found through late August. They are one of a number of species in the ravine whose bloom times are late because of the heavy winter snow accumulation. The showy, purple flowers of purple-stemmed asters line streamsides in mid- to late summer. This aster has purple, hairy stems and wedge-shaped leaves. The yellow flower clusters of large-leaved goldenrod are a common summer sight around the base of the ravine.

Red squirrels are the most common mammalian inhabitants of the Hermit Lakes area, probably second only to campers and hikers. These squirrels are almost exclusively found in conifer forests, whereas gray squirrels are associated with broad-leaved forests.

## TRIP 38
## THE ALPINE GARDEN

**RATING:** Moderate with some steep sections
**DISTANCE:** 0.6–2.4 miles round-trip
**ELEVATION CHANGE:** 300-foot descent
**ESTIMATED TIME:** 2–3 hours
**MAPS:** AMC's *White Mountain National Forest Map and Guide*, F9
AMC's *White Mountain Guide*, 27th ed., Map 1: Presidential Range, F9
**WMNF PARKING FEE:** None (but note auto road fee)

**The Alpine Garden, located on a relatively flat area on a shoulder of Mount Washington, is an arctic outpost inhabited by rare wildflowers that normally live only in northern Canada, Greenland, or Alaska. Huge rock piles look like they were put there by giants.**

The most unusual and exciting landscape in the White Mountains (and arguably all of New England) is the land above treeline. Save this outing for a calm,
sunny day, so you can savor the flowers and the extensive views eastward to
the Carter Range. It is a long and arduous hike to reach this special place. Fortunately, there is an alternative. If you are not too proud a hiker, then use the
Mount Washington Auto Road to take you to trails that start above timberline.
The Alpine Garden Trail is one of the most attractive.

The walk begins with a short descent on the Huntington Ravine Trail.
You then walk along the Alpine Garden Trail until you decide it's time to turn
around and retrace your steps. The suggested trip is often used by organizations running botanical field trips because it allows people to spend more time
in the alpine zone (rather than hiking up to get there) and also opens up the
alpine area to those for whom the hike up from Pinkham Notch would be too
difficult.

If the weather is good, you have lots of time, and everybody is happy, energetic, and capable, you could extend the outing by hiking up to the summit
of Mount Washington on the Lion Head and Tuckerman Ravine trails. This
entails an elevation gain of 1,100 feet over 0.9 mile, much of which is scrambling on boulders. After a stop at the summit, hike back down to your car via
the Nelson Crag Trail (0.8 mile, 500-foot descent), which intersects the Huntington Ravine Trail just short of the auto road where you left your car at the
Cow Pasture.

*Caution:* Check at Pinkham Notch Visitor Center (PNVC) for the weather
conditions on the summit of Mount Washington before beginning, since it is
likely to be about 20 degrees Fahrenheit colder and much windier there than in
the valley. The Alpine Garden is slightly more benign than the summit, since
it is about a thousand feet lower and somewhat protected from the westerly
winds. But remember, the weather here is notoriously fickle and can change
rapidly even with a good forecast. Don't fool with this trail if the weather is
questionable, since it is very exposed and rugged. Be prepared to turn back
if the weather changes during the hike, particularly since you have to hike up
from the Alpine Garden to return to your car.

Make sure everyone has sturdy shoes and extra clothes. This trail is not appropriate for anyone who is uncomfortable hiking on rocks.

The Governor Sherman Adams Summit Building at the top of Mount
Washington is 1.1 miles beyond the trailhead and has rest rooms, food service,
snacks, souvenirs, telephones, a post office, a museum, and lots of tourists.
There are also rest rooms at Glen House where the auto road begins.

## DIRECTIONS

Getting there can be half the fun, because the views from the auto road are phenomenal. There are so many signs for the Mount Washington auto road, a major tourist attraction, that you can't miss it. It is about 2.5 miles north of the AMC's Pinkham Notch Visitor Center along NH 16.

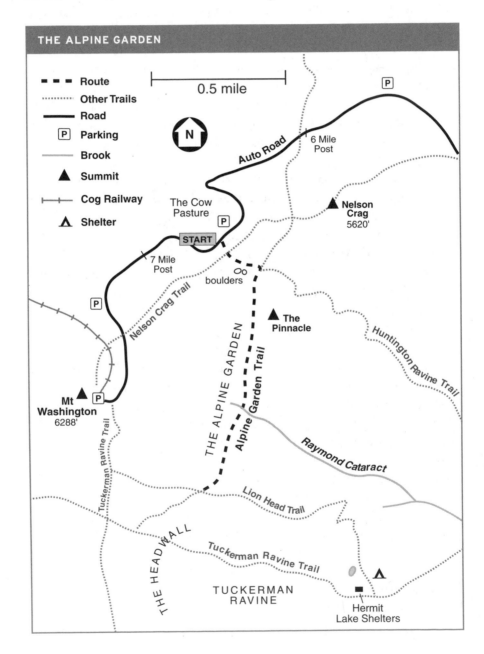

The auto road is not cheap. At the time of this writing, the auto road was charging $17 for a car and driver, $7 for each additional adult passenger, and $4 for children 5–12. It is a steep, winding road, not meant for drivers with vertigo. Campers and trailers are not permitted on the road.

The auto road is about 8 miles long and is conveniently marked with mile markers. Park at the turnoff below the 7-mile marker in a relatively flat area called the Cow Pasture. Look for the signs for the Huntington Ravine Trail, which descends east (left as you ascend) from the auto road.

## TRAIL DESCRIPTION

Note: Since this hike is in open terrain, there will be a great temptation to wander off on the tundra. Alpine vegetation can withstand the rigors of arctic conditions but cannot tolerate the pounding of hikers' feet. It is imperative that everyone stays on the trails. Alpine plants grow very slowly in these harsh conditions; therefore, it may take hundreds of years for plants to regrow in areas where they have been killed by trampling. And picking alpine plants is both illegal and extremely bad form. (You have our permission to severely chastise and report anyone engaged in such activities.) Everyone who enjoys the Alpine Garden is also responsible for protecting it.

From the parking area descend steeply over rocks on the Huntington Ravine Trail for 0.3 mile. When it levels out, turn right (south) onto the Alpine Garden Trail. Don't continue down the Huntington Ravine Trail any distance beyond this junction unless you are prepared for an extreme hiking experience. The AMC's *White Mountain Guide* calls the Huntington Ravine Trail the most difficult trail in the White Mountains, and it is particularly difficult on the descent. It is not a family hike. Instead, enjoy the relatively flat meander of the Alpine Garden Trail through alpine vegetation. Depending on how everyone is feeling, you could turn around after a short walk and ascend back to your car or hike completely across the Alpine Garden. The Alpine Garden Trail ends at the Lion Head Trail (1.2 miles), near the edge of Tuckerman Ravine. Retrace your steps back to the trailhead (unless you have plenty of time and energy to hike the loop over the summit described above).

## NATURE NOTES

A thorough description of the alpine area is a whole book in itself, so only a brief introduction is given here. For a more in-depth view see the *AMC Field Guide to the New England Alpine Summits*, 2nd ed., by Nancy G. Slack and Allison Bell.

On your drive, you will share the auto road with all sorts of vehicles. You may feel that this is not exactly the "natural experience" you wanted in the

White Mountains. Comfort yourself with the knowledge that this was the same route Henry David Thoreau used in a botanical excursion in 1858.

The auto road begins at 1,563 feet, reaches timberline at about 4,000 feet (just past Milepost 4), passes the trailhead to the Alpine Garden at about 5,700 feet, and ends at the Mount Washington summit at 6,288 feet. It's fascinating to travel first through a dense forest, then past shorter and shorter trees until spectacular mountain vistas open up before you.

The drive up the auto road takes you through three ecological zones: the broad-leaved deciduous forest (or northern hardwoods), the boreal forest, and the alpine tundra. This is a response to the change in climate with elevation. On average, the temperature drops about 1 degree for every 350 feet you climb, so it will be about 12 degrees cooler at the trailhead than at the beginning of the auto road, and a lot windier too. By driving a mere 7 miles on the auto road, you have driven the ecological equivalent of about 1,000 miles north.

We think of rocks as the very essence of unyielding, enduring solidity, but the auto road is a great place to observe that even rocks can be bent and folded. Between Mileposts 5 and 6 on the small cliff faces that border the road, you can see how distinct layers of rocks have been folded. This happened about 400 million years ago when these rocks were under intense heat and pressure and actually became flexible as they were compressed between two moving continents.

As you walk down the trail to the Alpine Garden, you may wonder who piled up all of the big boulders in such a jumble. The rocks were actually put there by water. Water, freezing and then expanding in cracks in the bedrock, caused chunks of bedrock to break off into the rock pile. On the summit cone of Mount Washington nearby, boulders are piled so deep that it is hard to find the underlying bedrock.

New Hampshire may be the Granite State, but the rocks that form its highest mountain range are not granite but schist and gneiss. Schist and gneiss are metamorphic rocks, so called because they are formed by the transformation of other types of rocks. In the Presidential Range the same intense heat and pressure that caused the folding of rocks along the auto road transformed sedimentary rocks (produced from compacted sand and mud under the sea) into schist and gneiss. This highest part of New England was once under the sea.

Many of the rocks are covered by yellow-green splotches that look like someone threw some paint at them. These are map lichens, whose scientific name, *Rhizocarpon geographicum*, also stresses their resemblance to a map. Lichens produce acids that break down the rocks upon which they reside, thus they are an initial step in soil formation.

The peak time to observe flowers of the alpine tundra in bloom is early to mid-June. This is early in the season for many hikers, but don't be disheartened; there are still many interesting plants to see all summer.

The first thing to notice about plants in the Alpine Garden is their small stature. Most never rise more than a few inches above the ground because of the fierce winds. Taller ones are likely to be found only where they are protected from the wind; for example, in the lee of rocks. Balsam fir and black spruce grow as low, gnarled shrubs called krummholz, a German word meaning crooked wood.

While hiking through the Alpine Garden, you will notice cushions of dark green, tightly packed, tiny leaves that hug the ground throughout the tundra. These "pincushions" are diapensia, a native of North American and Scandanavian arctic realms as well as the high peaks of New England.

**Diapensia and Lapland rosebay bloom in the Alpine Garden.**

If you are lucky enough to be on the Alpine Garden Trail in June and the wind and temperature have been cooperative, you will be treated to a profusion of its small, white flowers with five petals. The dark green leaves act as passive solar collectors, absorbing solar radiation and ensuring that the plant stays warmer than the surroundings. Insects find warmer temperatures and protection from the wind within the tight bundle of diapensia leaves.

Alpine azalea also grows as a cushion plant. Its leaves resemble diapensia, but its pink flowers are even smaller—no larger than the head of a matchstick. They still put on a great show when they all bloom together.

A flower that is bound to catch your eye in June because of its relatively large magenta blossoms is the Lapland rosebay. The flowers may bring to mind a small rhododendron, and in fact the Lapland rosebay is a very small species of rhododendron.

In keeping with the theme that small is beautiful in the Alpine Garden, there are tiny willows that never get more than 2 inches high. In June you might find pussy-willow-type "buds" coming right out of the ground. These are the male and female catkins of the bearberry willow.

Big yellow flowers blooming from late June throughout the summer are mountain avens. This plant, with relatively large scalloped leaves, grows in only two places in the world: in the White Mountains (where it is reasonably common) and on an island off Nova Scotia. You can sometimes find mountain avens along streams at lower elevations (see Trips 27 and 48).

In July delicate, white flowers with five petals on small plants with thin, grassy leaves are particularly abundant alongside the trail. This is mountain sandwort, a plant whose affinity for growing near trails in the White Mountains suggests that it is better adapted to Vibram soles than all others.

In July and August, the showiest flower in the Alpine Garden is the bluebell (harebell). This flower is common at lower elevations and may not have been native to the Alpine Garden. There is some speculation that its seeds may have been carried up the mountain in the droppings of donkeys that were used as pack animals in the nineteenth century.

You will not see many animals at the Alpine Garden. The alpine areas of the Rocky Mountains are blessed with herds of elk, deer, and bighorn sheep. In the White Mountains you will have to content yourself with wolf spiders, a large dark spider that scampers over the rocks; butterflies; other insects; and an occasional woodchuck or snowshoe hare. The only two species of birds that regularly build nests above the timberline are dark-eyed juncos and white-throated sparrows. The junco is a perky, gray bird with a white belly that flashes white outer tail feathers when it flies. The white-throated sparrow is famous for its song, a series of clear whistles. American pipit, a small, streaky sparrow-like bird with white outer tail feathers occasionally nests at the Alpine Garden. Watch also for ravens cavorting in the air, with their characteristic throaty call which sometimes sounds like the snorting of a hog. Admire their ability to soar over this unique and dramatic habitat.

# 6

# EVANS NOTCH

## LAY OF THE LAND

Evans Notch is the farthest east of the four major north–south notches that run through the White Mountains. It straddles the New Hampshire–Maine border for much of its length. The mountains on its western border include the Baldfaces, the Basin Rim, and the Royces, generally ranging from 3,000 to 3,500 feet in elevation. The hills on the east side of the notch are lower (1,000 to 2,900 feet), and include Caribou, Speckled, and Blueberry mountains and Deer Hill.

Evans Notch provides excellent family hiking opportunities. It is less crowded than other regions, and the lower elevations are ideal for children. Most of the summits have great views, flowing water abounds, and there are ample places for picking blueberries.

ME 113 provides access to most of the hiking trails. Approaching from the south, you pick up ME 113 in Fryeburg. Fryeburg is approximately 8 miles east of Conway and North Conway along NH 113 and US 302, respectively. Keep in mind, particularly when returning to New Hampshire, that NH 113 and ME 113 are two different roads. Heading north from Fryeburg, ME 113 passes through Chatham, North Chatham, and Stow. From the north ME 113 is reached by traveling east on US 2 about 10 miles from Gorham to the former logging town of Gilead.

## LOGISTICS AND SUPPLIES

The Basin is a National Forest Recreation Area named for a glacially carved bowl between West Royce Mountain and Mount Meader. Basin Pond offers fishing, canoeing, picnicking, swimming, and a great chance to spot moose and other wildlife. The most accessible rest rooms in the notch are there too. Other public rest rooms are at the campgrounds.

The WMNF's Androscoggin Ranger Station on NH 16 in Gorham and Evans Notch Information Center on US 2 east of Bethel have pamphlets on a number of the trails in Evans Notch as well as information on rock-collecting opportunities for young miners.

The towns closest to Evans Notch—Chatham, North Chatham, Stow, and Gilead—are small, so you may want to pick up supplies you need for your hike at the larger communities farther away (e.g., Bethel, Fryeburg, Gorham). The Chatham Trails Association has produced a detailed trail map of the Cold River valley and Evans Notch.

## NEARBY CAMPING

There are four national forest campgrounds in and around Evans Notch: the Cold River, Basin, Hastings, and Wild River campgrounds. The Cold River and Basin campgrounds are both at the Basin. The Hastings Campground, with 24 sites, is located between the two ends of the Roost Trail just off ME 113. It has limited accessibility for people with disabilities. The Wild River Campground, also with 24 sites, is reached by a 5-mile drive down Wild River Road, a dirt road off ME 113.

## TRIP 39
## DEER HILL AND DEER HILL SPRING

**RATING:** Deer Hill Spring only is easy; Deer Hill is moderate
**DISTANCE:** 1.6 miles round-trip to Deer Hill Spring; Deer Hill is 4.0 miles round-trip
**ELEVATION CHANGE:** Deer Hill Spring: minimal elevation gain; Deer Hill: 850-foot elevation gain
**ESTIMATED TIME:** 1 hour to Deer Hill Spring; 3–4 hours round-trip to Deer Hill
**MAPS:** AMC's *White Mountain National Forest Map and Guide*, G13 AMC's *White Mountain Guide*, 27th ed., Map 5: Carter Range–Evans Notch, G13
**WMNF PARKING FEE:** Yes

**The hike up Deer Hill is a pleasant half-day outing through forests of maple, beech, birch, and hemlock, and takes you from New Hampshire into Maine. Deer Hill Spring "quicksand" is an unusual phenomenon that should not be missed.**

These are actually two separate hikes that can be combined into one if you have two cars or are willing to hike about 2 miles along a road. The 850-foot rise in elevation during the hike up Deer Hill is definitely manageable for most families with children but still enough to make you feel like you have gotten a good bit of exercise. Blueberries are abundant and the views are great. The bubbling sands of Deer Hill Spring look like they belong more at Yellowstone National Park than the White Mountains.

## DIRECTIONS
From the North Conway area, follow ME 113 north from Fryeburg, along the Maine–New Hampshire border. The parking area for the trail is on the right about 6.5 miles north of the village of Stow, Maine, and 0.2 mile north of the AMC's Cold River Camp (facilities for registered guests only). It is also the parking area for the Baldface Circle Trail. For those approaching from Gorham or Bethel, take ME 113 south from US 2 in Gilead. The trailhead is about 2 miles south of the turnoff to the Basin Pond parking area.

## TRAIL DESCRIPTION

From the parking area take the Deer Hill Connector about 0.4 mile to a point where there is a small dam over the Cold River and the Conant Path goes off to the right. Take the Deer Hills Trail (no markers yet) across the dam.

After crossing the river bear right at the double yellow marker, pass the stone that indicates the border of New Hampshire and Maine, then look for

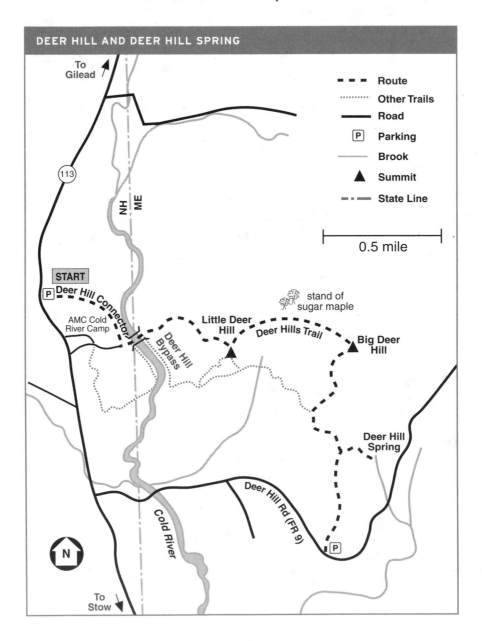

the sign for Little Deer Hill after the old logging road. Yellow blazes mark the trail as it goes uphill at a moderate grade through a northern hardwood forest, eventually passing over several ledges with blueberries and nice views, and reaching Little Deer Hill (1.3 miles). The views and blueberries are great here, so it is a possible turnaround spot. The summit of Big Deer Hill is another 0.7 mile beyond (20 to 30 minutes). The trail descends about 100 feet into the col between Little and Big Deer hills in a forest dominated by sugar maple, crosses a stream, then ascends about 400 feet to the summit of Big Deer Hill.

The trail is in relatively good condition and is easy to follow with some moderately steep, rocky sections and a few sections with roots. A heavy layer of leaves in some steep sections may make the trail slippery when wet.

You can get to Deer Hill Spring by continuing on the Deer Hills Trail 20 to 30 minutes (0.7 mile) beyond Big Deer Hill and turning left at the

These holes were created by a yellow-bellied sapsucker, a type of woodpecker.

short, 0.2-mile spur trail to the spring. This requires some prior planning, since you then either have to retrace your steps to the trailhead over both Deer Hills (about 2.9 miles), have previously left a second car on Deer Hill Road near the spring, or be willing to walk 2 miles back to the trailhead along roads. An alternative is to do Deer Hill Spring as a separate hike. For the closest access to the spring, drive south on ME 113 from the Baldface Circle/Deer Hill Connector parking lot for about 1 mile, turn left on Deer Hill Road (Forest Road 9) for 1.3 miles, and park where you see the signs for the trail on the left. Walk along the old logging road 0.6 mile (still part of the Deer Hills Trail), and then turn right on the 0.2-mile spur trail to the spring. That easy walk should take about 30 minutes.

## NATURE NOTES

The border of New Hampshire and Maine is noted with an impressive stone bench marker. Not many can resist the temptation to have one foot in New Hampshire and the other in Maine. Painted trillium, clintonia, and hobble-bush grow abundantly here.

Beyond the bridge the river has formed flat parallel terraces at different heights above its current banks. Each terrace was built up when the river flooded its banks and deposited sand, silt, and mud along its shores. During the melting of the last glacier about 12,000 years ago, Cold River was much deeper and wider than it is today. The terraces it formed at that time are now stranded high above the present water level.

Several dead wildlife trees stand along the trail between Cold River and Little Deer Hill. Observe the softball-sized holes in these trees and the large wood chips at the base, both the handiwork of pileated woodpeckers.

About halfway up the trail to Little Deer Hill on the right side, look for a hemlock with four separate trunks united at the base. More than likely, the original trunk was damaged by insects or wind, and none of the four branches could dominate and take over. Other trees in the area have double trunks for the same reason.

Many wildflowers grow alongside the trail, but unfortunately for summer visitors, most bloom in May and June. In the woods you can see clintonia, painted trillium, Canada mayflower, Indian cucumber-root, pink lady's slip-per, wild anemone, dwarf ginseng, partridgeberry, and wild sarsaparilla. The dominant understory shrub is hobblebush. Trailing arbutus and flowering wintergreen are common where the woods thin out near ledges. Blueberries are abundant on the ledgy areas, as are chokeberries and reindeer lichen. The trail is also a good one to learn to identify the different types of conifer trees: hemlock, red spruce, balsam fir, white pine, and red pine.

The summits of Little Deer Hill and Deer Hill are great for scenic vistas, picnics, and midsummer blueberry picking. From Little Deer Hill, the bare summits of the Baldface Range and the impressive cliff face of the Basin Rim are to the west. The best vista from Deer Hill is about 50 yards east of the true summit. Looking eastward you'll see hills, lakes, and bogs of Maine. With bin-oculars you may get lucky, as we did, and see a moose in one of the bogs.

Deer Hill Spring is a must. It is in a shady hemlock grove where you are likely to be serenaded by the beautiful flutelike sounds of the hermit thrush or the energetic song of the winter wren. Before you actually see it, there is noth-ing to alert you that something odd is nearby. Then you notice a porridge of bubbling yellow sand contrasting sharply with the dark surroundings. Water percolates out of the side of the mountain with enough force to keep sand constantly in suspension. Finer particles pass out of the spring with the outflow. There is a story that a horse was swallowed up by the quicksand years ago, and its remains still lie somewhere below. That would be a hard rumor to verify.

## TRIP 40
## LORD HILL

**RATING:** Easy
**DISTANCE:** 2.8 miles round-trip
**ELEVATION CHANGE:** 650-foot elevation gain
**ESTIMATED TIME:** 2–4 hours, depending on how long you spend at the mine
**MAPS:** AMC's *White Mountain National Forest Map and Guide*, G13
AMC's *White Mountain Guide*, 27th ed., Map 5: Carter Range–Evans Notch, G13
**WMNF PARKING FEE:** None
**OTHER ACTIVITIES:** Rock collecting, birding (nearby)

**The excursion to Lord Hill's summit on the Horseshoe Pond and Conant trails combines excellent views and a visit to an abandoned mine where amateur rock hobbyists are still permitted to collect.**

The view from the 1,257-foot summit includes Horseshoe Pond immediately below; long, sinuous Kezar Lake a little farther; and the hills and forests of this easternmost section of the national forest. Lord Hill is a little off the beaten track, but it is a great place to escape the crowds and get a sense of what the White Mountains were like in earlier times.

At a leisurely pace it should take about an hour to reach the summit of Lord Hill. With an hour or more of enjoying the view and poking around the mine and another hour back, plan on a half-day or more, especially if you bring a picnic.

The Forest Service has set up a wildlife viewing area on the shores of a wooded pond, Deer Hill Bog, along Deer Hill Road (Forest Road 9), not far from the Horseshoe Pond trailhead. Moose, great blue herons, and a variety of waterfowl frequent this pond. It makes an excellent stop before or after your hike.

## DIRECTIONS

From the Conway/North Conway area, take US 302 to Fryeburg, then head north on ME 113. Turn right (east) on unpaved Deer Hill Road (Forest Road 9), approximately 4.9 miles north of the little village of Stow. (If you pass AMC's Cold River Camp (0.8 mile beyond that), you have gone too far.) Fol-

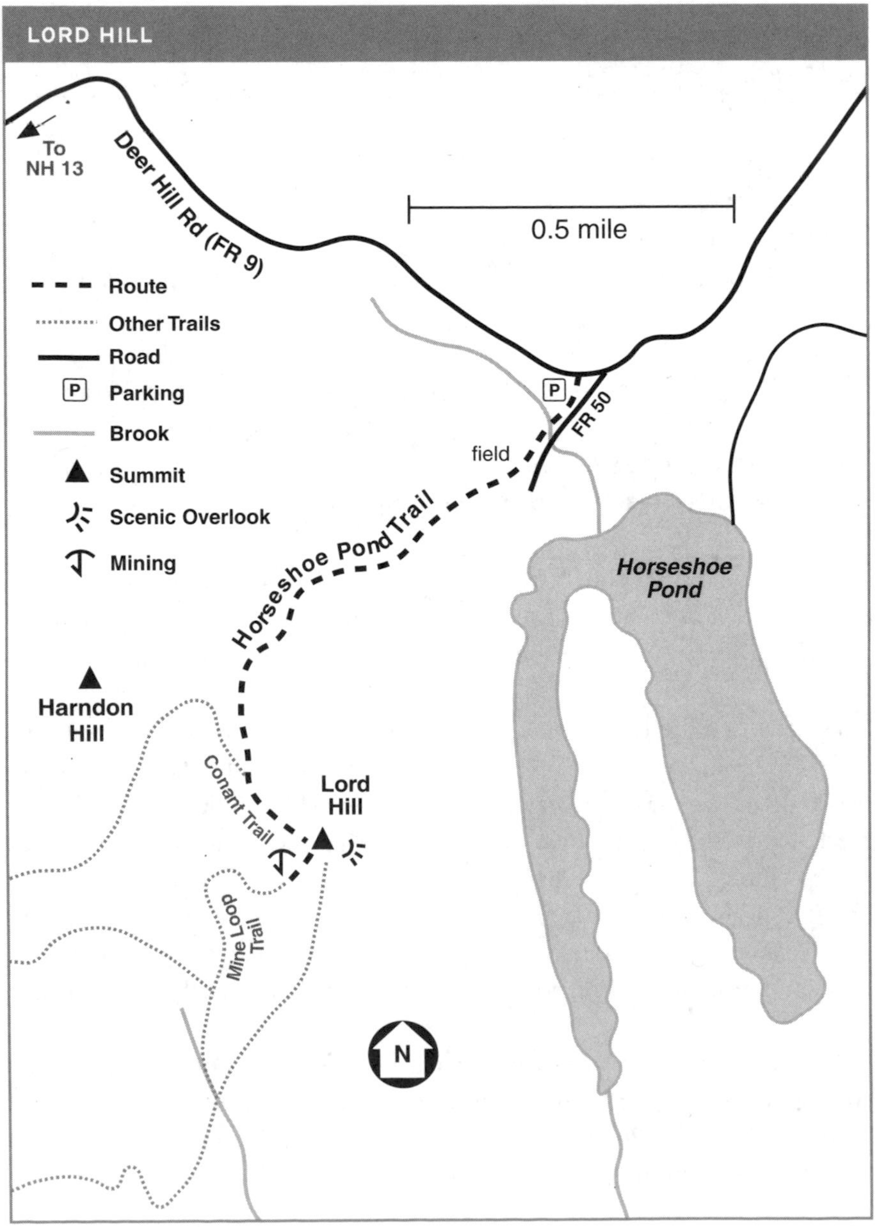
LORD HILL
To NH 13
Deer Hill Rd (FR 9)
0.5 mile
Route
Other Trails
Road
Parking
Brook
Summit
Scenic Overlook
Mining
P
FR 50
field
Horseshoe Pond Trail
Horseshoe Pond
Harndon Hill
Conant Trail
Lord Hill
Mine Loop Trail
N

low Deer Hill Road past the wildlife-viewing area (at 2.6 miles from ME 113) to the Horseshoe Pond trailhead on the right, 4.4 miles from ME 113. It is located in a bend in the road where there is room for cars to park. If you reach an unpaved road heading sharply to the right (Forest Road 50), you have gone about 0.1 mile too far.

If you are approaching from the north or west, take US 2 through Gorham and turn south on ME 113 about 10 miles east of the junction of US 2 with NH 16. Travel 13.7 miles on ME 113 through Evans Notch. Turn left on Deer Hill Road approximately 0.8 mile south of the AMC's Cold River Camp and follow the above directions.

## TRAIL DESCRIPTION

The Horseshoe Pond Trail, marked with yellow metal rectangles, starts off with a short downhill section through a beautiful white pine forest. The Horseshoe Pond Loop, which provided access to the shore of Horseshoe Pond near this section of the trail has been closed. There is no public access to the pond as of this writing.

The trail continues past the Styles gravesite (1851) in the pines. Rocks along the trail that are laden with crystals of quartz and mica hint at the riches you will find later. After 1.1 miles of a gradual uphill through a mixture of fields, open woodlands, and evergreen forests, the Horseshoe Pond Trail ends at a T intersection with the Conant Trail (also called the Pine–Lord Loop Trail or the Pine-Lord-Harndon Loop). Turn left and follow the Conant Trail for about 0.2 mile. At the summit go left to reach the best views from open ledges. Take the Mine Loop Trail to the right for the short (0.1 mile) walk to the abandoned mine.

The White Mountain National Forest has produced a flier on looking for minerals at Lord Hill and Deer Hill. Stop in at the National Forest Evans Notch Information Center in Bethel (on US 2) or other ranger stations for a copy.

## NATURE NOTES

Visiting the old mine on Lord Hill is a dream come true for rock hunters, both young and old. Many early explorers of the White Mountains came seeking riches from minerals locked up in the rocks. Although there is little commercial mining in the White Mountains now, in the past mining probably ranked number two behind lumbering in local commerce. Lord Hill is one of a number of mines in western Maine, some of which are still in commercial operation. The region is still a major source of amethyst and other semiprecious gems.

**A young miner at Lord Hill.**

The White Mountain National Forest allows you to dig for common minerals for your own use without a permit (except for smoky quartz in the Saco Ranger District). Power tools and explosives are forbidden, and a prospecting permit is required if you plan to sell the minerals.

The Lord Hill mine is actually an open depression in the hill, rather than a deep, dark shaft. It can be hot and sunny there on summer days, so bring sun hats and plenty of water. The floor of the hole is littered with small pieces of rock, the remnants of past blasting.

Miners at Lord Hill were particularly interested in the large chunks of muscovite, a silvery mica that can be divided into paper-thin crystals like the pages of a book. These crystals were used for capacitors. Although mica crystals are common in the granitic rocks throughout the White Mountains, the large, striking "books" at Lord Hill are particularly impressive. The opaque, whitish feldspar is not as striking, but at one time this mineral was mined here for use as a porcelain-like material for sinks and bathtubs.

Two gems found at Lord Hill are beryl, a greenish quartz that is high in the element beryllium, and topaz. Beryl crystals 10 to 12 feet long have been found in this part of Maine—one is now at the American Museum of Natural History in New York City. You might initially mistake the clear topaz for a quartz since it is also uncolored and translucent, but notice the difference in the arrangement of the angles of the crystals. Topaz has a smoother feel to it. Smoky quartz is also common at Lord Hill, and purple amethyst can be found as well.

These beautiful crystals were formed beneath the earth within the granite that makes up much of the White Mountains. Eons ago, molten rock bubbled up through cracks in the granite, forming pegmatite dikes of feldspar. Within the feldspar, crystals of the minerals formed, becoming large because they cooled very slowly. Later, erosion from water and ice and scouring by glaciers broke up the rock, revealing the minerals to future generations.

The scenery at the summit of Lord Hill is also striking. The view from the ledge at the summit includes Horseshoe Pond nearby and part of Kezar Lake in the distance. You also look out to a ridge that includes Speckled Mountain (2,906 feet), Red Rock Cliff, and Blueberry Mountain.

Observe the interesting forest dynamics as you climb up the hill. Stone walls indicate that the area was farmed at one time, and you also may find an old house foundation in the woods. The forest returned after the farms were abandoned. In December 1980, an intense windstorm hit the area. The storm was very patchy in its effects, so the forest now alternates between older stands of white pine, hemlock, and sugar maple and newer patches of aspen and birch.

Lord Hill also is a good low-elevation spot for red spruce, a tree that at one time covered much of the lower elevations in the mountains before it was intensively logged. If you feel so inclined, you can make spruce gum out of globs of the resin sticking to the bark. This used to be a popular treat before Mr. Wrigley. You'll need to work it over in your mouth, spitting out the grit. Eventually it will soften up and look like regular chewing gum.

For those with less adventurous gustatory and olfactory inclinations, raspberries grow in open areas near the base of the hill, and blueberries around the summit.

Look for piles of hemlock bark that somehow never made it to the tannery. Hemlocks, identified by their short flat needles (only one per bunch), were extensively logged for tannins before the advent of synthetic substitutes. After trees were cut, the bark was stripped and placed in piles in the woods before being transported to tanneries. Tannins extracted from the bark were used to preserve leather.

At the summit of Lord Hill there is a nice stand of red pine, a tree with distinctive reddish bark in "plates" and two long needles per bunch.

Keep your eyes open for the evidence of the pileated woodpeckers that live in the area. If you are lucky, you might catch a glimpse of this crow-sized woodpecker with a flaming red crest. If not, there are a number of trees with softball-sized holes chiseled out and large flakes of wood piled up on the ground below. One of these pileated woodpecker trees is located near the junction of the Horseshoe Pond and Conant trails.

Stop at the wildlife-viewing area on Deer Hill Road, either before or after your hike. A blind set up by the Forest Service looks out over a wooded swamp and provides a great opportunity to see moose, great blue heron, wood duck, hooded merganser, Canada goose, tree swallow, kingbird, red-winged blackbird, and warbler. Bring your binoculars.

## TRIP 41
## MOUNTAIN POND

**RATING:** Moderate

**DISTANCE:** 2.7-mile loop

**ELEVATION CHANGE:** Minimal elevation change

**ESTIMATED TIME:** 2–4 hours

**MAPS:** AMC's *White Mountain National Forest Map and Guide*, G12
AMC's *White Mountain Guide*, 27th ed., Map 5: Carter Range–Evans Notch, G12

**WMNF PARKING FEE:** Yes

**OTHER ACTIVITIES:** Birding

**A clear, quiet body of water 0.75 mile long by 0.5 mile wide, Mountain Pond evokes images of what many ponds in northern New England must have looked like before lakeside cottages and No Trespassing signs. Beaver houses, loons, a dense spruce-fir forest, and jumbles of rocks dot the shoreline.**

Mountain Pond Trail is south of the Baldface Range in the valley of Slippery Brook, east of Jackson and Wildcat Mountain. Mountain Pond is in a beautiful, secluded part of the White Mountain National Forest, yet it is accessible enough to be a fine family destination. Plan at least a half-day. Families with young children can take a very pleasant short walk, even if they decide not to hike the entire loop.

A shelter on the north side of the pond is a great place to stop for a picnic lunch. The latrine there is the only rest room in the area.

One caveat: This is not a great trail in damp weather. The numerous rocks on the trail become slippery and much of the rest of it gets muddy.

## DIRECTIONS

From North Conway head north on NH 16/US 302 and turn right on Town Hall Road in Intervale (left if you are coming south from Jackson or Glen). After 0.1 mile the road crosses NH 16A and becomes Slippery Brook Road (unmarked), which becomes Forest Road 17. The trailhead is 6.4 miles past 16A, the last four of which are unpaved (but hard packed) through the national forest. Ignore the small road going off to the right where the pavement ends at 2.4 miles. Plan on a fifteen-minute drive after leaving "civilization." The parking lot and trailhead are on the right of FR 17, about 0.6 mile past the junction with Forest Road 38.

Only about the first half of the distance to the trailhead from NH 16 is plowed in winter, so access to the trail is dubious at that time. The unplowed part of the road is popular with snowmobilers.

## TRAIL DESCRIPTION

From the parking lot follow the short, wide path marked with yellow blazes 0.3 mile to the Mountain Pond Loop Trail. The trail is deceptively long because you can easily see across the pond, yet it takes awhile to get around. Besides, it is such a lovely and interesting spot that you will naturally slow down. The trail is rocky in some sections, so expect tired feet at the end.

Although you could walk in either direction around the pond, we suggest walking counterclockwise by turning right at the fork. You will come quickly to the outlet of the pond, which could be muddy during spring thaw or right after heavy rains. If passage over this damp area looks doubtful, turn around and walk the shorter walk described below. It would be frustrating to start out clockwise, walk almost the entire loop, and then get to the outlet, only to discover that it is too muddy to cross comfortably.

The remainder of the loop is never far from the pond shore. The shelter is reached at 1.7 miles and the end of the loop at 2.4 miles.

A shorter walk suitable for all ages is to go clockwise (left) at the fork, walk to the shelter, have a nice relaxing picnic, and then return the way you came (total distance about 2 miles). There are several short spurs that lead down to

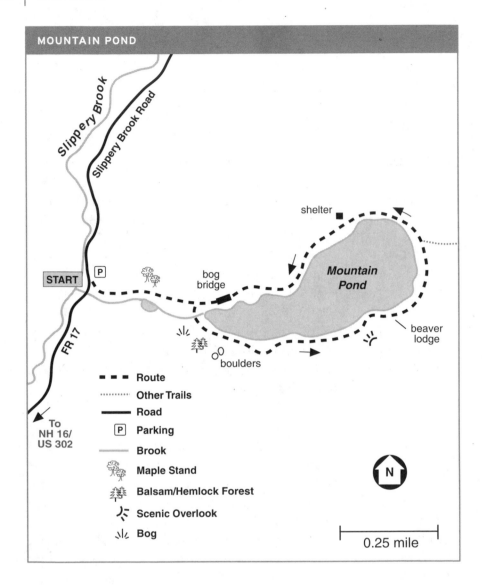

MOUNTAIN POND

**Legend:**
- Route
- Other Trails
- Road
- P Parking
- Brook
- Maple Stand
- Balsam/Hemlock Forest
- Scenic Overlook
- Bog

0.25 mile

the shore of the pond along this section of the trail and a wooden bog bridge across a wet area.

## NATURE NOTES

Not far from the parking lot, even before you get to the loop path, you can find four different kinds of maple tree. Striped maples are particularly striking and easy to identify. These small trees are named for the distinctive white striping along their bright green young stems and branches. Their large leaves (up to 10 inches across), with three relatively small pointed lobes, resemble the webbed foot of a goose, which is why they are also called goosefoot maples. Another name for striped maple is moosewood, a name that predates the popular vegetarian cookbook. Beneath these leaves in early summer one can occasionally find drooping flower clusters or the familiar winged seeds of maples. The striped maples you see along the trails are usually part of the understory, not more than 10 feet tall.

Unlike their smaller cousins, sugar maples are trees of the forest canopy at this elevation. Their leaves are smaller than those of the striped maple and have five pointed lobes. (Here is a good place to observe how sunlight affects leaves: Understory trees, like striped maples, that grow in the shade have larger leaves than trees such as sugar maples, which get more direct sunlight. Even on the same tree, leaves in the shade will tend to be larger than those in direct sunlight.) Sugar maple leaves turn brilliant yellow and orange in fall. And, of course, the concentrated sap of this tree is something everyone adores, particularly on blueberry pancakes.

**Mountain Pond.**

Red maples are equally at home in wetlands and on mountain slopes. Their leaves are smaller than striped maples' and are three-pointed, with sharp angles between the lobes. Red maples turn spectacular shades of red in fall. Their wine-colored flowers in spring bloom before their leaves come out and add a splash of color to wetlands early in the season.

Mountain maples are the most inconspicuous of our four maples, growing as understory shrubs. Their leaves tend to be three-pointed and rounded, and their twigs are hairy. Long clusters of flowers may be present in spring and early summer, and the familiar winged maple seeds can be seen in mid- to late summer.

Beyond the outlet, the trail is dominated by balsam fir and hemlock, with large boulders strewn about. There are many holes under the rocks and along the trail. Imagine the kinds of animals that may be using these as dens. Trees grow directly on top of the boulders, their roots snaking down to reach the soil below. Dense growth of moss, mountain wood sorrel, and other plants of the forest floor add to the magical atmosphere.

Two small plants common here, wintergreen and snowberry, are distinctive for their sweet, minty odor. Both have thick, glossy leaves that remain on the plant throughout winter (hence the name wintergreen). Wintergreen (also called teaberry or checkerberry) is the larger of the two plants, growing as high as two inches off the ground. You can crush a leaf to evoke its pleasant aroma, reminiscent of chewing gum. As a conservation lesson, pick a leaf only where the plant is abundant. The trailing vines of snowberry really hug the ground. Its tiny, rounded leaves are stalkless and seem to come off the stems in pairs. The "wintergreen" smell produced by snowberry is not as overpowering as that produced by wintergreen itself.

Mountain Pond is one of the best spots to find water birds in the White Mountains. Look for loons, ducks, and other water birds whenever you pass an opening along the pond shore. If you are fortunate enough to see loons, take the time to watch these large, handsome birds for a while as they swim silently across the pond, dive for fish, or sound their eerie cry. In summer the loon is unmistakable with its dark head, checkered necklace, speckled back, and large, daggerlike bill.

Common mergansers fish along the shores of the pond. These diving ducks have thin bills with serrated edges. This enables the birds to grasp more easily their slippery prey. Mergansers can be fascinating to watch because small groups use teamwork to capture fish. A merganser team swims in a line to drive the fish toward shore and then dives in tandem to prevent fish from escaping.

You might also spot black duck, hooded merganser, ruffed grouse, hairy woodpecker, rusty blackbird, purple finch, and a number of warblers.

From the south end of the pond looking north there is a view of South Baldface. The bald summit of this 3,500-foot mountain is the result of past wildfires. Back across the pond to the west are the twin peaks of the Doubleheads. There might be a beaver lodge right by the shore.

## TRIP 42
## THE ROOST

**RATING:** Moderate; steep but short

**DISTANCE:** 2.1 miles round-trip

**ELEVATION CHANGE:** 550-foot elevation gain

**ESTIMATED TIME:** 1–1.5 hours

**MAPS:** AMC's *White Mountain National Forest Map and Guide*, E13
AMC's *White Mountain Guide*, 27th ed., Map 5: Carter Range–Evans Notch, E13

**WMNF PARKING FEE:** Small parking area right at trailhead with no fee; larger area about 0.1 mile south with fee

**The Roost, a small hill north of Evans Notch, provides terrific views of the Wild River and Evans Brook valleys. Find the short, steep trail off ME 113 near the Hastings Campground at the abandoned village of Hastings.**

The ascent takes only about a half-hour from the north trailhead, so it rewards you with great views for relatively modest effort. (When you are walking up, you will probably question the use of the term "modest," but it is quick.) Either return the way you came or complete a loop by hiking the 1.2-mile trail and then walking back to your car 0.7 mile along ME 113.

### DIRECTIONS

The Roost Trail forms a semicircle with two trailheads on the east side of ME 113. The north trailhead is about 2.7 miles south of US 2, about 100 yards north of the bridge over Evans Brook and the junction of ME 113 with Wild River Road. This is 7 miles north of the Basin and Cold River campgrounds. There is only space for a few cars opposite the trailhead, so you may need to park at the more substantial turnoff on the south side of the bridge. The south trailhead is 0.7 mile south of the north trailhead on ME 113, about 0.1 mile north of its intersection with Forest Road 8.

### TRAIL DESCRIPTION

The distance to the summit of the Roost is 0.5 mile from the north trailhead and 0.7 mile from the south trailhead. From the north trailhead the trail

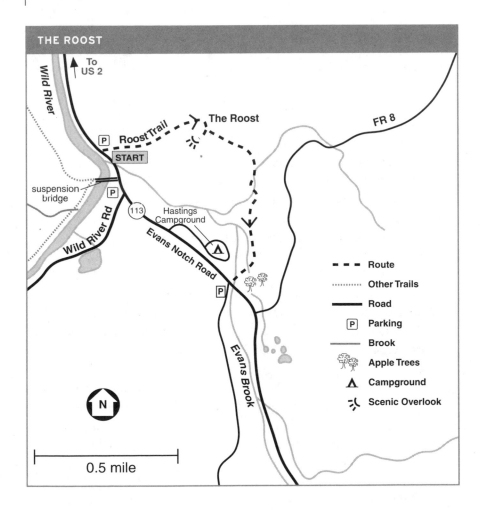

THE ROOST

To US 2

Wild River

Roost Trail

The Roost

FR 8

P

START

suspension bridge

P

113

Hastings Campground

Evans Notch Road

Wild River Rd

P

Evans Brook

N

Route

Other Trails

Road

P Parking

Brook

Apple Trees

Campground

Scenic Overlook

0.5 mile

immediately climbs some stairs. After about twenty minutes of hiking through a forest of mostly paper birch and aspen, you reach the summit. The summit has only a restricted view, so follow the sign To The Scenic View. This leads you downhill to the right on a rather steep side path 0.1 mile to open ledges that overlook the Wild River and the Evans Brook valleys.

After climbing back up to the main trail, either return the way you came or turn right for the rest of the loop. The trail descends through birch, beech, and sugar maple and then crosses a stream 0.3 mile from the summit. Like most streams in the White Mountains, this one could be trouble early in the season when water levels are high. The trail then turns right on a dirt road, crosses a second stream, and passes through an area of small balsam fir. The main road is just after an old apple grove. Turn right onto ME 113 for the walk back to your car.

## NATURE NOTES

The Roost is strategically situated right above the confluence of Evans Brook and the Wild River, enabling you to see both valleys. The Wild River valley, angling off to the southwest, is broader, looking as if glaciers did not carve it quite so deeply as they carved the Evans Brook valley. The tall peaks on the west slope of the Wild River valley are the Carter-Moriah Range. Since the panorama is to the west of the Roost, hike this trail in the morning if you want to take photographs without looking into the sun.

From the Roost, look down and see the leaves of trembling aspen shimmering in the breeze. These trees have smooth, light grayish green bark, but their most notable feature is their leaves. A very gentle wind that hardly even ruffles the leaves of other trees induces aspen leaves to shake violently and evoke the sound of the wind. This is because the leaf stalk is flattened rather than rounded as in most trees. The flattened stalks enable aspen leaves to bend more readily during even the slightest breeze. What function this serves for the aspen is anybody's guess, but what it does for us is to reveal even the slightest breeze.

Aspen, like paper birch, is an early colonizer of land where the trees have been cut or blown down. The aspens on the Roost probably moved in after the area was heavily logged from 1891 to 1917. You can read about the history of this area in *The Wild River Wilderness* by D. B. Wight (Courier Press, 1971)

**Suspension bridge over Wild River near the Roost.** Photo by Nancy Schalch.

and *Logging Railroads of the White Mountains* by C. F. Belcher (AMC Books, 1980).

The flood plain of the rivers that you see below from the Roost is one of the few level areas in this mountainous region. In the mid-nineteenth century it had been farmed by a runaway slave who, as legend has it, had to abandon his farm and flee the area when his former master came looking for him. Then the loggers came.

Before 1890 logging operations had been small. Logs were either floated down the Wild River or dragged by teams of horses to a mill at the village of Gilead. In 1891 the Wild River Railroad was built to transport wood products down the valley, and logging efforts began in earnest. Hemlock bark was taken for tanneries and red spruce for pulp. The village of Hastings, with a population of more than 300, sprang up almost overnight in the V between the two rivers. The village had sawmills, a school, a post office, houses for workers, and a plant that produced wood alcohol. The Wild River Railroad ran alongside the Wild River about 15 miles south into the valley, following the course of present-day ME 113 south from Gilead, then Wild River Road and Wild River Trail. Like Zealand Valley, there were a number of logging camps, trestles, railroad yards, and spur lines along the railroad. Also like Zealand, the logging activity removed many acres of trees and spawned fires and erosion, causing devastation where a few years before a wilderness had existed.

Disaster came in 1903 when the Wild River lived up to its name. A tremendous flood from March 11 to 20 inundated Hastings and destroyed much of the Wild River Railroad. This was followed in 1904 by a very dry year with many forest fires.

When the loggers left, the wilderness returned and prevails today. Now, looking down from the Roost, it is hard to imagine a thriving village had been there. The abandoned apple grove near the south trailhead is one of the few reminders of that once-thriving community.

Note the difference in the forest in the north and south parts of the trail. As you ascend from the north trailhead, you pass through a diverse forest of beech, sugar maple, paper birch, white ash, hop hornbeam (note vertically scraggly bark), and aspen. There is a red spruce forest near the summit, then, when you descend south, typical northern hardwoods, dominated by yellow birch, beech, and sugar maple. Along the dirt road, you pass some very big white pine, hemlock, and red spruce.

Take a detour along ME 113 to walk out on the 180-foot suspension bridge over the Wild River near the parking area for the north trailhead. This narrow footbridge bounces with your steps, which is either very exciting or terrorizing, depending on your point of view. There is a good sitting log near the water on the opposite side of the river, a great place to end your hike.

## TRIP 43
## BASIN TRAIL TO BASIN RIM

**RATING:** Moderate

**DISTANCE:** 4.6 miles round-trip

**ELEVATION CHANGE:** 800-foot elevation gain

**ESTIMATED TIME:** 4–6 hours

**MAPS:** AMC's *White Mountain National Forest Map and Guide*, F12
AMC's *White Mountain Guide*, 27th ed., Map 5: Carter Range–Evans Notch, F12

**WMNF PARKING FEE:** Yes

**OTHER ACTIVITIES:** Swimming, birding

**The Basin is an impressive glacial cirque (bowl-shaped ravine carved out by a glacier) in the Evans Notch region. The best view, which includes impressive cliffs and Basin Pond, is from the Basin Rim, a ridge in the Baldface-Royce Range.**

The Basin Trail runs 4.5 miles from the Wild River valley up and over the Basin Rim and then down to Evans Notch by the Basin Campground and Recreation Area, so you can ascend to the Rim from either direction. The approach from the Wild River valley is more gradual and allows you to hike along Blue Brook for a good distance, so we feature that part of the trail here. With two cars you could hike the entire trail.

## DIRECTIONS

The drive to the trailhead includes a 5.2-mile stretch on Wild River Road (Forest Road 12), a dirt road (well packed) that follows the route of the former Wild River Railroad. Wild River Road heads southwest off Evans Notch Road (ME 113) 2.8 miles south of the town of Gilead (where 113 intersects with US 2) and about 7 miles north of the Basin and Cold River campgrounds. It is marked by signs to the Wild River Campground. There is a parking area for hikers just before you actually enter the campground.

## TRAIL DESCRIPTION

The Basin Trail, marked by yellow blazes, starts out as a gentle path through
a rich, deciduous woodland full of wildflowers and a number of bog bridges.
Expect some muddy spots in spring or after rain. At 1.3 miles, the trail crosses
Blue Brook at a good lunch or snack spot, and then begins to ascend on the
east bank of the brook. This 0.3-mile part of the trail is exceptionally nice, with
rushing water, small ravines, and an impressive cliff. It could be a turnaround
point. In drier weather, there are ample places to walk on the flat rocks of the

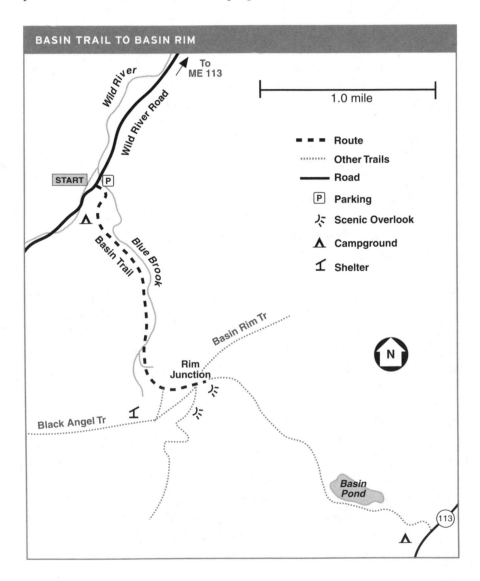

BASIN TRAIL TO BASIN RIM

Wild River

Wild River Road

To
ME 113

1.0 mile

- - - Route
.......... Other Trails
——— Road
P  Parking
⅄  Scenic Overlook
⛺  Campground
⌂  Shelter

START  P

Basin Trail

Blue Brook

Basin Rim Tr

Rim
Junction

Black Angel Tr

N

Basin
Pond

113

stream bed, and a few deeper pools for experiencing the water more directly. The trail then turns away from the brook, ascends more steeply and passes a trail leading to the Blue Brook Shelter (2.0 miles). It then reaches the Rim Junction at 2.2 miles where the Basin Rim Trail intersects. Continue on the Basin Trail for about another 0.1 mile to a small, open ledge facing eastward, slightly off the trail and just before it begins to descend into the Basin. This vista is a good lunch spot before retracing your steps. There is also a great overlook about 0.1 mile south of Rim Junction on the Basin Rim Trail.

(For those who have spotted a second car at Basin Pond and are hiking the entire Basin Trail, it is a 1,300-foot descent and 2.3 miles from Rim Junction to the parking area at Basin Pond.)

On the way back, follow the sign for the Basin Trail (not to be confused with the Basin Rim Trail) and Wild River Campground at Rim Junction. About 0.2 mile from the parking lot, be sure to follow an arrow pointing to the right at a fork with the old trail.

## NATURE NOTES

The view from the Basin Rim, which includes the cliffs of West Royce, the Basin Pond, Blueberry Mountain, and other peaks in Maine, allows you to contemplate the glacial geology of the Basin. The Basin is the Evans Notch counterpart

**West Royce Mountain, Basin Pond, and Blueberry Mountain from the Basin Rim.**

to Tuckerman Ravine, an eastward-facing bowl created by a mountain glacier during the last ice age (1 million to 12,000 years ago). The carving of the steep headwall occurred over a long period of time as a result of the abrasive action of small stones, pebbles, and sand within the ice. Also, rocks were plucked from the side of the mountain when water under the glacier thawed, flowed into cracks in the rocks, and then refroze. The rocks removed collect in a heap toward the bottom of the bowl. The flat bottom of glacial cirques are frequently filled with ponds, which geologists have termed tarns.

The Basin Rim provides a bird's-eye view of birds too. Watch for turkey vultures soaring majestically with outstretched wings at eye level over the valley. These birds are master gliders, riding warm thermal air currents created as the day heats up. It enables them to save energy that would be required for flapping while they search for their lunch of dead animals. You might also see ravens and swifts, both of which build nests on the cliffs. Warblers such as yellow-rumped magnolia, black-throated green warbler, black-throated blue warbler, and redstarts flitter around the trees on the ridge.

Signs of moose are everywhere, particularly on the lower part of this trail. Look for their very large hoof prints in muddy parts of the trail and their droppings in piles scattered here and there. If you are lucky and have a pair of binoculars, you may even be able to spot one from the viewpoint in the marshy areas of Basin Pond down below.

The walk along Blue Brook may delight you even more than the vista. The water rushes through some small canyons, forming miniature waterfalls and quieter pools. When water levels are low, there are places where you can walk across the brook by hopping from rock to rock. Small caves and passageways between large boulders invite exploration. Bring a bathing suit if you want a chance for the brook to turn you into the color of its namesake. One particularly good spot to explore is where the brook flows near an impressive cliff face that rises up on the opposite bank.

Wildflowers are abundant, particularly along the first part of the trail. Look for the cloverlike three-leaflets of the mountain wood sorrel. It produces white flowers lined with pink from late June through early August. Bunchberry, trillium, clintonia, Indian cucumber-root, and pink lady's slipper may be in bloom, depending on the time of year. Cinnamon fern is common in damp areas. These large ferns are named for their cinnamon-colored fertile frond (the part that bears the spores) rising straight up from a circle of green fronds. Its stipe (stalk) is covered with cinnamon-colored chaff.

Basin Pond itself invites exploration, either by driving there after the hike or, for those who have spotted a second car, by continuing on the Basin Trail down the steep headwall to the Basin Recreation Area (picnic tables, rest rooms, campground, and canoe access) off ME 113. Walk out on the dam, stroll along the shoreline, or look out over the pond for ducks, spotted sandpipers, swallows, signs of beavers, and an elusive moose. Bring your canoe if you have one. It makes a fitting end to a great day of hiking.

## TRIP 44
## BLUEBERRY MOUNTAIN VIA STONE HOUSE TRAIL

**RATING:** Moderate with some steep sections
**DISTANCE:** 4.7 miles round-trip
**ELEVATION CHANGE:** 1,150-foot elevation gain
**ESTIMATED TIME:** 3–5 hours
**MAPS:** AMC's *White Mountain National Forest Map and Guide,* F13
AMC's *White Mountain Guide,* 27th ed., Map 5: Carter Range–Evans Notch, F13
**WMNF PARKING FEE:** None
**OTHER ACTIVITIES:** Swimming

**Blueberry Mountain is loaded with blueberries and commands great views of the Baldface Ridge and the hills around the Cold River valley. Stone House Trail passes a gorge and a deep pool in Rattlesnake Brook.**

The name of this trail conjures up images of an August afternoon blissfully spent picking sweet blue morsels from low shrubs while looking out over a pretty valley and surrounding mountains. Most of the trail is a soft, gradually ascending path, but the upper part is steeper and has a few rocky sections.

A 0.7-mile loop around the summit gives you access to several outlooks. Plan on at least a half-day outing to hike the entire walk plus the loop. It can be a full day if you stop at the gorge and the pool, have a picnic lunch, and do some serious blueberry picking on the summit. If you do not have much time or energy, a hike only as far as Rattlesnake Pool would still be a satisfying one-to-two-hour outing.

The Stone House Trail provides the easiest ascent of Blueberry Mountain and is the most suitable for young children, but there are several other ways to hike up or down. The Stone House Trail can be combined with the Blueberry Ridge and White Cairn trails to make a nice loop, but be aware that the White Cairn Trail has some steep, rocky sections that could be a problem in wet weather. Check the AMC's *White Mountain Guide* or the Chatham Trails Association (CTA) map if you want to explore more.

## DIRECTIONS

If you are coming from NH 16 in Conway or North Conway, pick up ME 113 in Fryeburg either by taking US 302 or NH 113, and head north. From Gorham, N.H., or Bethel, Maine, take ME 113 south from its junction with US 2.

The trailhead for the Stone House Trail is off an unmarked dirt road (Forest Road 16/Stone House Road) that heads east from ME 113 about 1.3 miles north of the AMC's Cold River Camp, 7 miles north of the Stowe Corner Store, and about a mile south of the Basin Recreation Area.

Forest Road 16 crosses a small stream and then makes a sharp right and then a sharp left. Park on the side of the road at a closed gate about 1.1 miles from ME 113. Continue walking on the road past the trailhead for the White Cairn Trail (0.3 mile) until you reach the Stone House Trail going off to the left, about 0.5 mile from the gate. The road continues on as the Shell Pond Trail, past the Stone House and a private airstrip.

## TRAIL DESCRIPTION

The Stone House Trail is named for the Stone House, which was built from granite carted down from the Baldface Ridge by oxen about 200 years ago. The trail is well marked with CTA signs and some yellow blazes. The trail passes through private land for the first mile, so stay on the main trail marked by the CTA signs and blazes, except for the detours to Rattlesnake Flume and Pool.

The first part of the trail is wide, like an old logging road, and is a very gradual uphill. After 0.2 mile, a private path from the Stone House enters right. A few paces beyond, a spur trail to the right marked with an arrow leads you to the gorge. It is definitely worth the 30-yard detour to the little wooden bridge over Rattlesnake Flume. There is a whole network of trails beyond that bridge which could easily get you lost, so return back to the main trail the way you came and continue uphill.

After 0.5 mile, the trail crosses a small wooden bridge and then passes a sign saying Stone House Trail to Blueberry Mountain. Shortly after, another spur trail on the right leads you 0.1 mile to Rattlesnake Pool.

After the pool, return to the main trail. This is a logical place to turn back if you have had enough hiking. If not, continue uphill on the Stone House Trail, being sure to stay left at a fork as indicated by a CTA sign.

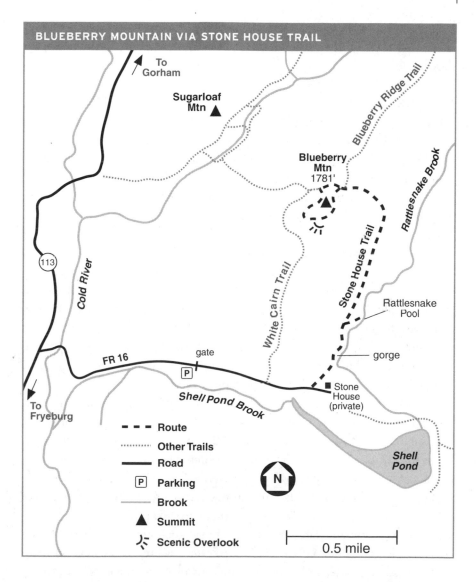

At 0.8 mile, the trail enters the Caribou–Speckled Mountain Wilderness and becomes steeper, passing through a thick forest of beech. Near the summit of Blueberry Mountain, red spruce and balsam fir take over. Make sure to follow the yellow blazes carefully at this point. The trail reaches the junction with Blueberry Ridge Trail 1.5 miles from the start of the trail (2 miles from your car).

For the best vistas and blueberries, take a left (west) on the Blueberry Ridge Trail and follow it past a few small cairns for about 50 yards to its junction with the Overlook Loop. The Overlook Loop goes off to the left, winding past ledges and a small bog for 0.5 mile before ending back at the Blueberry Ridge Trail. Turn right for the 0.2-mile walk back to the Stone House Trail and your descent.

## NATURE NOTES

Rattlesnake Flume is the first highlight of the Stone House Trail. Here you can stand on a wooden bridge and watch the waters of Rattlesnake Brook rushing through a narrow gorge with straight walls rising about 25 feet above the water. Rock fern and rock tripe cover the damp walls of the flume. On the opposite side of the brook look for the exquisite flowers of trailing arbutus (in May) and twinflower (in July). Like the well-known Flume Gorge of Franconia Notch, Rattlesnake Flume was created by the erosion of a narrow dike of softer rock that had intruded into the granite.

Rattlesnake Pool is actually a series of small pools connected by cascades and chutes. The setting is a shady woods of hemlock, beech, yellow birch, and striped maple. This is a good spot for a snack, lunch, or if you are truly daring, a plunge into the icy waters. The first pool is fairly deep (probably about fifteen feet) and is remarkable for its very clear water. The pools farther downstream are shallower and more suitable for young children, but be prepared for some scrambling over boulders that may be slippery.

The Overlook Loop around the summit of Blueberry Mountain has great views from a number of open, rocky ledges. We first visited the summit on a magical day in fall when the scene was at first muted and dull because of fog. Then the fog began to lift, unveiling incredibly vivid fall foliage. The peaks of the Baldface Range slowly came into view and eventually loomed over everything. Special moments like this can make you forget all the damp days of hiking in the mist, when you cannot see much past your own nose.

The most abundant plants around the Overlook Loop are blueberry, huckleberry, and sheep laurel. Lowbush blueberry shrubs are everywhere on Blueberry Mountain, so bring a container for your mid-July through late-August hike. Do not ignore the darker, blue-black huckleberries—they are "seedier" but also quite tasty. The huckleberry can be distinguished from blueberry by their leaves; huckleberry leaves are covered by small, yellow resin dots on their undersides (easier to see if you have a hand lens).

Other plants to note around the ledges are rhodora, which has beautiful, large pink flowers around Memorial Day weekend, three-toothed cinquefoil, red pine, white pine, and red spruce.

The small bog along the Overlook Loop provides a good illustration of why bogs form where they do. The water that collects in this depression is

**Rattlesnake Pool.**

stagnant, having no flow of water to replenish nutrients once they are used up by plants. The sphagnum moss that grows so abundantly in the bog make life even more difficult for plants and for the fungi and bacteria that decompose dead leaves and recycle nutrients, because they increase the acidity of the water. As a result, plants that live in bogs have to be able to survive on very low levels of nutrients.

One beautiful tree that manages to grow quite well in this and other bogs is larch, a conifer whose gracefully curved branches and light, airy appearance make it seem lacy and oriental. You may spot cotton sedge, with its unmistakable white cottony balls at the top of leafless, grasslike stems. Bog bilberry, rhodora, and mountain holly also grow here.

Beechdrops is a unique plant that grows only under beech trees. All you ever see of this 6-to-18-inch plant are its small white flowers with reddish

**Hermit thrush, a beautiful songster of lower elevations.**

brown splotches scattered along a colorless stalk. It has no green leaves because it gets all its nutrition by parasitizing the roots of beech trees. Beechdrops do no obvious damage to their host beech trees. Whenever there are beechdrops, you are bound to find some beeches present.

If you are listening for birdsongs as you ascend in June and July, you are likely to hear the flutelike songs of hermit thrush as you start the trail and Swainson's thrush higher up. Also, keep your eyes open for a guild of forest birds, including chickadee, nuthatch, downy woodpecker, blue jay, and some finches. Ravens, dark-eyed juncos, and snowshoe hares are all possible at the summit.

# 7

# KILKENNY REGION

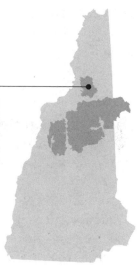

## LAY OF THE LAND

The Kilkenny Region lies north of the major White Mountain areas, above US 2 and Gorham. It tends to be less crowded than the busy notches farther south, probably because it is a longer drive for visitors from the south; its mountains are not as tall as the Presidential or the Franconia ranges; and the area is still a center of logging operations. Nevertheless, the Kilkenny Region has a certain mystique for backpackers and others who want to escape the crowds. It is the White Mountains as they might have been 50 years ago. Much of the area is wild and less developed for tourists. Several peaks in the Kilkenny Range, which forms the central "spine" of this region, are over 4,000 feet.

## LOGISTICS AND SUPPLIES

The South Pond Recreational Area (see below) has a bathhouse, rest rooms, and picnic tables. Berlin is the largest city in this section of the White Mountains. Pick up supplies there or in other towns you pass through on your way up, such as Gorham, Lancaster, or Twin Mountain. Stark, several miles west of the access road, is the nearest community to the South Pond Recreation Area.

## NEARBY CAMPING

There are no national forest campgrounds in this region. The Nay Pond Campground is in West Milan off NH 110. Moose Brook State Park in Gorham has 42 tent sites.

---

## TRIP 45
## LOOKOUT LEDGE

**RATING:** Moderate

**DISTANCE:** 2.6 miles round-trip

**ELEVATION CHANGE:** 450-foot elevation gain

**ESTIMATED TIME:** 1.5–3 hours

**MAPS:** AMC's *White Mountain National Forest Map and Guide*, E9 and Kilkenny inset

AMC's *White Mountain Guide*, 27th ed., Map 6: North Country–Mahoosuc Range, E9

**WMNF PARKING FEE:** None

**Lookout Ledge is a rocky outcropping on the side of Mount Randolph that affords a wonderful view of King Ravine and Mounts Adams and Madison, plus some of the peaks of the Carter Range.**

Lookout Ledge can be approached by a number of trails north of US 2 maintained by the Randolph Mountain Club (RMC). The Ledge Trail provides a relatively direct ascent, steep in a few places but for the most part well graded.

You could also think of this as the hay-scented-fern walk. The walk was described in the AMC's *White Mountain Guide*, 26th ed., as passing through a "beautiful forest," but the forest is now in transition. The ice storm in January 1998 knocked down an extraordinary number of trees. Sunlight that now penetrates to the forest floor has stimulated the rampant growth of hay-scented fern.

## DIRECTIONS

The trailhead for the Ledge Trail is at the Ravine House site on Durand Road in Randolph. From Franconia Notch, Crawford Notch, and Twin Mountain take US 3 north at its junction with US 302 in Twin Mountain. After about 2 miles, turn right on NH 115 and take it for about 10 miles to US 2. Turn right

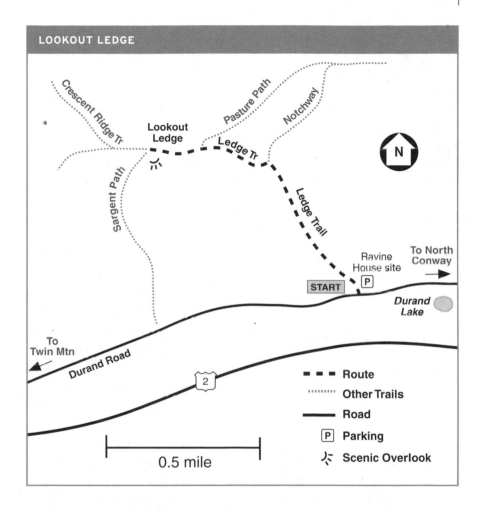

on US 2, take it for about 6 miles, then make a left onto Durand Road, which parallels US 2 closely. The Ravine House site is well marked on the left in about 2 miles. The trailhead is on the west side of the Ravine House site, where there is room for several cars. (Durand Road eventually rejoins US 2 about 1 mile east of the Ravine House. John Durand, for whom the road was named, was a Londoner who received the original grant to settle in the region. The town of Randolph was originally known as Durand.)

From North Conway and Pinkham Notch, take NH 16 into Gorham, where it meets US 2. Travel west on US 2 for about 4 miles past its split with NH 16. Make a right at the east intersection of Durand Road with US 2 and take it for 1 mile to the Ravine House site on the right.

## TRAIL DESCRIPTION

The Ledge Trail is not heavily used, so may be overgrown in sections, but it is well marked with orange blazes. The first few paces are on blacktop, then on a steep, old logging road. At a small stream it turns right and leaves the logging road and parallels the small stream uphill. In 0.6 mile, the trail makes a sharp bend to the left where the Notchway comes in. It then climbs steeply, joins another overgrown logging road for a time, and reaches a junction with the Pasture Path at 1.1 miles. Follow the Ledge Trail for another 0.2 mile to Lookout Ledge, where it meets the Crescent Ridge Trail and Sargent Path.

## NATURE NOTES

The most striking view from Lookout Ledge is of the glacial cirque of King Ravine on the upper slope of Mount Adams. It is a classical bowl-shaped ravine, as if it were taken straight from the pages of a geology textbook. With binoculars you can easily see the boulders that fell from the sides of the ravine and now litter its floor. Although the boulders look small from Lookout Ledge, they present a serious challenge to hikers into King Ravine. Look for Crag Camp, an RMC-operated cabin overlooking King Ravine on its right wall.

Lookout Ledge is a great place to bring out your compass and a map of the region in order to identify mountains, ridges, valleys, and streams. Any of the AMC's maps of this area would be perfect for this task, including the *White Mountain National Forest Map and Guide* (which provides a landscape-level view of the forest), the Brad Washburn map "Mount Washington and the Heart of Presidential Range," or the North Country–Mahoosuc Range map that accompanies the 27th edition of the *White Mountain Guide*. Mounts Adams and Madison, with their pointed, picturesque summits, loom large in the foreground. From west to east are Castellated Ridge, Nowell Ridge, King Ravine, Durand Ridge, Snyder Brook, Gordon Ridge, and Howker Ridge. The col between the two peaks is the location of the AMC's Madison Hut. To the southeast are Pine Mountain and Imp Mountain of the Carter-Moriah Range. The Mahoosuc Range and the Androscoggin River Valley are to the east. Durand Lake is right below.

The forest gap dynamics as you hike up the Ledge Trail provide an interesting ecological lesson in succession. What had once been a closed canopy of northern hardwoods has been opened up by blowdowns resulting from the 1998 ice storm. Where trees have been thrown over, sunlight now penetrates to the forest floor. The most immediate beneficiary is hay-scented fern, a plant that thrives in openings within the forest and has taken over large sections of the understory. These ferns are able to exploit forest gaps because once they

**Hay-scented fern along the Lookout Ledge Trail.**

take root, they spread rapidly. All the hay-scented ferns in one forest opening may actually be connected by underground rhizomes and therefore be one individual plant. Eventually, saplings of sugar maple, yellow birch, and American beech, spawned from nearby trees that survived the storm, will likely fill in the open patches, perhaps preceded by paper birch. For the trees, periodic setbacks from storms, harsh winters, drought, flooding, disease, and insect outbreaks are part of what they must tolerate if they are going to thrive in the White Mountains.

Two other types of ferns grow in an obvious place along the Ledge Trail. Look for New York fern, with its smallish, lacy frond tapered at both ends, and sensitive fern along the driveway at the beginning of the trail. Sensitive ferns produce clusters of small round spore cases (sori) on a stem separate from its leafy frond. You might have seen these "fertile fronds" in dried flower arrangements, where they are usually spray-painted silver.

A wildflower that grows in abundance along the Ledge Trail is Solomon's seal. This member of the lily family has unbranched arching stems with broad, lance-shaped leaves. In spring pairs of small, greenish-yellow flowers hang down underneath the stem. In summer these turn into blue-black berries. The name Solomon's seal is derived from the pattern of the scar left on the rootstock when the stem is broken off. It presumably resembles the official seal of the ancient king.

The Ravine House site at the trailhead should be a place of pilgrimage for anyone interested in the history of trail-building. First opened for guests in 1877, it became a summer hangout for people who built and hiked trails in the Northern Presidentials and the Randolph area. According to Guy and Laura Waterman's *Forest and Crag: A History of Hiking, Trail Blazing, and Adventure in the Northeast Mountains* (AMC Books), the Ravine House was not an opulent hotel cut from the gilded age, such as the still extant Mount Washington Hotel in Bretton Woods, but rather a comfortable, rambling inn, grand in its own way. Like visitors today to AMC Huts, the hikers of those days must have looked forward to returning to the Ravine House each evening for dinner and discussion with the other guests about the trails they had hiked that day and what they were planning next. The Ravine House closed its doors in 1960, but the town of Randolph continues the tradition of trail work and community spirit fostered by the Ravine House and several other now defunct hotels in the area.

## TRIP 46
## DEVIL'S HOPYARD

**RATING:** Easy

**DISTANCE:** 2.0 miles round-trip

**ELEVATION CHANGE:** Minimal elevation change

**ESTIMATED TIME:** 1–2 hours

**MAPS:** AMC's *White Mountain National Forest Map and Guide*, Kilkenny inset

AMC's *White Mountain Guide*, 27th ed., Map 6: North Country–Mahoosuc Range, B8

**WMNF PARKING FEE:** Yes

**OTHER ACTIVITIES:** Fishing, swimming

**The Devil's Hopyard gorge is otherworldly. The cold water of the rushing stream below the boulders and the dense shade within the steep walls of the gorge create a cool, lush, and rocky landscape.**

The South Pond Recreation Area is ideal for families—an easily accessible, developed Forest Service recreational area with picnic tables, a swimming beach, a bathhouse, and boater access. South Pond itself hosts lake trout and loons and serves as a jumping-off point for a short walk to a narrow, deep gorge called the Devil's Hopyard or for longer backpacking trips along the Kilkenny Ridge.

The beginning section of the trail to the Devil's Hopyard is a wheelchair-accessible path, which means it is also ideal for strollers and very young walkers. Within the Devil's Hopyard itself, the trail requires some scrambling on rocks, so this section is not recommended for families with young children (two to five years). Caution is required at all times for everyone because the rocks in the shady gorge are wet and slippery. The Devil's Hopyard is an exquisite spot, however, and it is certainly worth the walk, even if you don't get very far into it.

The recreation area is open roughly from 9:00 A.M. to 8:00 P.M. during the summer season, and an entrance fee is charged. During the off-season a barrier blocks the access road about a mile from the parking area. Hikers can go around the barrier but need to walk about twenty minutes to get to the pond itself and the Hopyard trail.

The trail should take about an hour, but add more time if you walk farther into the Devil's Hopyard or if you need to park at the gate. You can spend a whole day in the area, hanging out at the beach and picnic area for part of the time and hiking for the remainder.

## DIRECTIONS

Take NH 16 north from Gorham 4.5 miles to Berlin. Bear left on NH 110 heading north (to West Milan). It is a little tricky following NH 110 as it winds its way through Berlin, since the directional arrows are rather tiny. It makes a left on Madigan Street and then a right on Wight Street. Stay on NH 110 past Ducky's Minimart and the Nay Pond Campground through West Milan. South Pond Road is on the left 14.7 miles after turning onto NH 110 in Berlin. There are a number of mailboxes and a hiking sign at the intersection, but the sign for the South Pond Recreation Area may not be there in the off-season. Bear right in 0.7 mile, where South Pond Road forks. If you visit when the barrier is across the road a short distance after the fork, you will need to leave your car there and walk the remainder of the distance to the pond (about a mile).

From Franconia Notch or Twin Mountain, take US 3 north about 25 miles past Twin Mountain to its intersection with NH 110 in Groveton. This drive will take you near the town of Guildhall, Vermont, notable as the ancestral home of the Crawford family before they settled in the notch that now bears their name. Follow NH 110 through Stark another 8 miles or so, and turn right on South Pond Road about 1.7 miles past a historic marker along the road.

## TRAIL DESCRIPTION

This is a dead-end trail, and you don't have to walk to the very end to enjoy it. Walk past the bathhouse at the South Pond Recreation Area, following signs to the Kilkenny Ridge Trail and the wheelchair-accessible trail. These start out together along South Pond as a level, flat gravel path for several hundred yards. Along the way there are benches at which you can stop and admire the

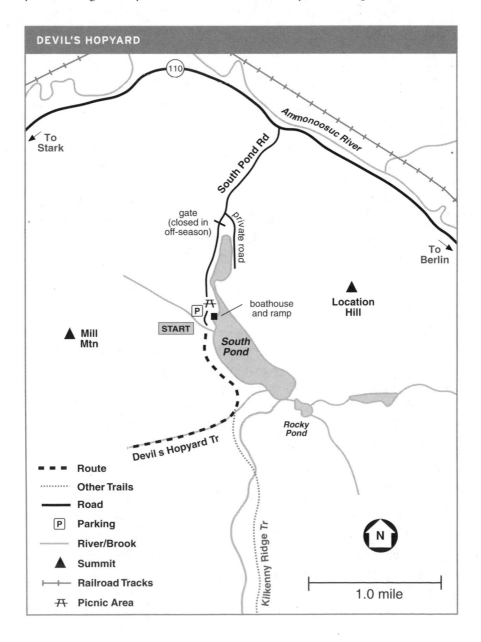

DEVIL'S HOPYARD

110

To Stark

Ammonoosuc River

South Pond Rd

gate (closed in off-season)

private road

To Berlin

P

boathouse and ramp

Location Hill

Mill Mtn

START

South Pond

Rocky Pond

Devil's Hopyard Tr

Kilkenny Ridge Tr

- - - Route

......... Other Trails

—— Road

P Parking

—— River/Brook

▲ Summit

+—+— Railroad Tracks

Picnic Area

N

1.0 mile

pond, pull out a fishing rod, or throw stones in the water. The trail extends as a path beyond the handicapped trail. At 0.6 mile, the trail to the Devil's Hopyard forks off to the right and the Kilkenny Ridge Trail continues on straight for 13 more miles. At 0.8 mile, the Devil's Hopyard Trail crosses a stream on a bouncy log bridge and shortly beyond enters the Devil's Hopyard itself. Here the trail changes from a flat woodland path to a rocky scramble.

Once in the Devil's Hopyard itself, the trail becomes increasingly steep before ending at 1.3 miles and climbing about 400 feet. The gorge is shady and remains damp long after rainstorms have passed. Use your judgment about how much farther everyone should clamber before turning around.

## NATURE NOTES

Before entering the Devil's Hopyard, the trail passes through a rich deciduous forest, the type that dominates the lower elevations of the White Mountains. Trees include American beech, sugar maple, and yellow birch. Beech trees have distinct smooth, gray bark that looks like it was meant for someone to carve their initials into (of course, you won't do that!). Sugar maples have the familiar five-lobed leaves. The bark of yellow birch, which peels naturally, is yellowish brown and marked with short horizontal lines.

Two shorter woody plants common along this part of the trail are striped maple and hobblebush. Striped maple is a small tree with large, lobed leaves that look like a goose's foot and distinctly green-and-white-striped bark. Hobblebush forms impenetrable thickets that will hobble anyone who dares to lumber through. It has large, rounded leaves that are arranged along its skinny branches in pairs. In May it produces striking, flat-topped clusters of white flowers, larger showy ones on the outside of the cluster and smaller ones inside. Its red berries in summer provide a nice splash of color to the forest understory.

The flowers of the hobblebush show a fascinating division of labor. The showy outer flowers are all show but no business. They serve to attract insects to the cluster but are themselves sterile. The innocuous-looking flowers in the center of the cluster lack the showy petals but have the stamens and pistils needed to produce fruits and seeds. Insects attracted to the cluster by the showy flowers brush up against the inner ones, pollinating them. Later on in the season clusters of fruits that start out red and eventually turn bluish-black, show that this unique arrangement does work.

This is a good place to observe the two different ways leaves arrange themselves around branches. Hobblebush and maples have "opposite" leaves, because two leaves are attached to branches in pairs at the same point. Yellow

**Hobblebush in midsummer.** Photo by Nancy Schalch.

birch and beech are "alternately" leaved, because individual leaves are attached singly and alternate along the stem.

Opposite- or alternate-leaved patterns are generally consistent within groups of plants. All maples and viburnums (of which hobblebush is a representative) have opposite leaves. Beeches, birches, oaks, and blueberries are always alternately leaved. The white ash, which grows along South Pond, not only has opposite leaves, but the leaves are compound, i.e., broken up into seven or so leaflets.

The small, delicate fern that covers much of the forest floor is New York fern, a misnomer since it is easily as common to New England as it is to New York. Note that its frond (the upright stem and leaflet combination) tapers sharply at the top and bottom.

Shiny club moss is abundant in the forest floor at the junction of the Devil's Hopyard and Kilkenny Ridge trails. It resembles an upright moss with erect, 6-inch stems. These are covered by tightly whorled "leaves," each from an eighth- to a quarter-inch long. They are easily overlooked, but millions of years ago their distant relatives were as large as trees. Much of the coal we burn for fuel came from the fossilized ancestors of the little club moss.

As you enter the Devil's Hopyard, the gradient steepens and the stream alternates between fast-moving riffles and calm pools. Notice how cool it is, as if you've just walked into a refrigerator. The cooler temperature results from the cold water of the rushing stream and the dense shade within the steep walls of the gorge. Even in midsummer, lingering ice can be found in holes between the rocks.

At times you might feel as if you are walking on top of the stream, and indeed you are. The stream is often hidden underneath a jumble of large rocks that are part of the trail. Gurgling sounds from holes between the rocks reveal that the stream has gone underground.

Mosses abound in this cool, damp habitat. One of the most abundant here is the common piggyback moss, named because the new, delicate ferny branches ride directly on top of the old. This moss is also called fern moss, so named because of its delicate, ferny appearance.

As for the name Devil's Hopyard, your guess is as good as ours. Someone must have considered the dark, misty gorge a sinister place, appropriate for a devil. That same person must have thought that labeling it a hopyard, after a cultivated vine found nowhere in the White Mountains, was a more powerful symbol than naming it a mossyard.

# 8
# HIKES TO HUTS

**IN 1888, THE APPALACHIAN MOUNTAIN CLUB** built a hut to provide overnight accommodations at Madison Springs high up in the Northern Presidential Range. Today, the AMC operates a network of eight mountain huts—each
a day's hike apart—that stretches 56 miles along the Appalachian Trail through
the White Mountains in New Hampshire. The huts are set amid some of the
most spectacular scenery in the East and have a long, cherished history of
providing hospitality to hikers.

By staying at an AMC hut you can extend your day hike over 2 days and reach
farther into the backcountry to explore trails, mountains, lakes, and waterfalls.
And at the end of the day, the hut provides hospitality, hearty meals, and clean,
comfortable accommodations. Guests can take part in a naturalist walk and
learn about natural history and local ecology from displays and books. Snacks
and hot drinks are available even for day visitors who stop to rest midhike.

The AMC huts are reached by hikes of varying difficulty, from gentle,
wooded trails to more rigorous above-treeline routes. The hut trips in this
book require only an easy to moderate hike and make fine destinations for day
hikes as well as overnight trips. For cold-weather hiking, snowshoeing, and
skiing enthusiasts, three of those four (Carter, Zealand, and Lonesome Lake)
are open in winter on a self-service basis. All other huts close in September or
October and reopen in May or June.

Reservations are required for an overnight stay. For more information or for reservations, call 603-466-2727 or go to www.outdoors.org/lodging. The website includes planning resources and lets you check availability, current weather and trail conditions, and more.

## TRIP 47
## LONESOME LAKE HUT

**RATING:** Moderate
**DISTANCE:** 3.2 miles round-trip
**ELEVATION CHANGE:** 950-foot elevation gain
**ESTIMATED TIME:** 4 hours
**MAPS:** AMC's *White Mountain National Forest Map and Guide*, H4
AMC's *White Mountain Guide*, 27th ed., Map 2: Franconia–Pemigewasset, H4
**WMNF PARKING FEE:** None
**WINTER NOTES:** Snowshoe to this hut in winter for a great adventure with family or friends.
**OTHER ACTIVITIES:** Swimming, fishing

**Lonesome Lake is a beautiful lake perched on a shoulder of the Kinsman Range on the west side of Franconia Notch. It is a good family destination because it rewards you with swimming and great views after a moderate effort.**

The AMC's Lonesome Lake Hut at the south end of the lake provides overnight accommodations and very hearty meals (reservations required). Day-hikers can use the rest rooms and buy trail snacks, hot and cold drinks, trail maps, T-shirts, and other supplies. Soup is sometimes available midday.

This hut is especially popular with families because it requires a relatively short walk and is laid out so that families staying overnight often can have a room to themselves. An AMC naturalist is usually there to present an evening program, lead a family-oriented nature walk, or discuss your questions about the mountains. Day hikes starting from the hut include a short, self-guided nature trail or a longer network of trails that take you around the lake to Cannon Mountain or other destinations.

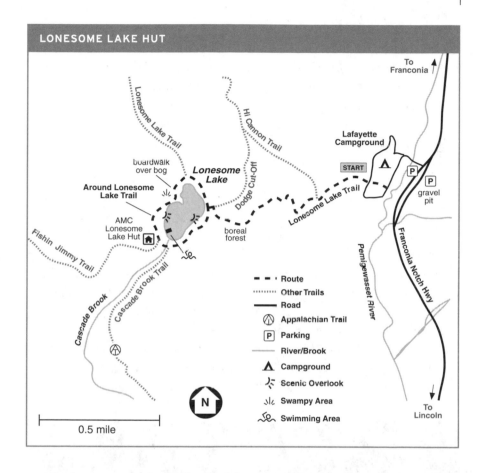

The Lonesome Lake Trail is a short, somewhat steep climb. The Around Lonesome Lake Trail then takes you past the hut on a complete loop around the lake. Allow about one and a half hours to ascend to the hut, about an hour or so to stroll around the lake, and one hour to descend. The Cascade Brook Trail, part of the Appalachian Trail, offers a longer, more gradual ascent from Franconia Notch.

## DIRECTIONS

The Lonesome Lake Trail starts at the Lafayette Place Campground in Franconia Notch State Park. From the north, take the Franconia Notch Highway through the notch to the exit for the campground, about 1.5 miles south of the former Old Man of the Mountain. If you are coming from the south through Lincoln and North Woodstock, exit at the trailhead parking, about 1.5 miles north of the Basin, then cross over to the west side through a foot tunnel.

## TRAIL DESCRIPTION

The trail begins at the picnic area at the campground's south parking lot on the west side of the highway. There is a large sign for the trail and yellow blazes to help you make your way past the picnic area, across the Pemigewasset River, and through the campground without getting off track. After leaving the campground, the Lonesome Lake Trail follows an old bridle path once used to reach a private camp on the lake. In ten minutes (0.3 mile), make a sharp left turn and cross a wooden plank bridge over a stream that tumbles down the mountainside. At 0.4 mile, the Hi Cannon Trail exits right toward the summit of Cannon Mountain. The Lonesome Lake Trail then ascends moderately steeply via three switchbacks, then descends slightly through a pretty boreal forest before reaching the lake at the junction with the Cascade Brook Trail (1.2 miles).

At this point, begin your loop around Lonesome Lake on the Around Lonesome Lake Trail. (This trail incorporates sections of the Cascade Brook, Fishin' Jimmy, and Lonesome Lake trails.) Since it's a loop, you can take it in either direction, but we describe it going clockwise. Turn left on the Cascade Brook Trail and follow the southeast shoreline of the lake toward Lonesome Lake Hut. From vantage points along the shore you can see North and South Kinsman mountains and the Cannonballs. At 1.4 miles, turn right on the Fishin'

A dock at Lonesome Lake.

Jimmy Trail. In another 0.1 mile you pass the outlet of the lake and then the dock area of the Lonesome Lake Hut (1.6 miles), where the best swimming is. On a hot summer day, after sweating mightily on the way up, there will be nothing better than a swim.

At this point you can visit the hut by following the Fishin' Jimmy Trail to the left. Ask at the hut for information on the self-guided nature walk, which uses the next portion of the Around Lonesome Lake Trail.

The Around Lonesome Lake Trail continues clockwise along the western shore of the lake. The trail goes through an open boggy area on split-rail bridges and planks, and at about 0.3 mile from the hut reaches the junction with the Lonesome Lake Trail. Turn right on the Lonesome Lake Trail to complete the loop in another 0.2 mile. From here you could either descend to your car at Lafayette Place on the Lonesome Lake Trail or walk back to the hut.

Parts of the Around Lonesome Lake Trail may be soggy, particularly in spring.

## NATURE NOTES

The highlight of this hike is Lonesome Lake. The ascent runs through a dense northern hardwood forest and includes a few stream crossings and some nice choruses of hermit thrushes and winter wrens. About 1 mile from the trailhead, the trail levels out. Here you walk through a beautiful boreal forest with red spruce and balsam fir and a lush understory of moss, goldthread, mountain wood sorrel, and clintonia. The terrain here is very hummocky—it looks like the kind of place where elves might pop out from behind the trees.

If the weather is cooperative, you should jump into the lake for a swim, but keep in mind that there are no lifeguards. The lake is about twenty acres in area and averages 3 to 6 feet in depth with a maximum depth of 12 feet. Technically it's a tarn—a mountain pond scoured out of the mountainside by the glacier. This may be the best place in New England to get a beautiful view while practicing your backstroke. Across the notch is Mount Lafayette and other peaks of the Franconia Range. Walker Ravine in Mount Lafayette appears as a deep V in the mountainside.

While sitting around the lake you will likely see dragonflies hovering and darting above the water. Dragonflies are strong flyers and active predators of other insects around the lake. Dragonfly behavior is fun to watch. Although you might see dragonflies chasing prey, much of their activity is related to mating. Territorial males alight on their favorite perches and chase intruding males away. Males and females mate on the wing, and you may even see two dragonflies in such a "tandem flight." The female then deposits her eggs in the water by hovering above the water and touching it periodically with the tip of her abdomen.

Look for dragonfly exuviae along the shoreline. These are the discarded exoskeletons of dragonfly nymphs (larvae). The nymphs live in water as voracious predators. When it is time to molt into adulthood, they crawl out onto vegetation, split their exoskeleton (skin), and emerge as adults, much like a butterfly emerging from a cocoon. The remaining exuviae are left behind on the vegetation and provide a nice record of successful breeding. The newly emerged adult, called a teneral, is soft and vulnerable for at least a few hours until its wings and new exoskeleton harden.

You can fish for brook trout at Lonesome Lake. Contact the New Hampshire Fish and Game Department for the appropriate license.

Very tame snowshoe hares hang out around the dock and the hut. These hares change colors to match the season, brown in summer and white in winter. This camouflages them, although their tameness around the hut leaves the impression that they are not too worried about predators. The grassy areas around the hut provide them with forage during the summer. In winter they feed on twigs and bark.

Shrubs growing by the dock include sheep laurel, wild raisin (witherod), sweet gale, and mountain ash. You may also observe the difference between red spruce (square needles) and balsam fir (flat needles).

If you stay at the hut in June, you will have a chance to awaken to a symphony of birdsongs. These include Swainson's thrush, winter wren, and white-throated sparrow. Yellow-rumped warbler, chickadee, and dark-eyed junco are also around.

Beaver have played a large part in creating the landscape around Lonesome Lake. As of this writing they no longer inhabit the lake itself, but their legacy remains in the extensive boggy wetlands created by their dams, particularly on the western and northwestern shore. You can still see the old dams too. Beaver are now active downstream from the outlet and upstream of the northwestern shore.

The wetlands on the west and northwestern shore support a number of wetlands plants. As the self-guided nature trail describes, the wooden planks protect your shoes from the dampness, while at the same time protecting the plants from your shoes. The most abundant shrubs are sheep laurel, sweet gale, and leatherleaf. The pink flowers of sheep laurel, produced in early July, look like smaller versions of those of mountain laurel, a close relative. The crushed leaves of sweet gale smell as sweet as those of its close relative, the bayberry.

Children might like to examine the undersides of leaves of several of the shrubs, with a hand lens if possible. Sweet gale leaves have tiny yellow resin dots. The undersides of the thick leaves of leatherleaf are covered by rusty scales. The best leaf "underside" to show them, however, is Labrador tea, a shrub with thick, leathery leaves, the undersides of which are covered with dense, reddish brown woolly hairs.

In the same area, look for larches between the plank trail and the lake. This relative of pine, spruce, and fir is partial to bogs. Unlike pines, which have needles in bunches of two to five, larches have needles in bunches of twenty or so, which give its branches a delicate, lacy appearance.

You may find carnivorous sundews in the wetland. These are tiny bog plants that capture small insects by using sticky hairs on the tips of spoon-shaped leaves. The insects are digested and provide nutrients to the plant. The low nutrient conditions of bogs make them a haven for carnivorous plants, but it takes a sharp eye to find sundews.

On the northwest shore, near the junction with the Lonesome Lake Trail, there are many upturned trees whose intricate root systems are exposed to view. It reveals graphically how shallow the root systems are, due to the thinness of the soil. Here you will also find the large, cabbagelike leaves of Indian poke and an extensive cover of peat moss.

When you are looking for various wetlands plants and other natural wonders, you may not be able to resist sitting for awhile on one of the shoreline rocks to contemplate the lake and the view across Franconia Notch to Mount Lafayette while imbibing music provided by thrushes and other birds. And you can top it off with a swim.

## TRIP 48
## ZEALAND FALLS HUT

**RATING:** Moderate

**DISTANCE:** 5.6 miles round-trip to the hut

**ELEVATION CHANGE:** 650-foot elevation gain

**ESTIMATED TIME:** 3–4 hours

**MAPS:** AMC's *White Mountain National Forest Map and Guide*, G7
AMC's *White Mountain Guide*, 27th ed., Map 2: Franconia–
Pemigewasset, G7

**WMNF PARKING FEE:** Yes

**WINTER NOTES:** Zealand Falls Hut is a popular cross-country ski
destination, and the hut is open on a self-serve basis in winter. The
trail follows an old logging road, which is not difficult except for
the last 0.1 mile, where you need to remove your skis. Keep in mind
that Zealand Road is closed from mid-November through mid-May,
adding 3.7 miles to the journey.

**OTHER ACTIVITIES:** Birding, swimming

**From the front porch of Zealand Falls Hut you get one of the most
spectacular views in the White Mountains and you can easily spend
hours at Zealand Pond and Falls nearby.**

The Zealand Trail takes you along a stream, over wooden bridges, past beaver
meadows, along a pond where moose may lurk, and eventually to Zealand
Falls and the AMC's Zealand Falls Hut. The hike is relatively easy, following
the bed of an old logging railroad for most of its length except for a steep climb
to the hut in the last 0.1 mile. Zealand Road is closed from mid-November
through mid-May, adding 3.5 miles to the journey in each direction.

Overlooking Zealand Notch at about 2,700 feet, Zealand Falls Hut offers
overnight lodging with breakfast and dinner (reservations essential). Since
sleeping accommodations are in two large rooms with eighteen bunks each,
the hut is not as comfortable for families with young children as Lonesome
Lake Hut. (The AMC encourages families with children under three to stay
only at huts that have small, family-sized bunkrooms, such as Lonesome
Lake—see Trip 47.) But even a day trip to Zealand Falls Hut is more than
worth the effort.

**The view from Zealand Falls Hut is one of the finest in the White Mountains.**

If you do stay overnight, the hut is a base for a number of wonderful day hikes. One of our favorites is the hike to Thoreau Falls, which takes you along the side of Whitewall Mountain on the Ethan Pond Trail to a waterfall named after the famous naturalist and philosopher. Another option is to hike up the Zeacliff Trail for wonderful views of the Pemigewassett Wilderness.

Rumor has it that the area was named "Zealand" after New Zealand as a testament to its remoteness. When you are there, contemplating the serene forest with delicate wildflowers and the melodies of birdsongs wafting gently through the air, you would never imagine that at the end of the nineteenth and beginning of the twentieth centuries, the Zealand Valley was ravaged by logging and two immense forest fires. Miraculously, it all came back, a testament to the amazing recuperative powers of nature.

## DIRECTIONS

The trailhead for the Zealand Trail is near Twin Mountain and Bretton Woods.

From the Conway-Jackson area: Take US 302 west through Crawford Notch. Turn left on Zealand Road at the Zealand Campground, about 6 miles north of the Crawford Notch Visitor Center. Follow Zealand Road for about 3.5 miles until its end and park in the lot. The trail is straight ahead, beyond the gate. Zealand Road is closed to vehicles from mid-November to mid-May,

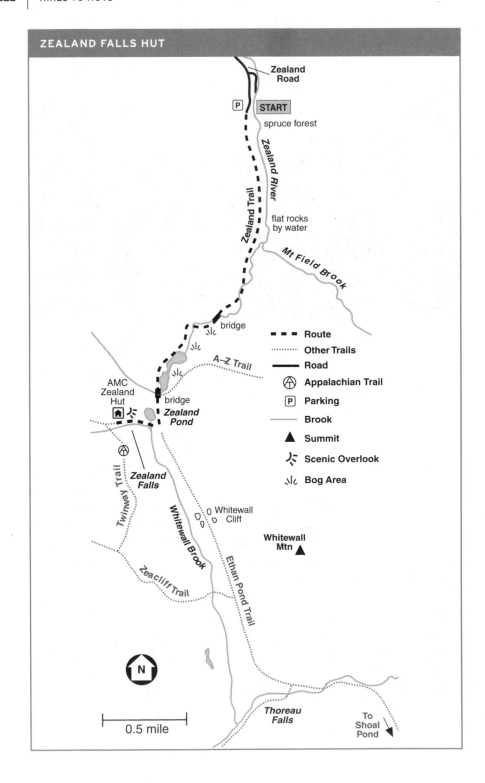

**ZEALAND FALLS HUT**

Zealand Road

P START

spruce forest

Zealand Trail

Zealand River

flat rocks by water

Mt Field Brook

bridge

A–Z Trail

AMC Zealand Hut

bridge

Zealand Pond

- - - **Route**
........... **Other Trails**
——— **Road**
Ⓐ **Appalachian Trail**
P **Parking**
——— **Brook**
▲ **Summit**
⅄ **Scenic Overlook**
⅄ **Bog Area**

Twinway Trail

Zealand Falls

Whitewall Brook

Whitewall Cliff

Whitewall Mtn ▲

Zeacliff Trail

Ethan Pond Trail

N

0.5 mile

Thoreau Falls

To Shoal Pond

and hikers and skiers must park across US 302 0.2 mile from Zealand Road.

From Franconia Notch: Take US 3 north to Twin Mountain. Turn right (east) on US 302 and follow it for 2 miles. Turn right at the Zealand Campground and follow Zealand Road till its end as above.

From points north: Follow either US 3 or NH 115 south to Twin Mountain. Turn left (east) on US 302 and follow the directions given above.

## TRAIL DESCRIPTION

The Zealand Trail is easy and well marked with blue blazes. Be aware that the winter ski trail crosses back and forth over the hiking trail. It does cross some soggy terrain, and despite wooden bridges and planks, it can still be a bit wet in spring or during wet weather.

The Zealand Trail follows the bed of an old logging railroad for much of its length. The first part of the trail is a slight uphill through a dense red spruce forest with very young trees lining the trail. Most of the rest of the walk is through northern hardwoods. See if you can observe when you are on the old railroad and when the trail diverts from that.

After about 20 minutes, the first of many wooden bridges crosses a wet area. At 0.8 mile, you approach the Zealand River, where several flat rocks are perfect for having a snack or lunch. At 1.5 miles the trail crosses the river. You pass through a very attractive balsam fir and white birch woodland with an understory of mountain wood sorrel, clintonia, and hobblebush.

After about 50 minutes (1.8 miles), the trail crosses an open beaver swamp. The Forest Service is in a constant battle with the beavers to keep the Zealand Trail above water, and the new elevated wooden walkway here is their latest response to beaver development projects. The trail then reenters the forest and skirts open wetlands and wet meadows. At 2.3 miles (about 1.5 hours) the A–Z trail enters from the left, just beyond a beautiful grassy beaver meadow with a view across to Mount Tom. The trail crosses the inlet to Zealand Pond, follows the shore of the pond, then ends at the junction of the Ethan Pond and Twinway trails. Turn right on the Twinway Trail to reach Zealand Falls Hut in another 0.3 mile. The last 0.1 mile is rough and steep but stone steps aid your ascent. The bottom of Zealand Falls is to the left near the base of this steep part.

A hike along the Ethan Pond Trail through Zealand Valley to Thoreau Falls could be combined with the Zealand Trail to make a very long day hike (greater than 10 miles) for those with lots of energy and time. Alternatively, Thoreau Falls is a nice half-day destination for those staying overnight at the hut. Like the hike to the hut, the Ethan Pond Trail in Zealand Notch follows an old logging railroad and is fairly level.

## NATURE NOTES

The Zealand Valley is one of the best places in the White Mountains to see wildlife. Beavers have had a major influence on the area. Their mud and stick dams alter the flow of the rivers, flooding the forest and creating a pond and wetland that serves not only the beaver but other wildlife as well.

Beavers are one of the largest members of the rodent family, which also includes mice and squirrels. Their webbed feet are perfect for swimming and their scaly flat tails, when slapped on the water, warn other beavers of danger. Beavers use their large front teeth to feed on the nutritious inner bark of trees, favoring aspen, birch, alder, willow, and maple. Look for stumps of beaver-chiseled trees along the Zealand Trail. Grasses and other vegetation are also part of their diets.

Beavers are one of the few animals (along with humans) that modify their entire habitat to suit their needs, building dams and conical houses of sticks and mud. A family of parents, kits, and one-year-olds occupies a lodge. Two-year-olds are booted out and may start their own colony nearby.

In winter, these rodents stockpile small branches underwater, then remain in their lodges for the most part, venturing out the underwater entrance only to grab something from their food cache under the ice.

**A beaver at home along the Zealand Trail.**

In the first few centuries of European settlement of this country, beavers were trapped in large numbers for their valuable fur. In many areas they disappeared. In the past 30 years, however, they have made a remarkable comeback and have been reintroduced successfully by wildlife management agencies in much of their former range.

Although you can find ample evidence of their presence, beavers themselves are hard to spot. The best time to look is in the half-light of early dawn or dusk.

Before passing the junction with the Twinway Trail (2.3 miles), note the pond on the left. A few years back, the old beavers had disappeared, the dam fell into disrepair, and the pond turned into a meadow. New residents restored the dam and reflooded the area again. In the late nineteenth century, this was neither a pond nor a meadow but a railroad yard servicing the logging industry.

Moose like to feed on tender submerged plants, so beaver ponds are good places to look. If you are not lucky enough to actually see one, look for evidence of their presence. Moose tracks, resembling large deer tracks, are likely to be in muddy areas around any of the wetlands; their rounded droppings may also be there. The sharpest-eyed member of your group may also find moose teeth marks on bark; they look like someone stripped the bark off the tree with a giant comb.

Along the shore of Zealand Pond you will see neat stacks of logs, and you might wonder what sort of animal put them there and why. The wood is used to heat the hut in winter.

Zealand Falls Hut is popular with birders. In June and July, you can hear the songs of winter wren, hermit thrush, and white-throated sparrow right from the porch. These birds, along with purple finch, black-throated blue warbler, black-throated green warbler, redstart, ovenbird, and red-eyed vireo, will be singing and calling along the trail, but spotting them in the dense forest is tough. It's easier to see black duck, wood duck, blue jay, swallow, and perhaps even a goshawk over the open areas around the beaver ponds.

While looking for birds and moose around the beaver ponds, listen for green frogs, which sound like someone plunking the string of a banjo. Dragonflies patrol for insects over the water. Tall meadow rue, a plant with fuzzy white flowers, is abundant on the shoreline.

The view from Zealand Falls Hut of Zealand and Carrigain notches is one of the most magnificent in the White Mountains. Zealand Notch, the closer of the two, is a classic U-shaped glacially carved valley. It is bounded on the left (east) by the impressive cliffs of Whitewall Mountain. Rock slides, logging, and fires have left much of Whitewall Mountain barren. The straight horizontal line on the mountainside is a former logging railroad that now is the Ethan Pond Trail. "Skid marks" heading down the mountain are sites where logs were dragged down to the railroad. The west side of Zealand Notch is bounded by Zealand Ridge, which can be reached by following the Twinway Trail very steeply beyond the hut. Carrigain Notch in the distance has an aura of remoteness.

The Zealand Valley was completely ravaged by the logging company of J. E. Henry (see also Trip 15), which conducted operations in this area from about 1880 to 1903. During this short period of time, there was a town with a sawmill, school, post office, and railroad yard just west of the present-day Zealand Campground. Loggers stayed at logging camps near the falls and sent the logs to the sawmill on the railroad. Sloppy logging practices spawned a number of devastating forest fires, as sparks from the railroad ignited dead branches, stumps, and other "waste" left from the logging operations. The loggers left Zealand Valley looking like a charred, barren moonscape.

The hut has a nice display of old photographs on the wall from this period. See also C. Francis Belcher's *Logging Railroads of the White Mountains* (AMC Books) for more details.

When the loggers left, nature began slowly repairing the valley through the process of ecological succession. First came smaller plants like fireweed, then raspberry, blueberry, and other small shrubs. The first trees to come back were paper birch. Large patches of the forest in the Zealand Notch are still dominated by this tree, its striking white bark giving a light, airy woodland feeling. Eventually, northern hardwood species will take over from the paper birch, but it is not clear if the red spruce—the tree loggers sought most eagerly—will ever again dominate this area.

While you are at the hut, stop in and ask for information on the self-guided nature walk. This takes you to eight stations that illustrate the geology and ecology of the area.

Just in front of the porch at the hut are a few red-berried elders. This distinctive shrub of wet areas and streamsides has compound leaves in pairs along branches. Red-berried elders produce clusters of small white flowers, which turn into small, colorful (but inedible) berries.

Explore the rocky riverbed of Whitewall Brook (except during extremely high water), a few yards beyond the hut. On a hot day, you will immediately feel the cool breeze streaming down the mountain by the brook. This natural refrigerator allows alpine plants to grow at a lower elevation than usual. The showiest is mountain avens, a wildflower with bright yellow flowers and rounded scalloped leaves that is found virtually nowhere else in the world but in the White Mountains. Mountain cranberry, a low plant with small, dark green evergreen leaves also is there, wherever there is enough soil for a root-hold. Other plants growing around the brook include three-toothed cinque-foil, meadowsweet, mountain ash, balsam fir, and red spruce.

Many people enjoy sitting on the flat rocks in Whitewall Brook above the falls. There are a number of pools within the brook that are deep enough for swimming or wading, particularly if you walk upstream. Hearty polar bears will jump right in; others will join them if the weather is hot enough. The screeches you hear are decidedly human.

## TRIP 49
## MIZPAH SPRINGS HUT

**RATING:** Moderate

**DISTANCE:** 5.2 miles round-trip, plus a number of possible side trips for views

**ELEVATION CHANGE:** 1,900-foot elevation gain

**ESTIMATED TIME:** 5 hours for the round-trip

**MAPS:** AMC's *White Mountain National Forest Map and Guide*, G8
AMC's *White Mountain Guide*, 27th ed., Map 1: Presidential Range, G8

**WMNF PARKING FEE:** Yes

**WINTER NOTES:** The hut is not open in winter, but the hike is still a great one-day snowshoe excursion.

**OTHER ACTIVITIES:** Birding

**Mizpah Springs Hut is set in the boreal forest at 3,800 feet elevation on the side of Mount Pierce. Side trips offer views of the Presidential Range and a mountain bog.**

This route follows the historic Crawford Path, first constructed as a footpath by Abel and Ethan Allen Crawford in 1819. In 1840, Thomas Crawford expanded it to serve as a bridle path, easing access to the mountains for a wider range of Crawford House guests. The Crawford Path is considered the oldest continuously maintained hiking path in America, and is now part of the Appalachian Trail.

The hike to the hut takes you through the watershed of Gibbs Brook, which features a beautiful cascade and an old growth red spruce forest. There are no views from the hut itself, but side trips can be taken to the summit of Mount

Pierce, from which there are stunning views of the Southern Presidentials, or to an interesting mountain bog on the side of Mount Jackson.

Completed in 1964, Mizpah Springs Hut was the last of the backcountry AMC huts to be constructed. It made a much more reasonable overnight stop for people hiking between Zealand Falls Hut and Lake of the Clouds near Mount Washington. Several tent platforms are near the hut.

With extra time, you can make an interesting, sporty loop by hiking to Mizpah Springs Hut on the route suggested below, then following the Webster Cliff Trail to Mount Jackson (wonderful views), and returning to Crawford Notch via the Webster-Jackson Trail. This takes you past Cloudwater Bog and over Mount Jackson, adding 2.4 miles and 500 feet to the hike described here. The Webster Jackson Trail comes out on NH 302 near the south end of Saco Lake, so it is about 0.5-mile walk north to get back to the trailhead for the Crawford Path. Keep in mind that the descent using this alternate route will take about twice as long as simply retracing your steps down the Crawford Path from the hut. Consult the AMC's *White Mountain Guide* for more details.

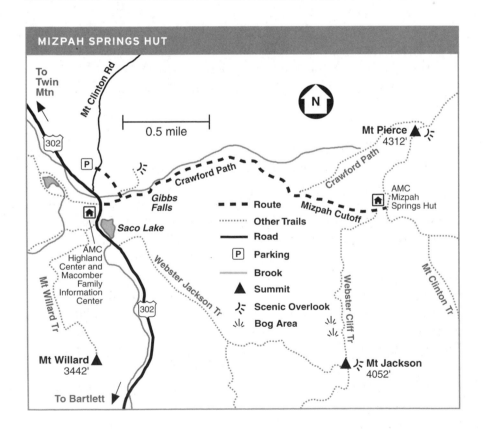

MIZPAH SPRINGS HUT

## DIRECTIONS

The trailhead for the Crawford Path is near the AMC's Highland Center at the head of Crawford Notch. See Trip 20 for directions. Hikers using the Crawford Path are requested to park in the hiker parking lot on Mount Clinton Road. This is a short (ca. 0.2 mile) distance off US 302 just beyond the center.

## TRAIL DESCRIPTION

Begin on the Crawford Connector, which links the parking area to the original Crawford Path. Just before the connector crosses Gibbs Brook, the Crawford Cliff Spur diverges to the left. This follows the north bank of the brook for a short distance to a pool and then ascends steeply and roughly to Crawford Cliff from which there are views of the notch and the Willey Range. The distance to the overlook is 0.4 mile.

The Crawford Connector ends at the original Crawford Path (coming up directly from US 302 opposite the Highland Center) at 0.4 mile. Turn left and start ascending the Crawford Path along the south bank of Gibbs Brook. At 0.6 mile, a short spur path leads left to Gibbs Falls. According to John Mudge in *White Mountains, Names, Places, and Legends*, the falls were a popular destination for guests from the old Crawford House. Men would hike in coat and tie, and women in hoop skirts. After passing the falls, you soon enter the Gibbs Brook Scenic Area. Take note of the old growth red spruce and some very large yellow birch. The trail eventually turns away from the brook and at 1.9 miles, the Mizpah Cutoff comes in from the right. The Crawford Path continues straight for the summit of Mount Pierce. For Mizpah Springs Hut, take the Mizpah Cutoff. This ascends about 400 feet steadily, and then becomes level, and passes across boggy sections on logs. The Cutoff intersects the Webster Cliff Trail at Mizpah Springs. The hut is just beyond.

After resting at the hut and having lunch or snacks, you will hopefully have time to explore the area further. Mount Pierce makes a nice destination. Formerly known as Mount Clinton after DeWitt Clinton, the governor of New York who built the Erie Canal, the peak was renamed to honor the only president who hailed from New Hampshire. The summit, reached by the Webster Cliff Trail, is above treeline and affords wonderful alpine views. The trail starts ascending steeply from the hut, passes through an open area with many dead balsam fir, and reaches the summit above tree line in 0.8 mile (500 foot elevation gain). Allow about 40 minutes for the ascent.

Cloudwater Bog, one of the finest examples of an alpine bog in the White Mountains, is about a mile in the other direction, i.e., toward Mount Jackson, along the Webster Cliff Trail. The hike to this bog is relatively level. You will see unique plants and get nice views of the Southern Presidentials at the bog. Please stay on the trail to avoid trampling the delicate vegetation.

## NATURE NOTES

Mizpah Springs Hut is one of the best locations in the White Mountains to hear and see birds of the boreal forest. Many migratory birds in North America breed in the boreal forest, a vast northern belt of spruce and fir dominated forest across the northern latitudes of the continent. Most of this habitat is in central Canada and Alaska, so most people only see these birds during migration, but the high elevations of the Northeast (as well as the Rocky Mountains) are southern outposts for these birds. You can pick up a bird list at the hut. If you are at Mizpah during June through mid-July, you will be treated to an enchanting chorus of these birds, particularly if you are there early in the morning or late in the afternoon. Swainson's thrush is one of the most accomplished songsters at Mizpah. Its song is flutelike, ethereal, and ascending in pitch, very appropriate for a bird of high elevations. Bicknells thrush and veery both sound like harpsichords giving a rolling series of notes, the former singing more or less on at one pitch and the latter modulated and typically ending with descending notes. Another amazing songster is the winter wren. This tiny bird is rarely seen, but it gives a loud, boisterous, very extended series of notes that include a number of different phrases. You'll wonder how such a small creature can hold its breath so long. White-throated sparrows give several clear, sweet whistles that have been described in words as "See old Sam Peabody Peabody Peabody." A musical trill at one pitch given from the top of a spruce or fir is likely to be a dark-eyed junco. The purple finch, the state bird of New Hampshire, gives a lively warble. Look and listen also for a number of species of wood warblers, boldly marked with yellow, black, and white patterns, that breed around Mizpah Springs. These include yellow-rumped, magnolia, and blackpoll warblers.

If you have time for the additional hike, the summit of 4,312-foot Mount Pierce has wonderful views of the Southern Presidentials and provides a representation of the White Mountain's special alpine (above timberline) habitat (see Trip 38 for a description of the alpine zone). The alpine zone of the Southern Presidentials has many small bogs. These are formed in areas where rainwater does not drain, such as in a col (saddle) between two peaks. Baked apple berry, also called cloudberry, is a specialty of these bogs. It is a type of raspberry that produces only one flower and fruit per plant. Baked apple berries are harvested commercially in Scandanavia, where they are turned into

**A boreal chickadee, one of the highest elevation birds inhabiting the forest around Mizpah Springs Hut.**

jam. Cloudwater Bog, which is along the Webster Cliff Trail between Mizpah Springs Hut and Mount Jackson, is a great place to see baked apple berry, as well as cotton sedge, bog laurel, and peat (sphagnum) moss.

On the hike up from the hut to the summit along the Webster Cliff Trail, you pass through a strange-looking area of dead trees called a fir wave. The larger balsam fir of the canopy are dead, but there are many small, healthy shrub-sized trees. For many years fir waves were a puzzle to both forest ecologists and hikers. Scientists now have concluded that fir waves represent a common pattern of forest regeneration in these high elevation forests. The wave occurs parallel to the slope and starts where the fir trees have reached the end of their life span (ca. 80 years). They die, get knocked down by winds (often bringing down their neighbors too), and are replaced by regenerating saplings. New fir waves are periodically forming in the balsam fir zone (roughly between 3,000 and 4,500 feet) when trees reach their age of senescence. These waves gradually move up the slope, much like a conveyer belt, ending only when they reach the end of the balsam fir zone.

## TRIP 50
## CARTER NOTCH HUT

**RATING:** Moderate with a few steep sections

**DISTANCE:** 7.6 miles round-trip

**ELEVATION CHANGE:** 1,900-foot elevation gain

**ESTIMATED TIME:** 7 hours

**MAPS:** AMC's *White Mountain National Forest Map and Guide*, F10
AMC's *White Mountain Guide*, 27th ed., Map 5: Carter Range–Evans
Notch, F10

**WMNF PARKING FEE:** Yes

**WINTER NOTES:** Carter Notch Hut is open in winter and is a great
destination for snowshoers looking for an overnight adventure.

**OTHER ACTIVITIES:** Fishing, swimming

**The AMC's Carter Notch Hut is in a remote col nestled between two
4,000-foot mountains in the eastern part of the White Mountains.
The notch features two pristine lakes and a stark field of boulders
called the Rampart.**

Carter Notch Hut is open all year on a self-service basis. There are two bunk-houses along with a dining and kitchen building. You provide your own food and bedding, but you have full use of kitchen facilities. Reservations are required (call 603-466-2727 or go to www.outdoors.org/lodging).

Carter Notch is most easily reached by the Nineteen Mile Brook Trail, an attractive trail that ascends moderately and follows the brook for much of its length. If you are not staying overnight at the hut, leave yourself lots of time so that you can enjoy the wildness and splendor of Carter Notch. The Nineteen Mile Brook Trail has many small waterfalls and pools that are satisfying destinations in their own right.

For those capable of an even longer outing, you can make a nice loop by taking the Nineteen Mile Brook Trail to the hut, and then hiking up Carter Dome via the steep Carter Moriah Trail. From there the Carter Dome Trail leads back down to the Nineteen Mile Brook Trail at its halfway point. That adds 2.6 miles, 1,500 feet, and 2.5 hours to the hike described here. Consult the AMC's *White Mountain Guide* for more details and for assistance with trip planning. A winter trip to Carter Notch Hut takes careful planning—consider the weather and bring cold-weather gear. For more information, see www. outdoors.org/lodging/huts/huts-carter.cfm.

## DIRECTIONS

The trailhead for the Nineteen Mile Brook trail is off NH 16, about 4 miles north of AMC's Pinkham Notch Visitor Center and 1 mile north of the Mount Washington Auto Road. If you are coming from the north, it is about 6.5 miles south of the intersection of US 2 and NH 16 in Gorham. The large parking area is on the east side of NH 16.

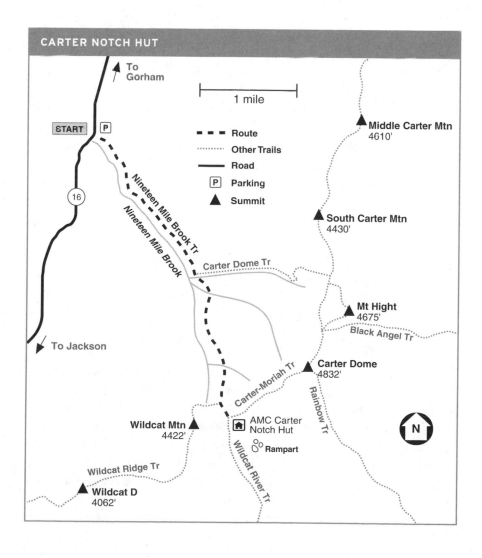

## TRAIL DESCRIPTION

The Nineteen Mile Brook Trail is marked with blue blazes and begins along the route of an old road. The trail ascends moderately and the sound of running water is your constant companion for the first 2.2 miles of this hike. At 1.2 miles the trail passes a small dam, which ponds up water, forming an inviting swimming hole. After this, the trail becomes rockier, but still ascends moderately. The Carter Dome Trail goes off to the left at 1.9 miles (1 hour). A few steps beyond that, the trail crosses a tributary of Nineteen Mile Brook on a wooden bridge. Another tributary is crossed at 2.2 miles on a somewhat shaky log bridge, and the trail then ascends away from the brook. You cross a third tributary at 3.1 miles. The trail ascends at a steeper pitch for a short distance and then becomes a level, pleasant boreal forest walk where you catch glimpses through the trees of Wildcat Mountain as it dramatically plunges down to Carter Notch. A final steep section takes you to the height of land (elevation 3,400 feet) at the junction with the Wildcat Ridge Trail (3.6 miles). The Nineteen Mile Brook Trail then descends steeply for 100 feet to the larger of the two Carter Lakes, and then passes the Carter-Moriah Trail, which departs to the left. You then pass the smaller Carter Lake to reach the hut at 3.8 miles.

While you are at Carter Notch, you should not miss the Rampart. Walk about 100 yards south of the bunkhouses on the Wildcat River Trail. A trail (signed) leads left to this incredible boulder field. Once you reach the boulders, the going is rough, but for those who are comfortable scrambling on uneven rocks, it is worth exploring this area further. You will be rewarded with a nice overview of the hut and the two lakes, an excellent vista to the south.

Another interesting side trip is to hike up the Carter-Moriah Trail for 0.3 mile to an excellent viewpoint of the Notch near an immense boulder named Pulpit Rock. This is a very steep ascent, but the view is tremendous.

## NATURE NOTES

The Nineteen Mile Brook Trail starts out in a hemlock forest. Hemlocks often dominate in the valleys of streams at lower elevations (see also Trip 32). Yellow birch is also common. Eventually hemlock gives way to a spruce-fir forest with scattered paper birch, the typical forest at elevations of greater than 2,500 feet.

A number of yellow birch and red spruce along the trail appear to be growing on stilts. In one form, roots snake down to the ground from a tree growing on top of a large boulder. In another, the base of the tree trunk is suspended above the ground with the roots forming the struts of a tower. These trees probably started growing on top of a log that subsequently rotted away.

About twenty minutes into the hike you pass a large rock outcropping along the side of the brook. This is schist, a metamorphic rock that underlies most of the Presidential Range (see Appendix B, Natural History of the White Mountains). Look for lines of quartz that formed in cracks within the schist.

The upper half of the Nineteen Mile Brook Trail, between 2.2 and 3.3 miles, may be the hobblebush capital of the world. This common viburnum has rounded leaves located in pairs in rows along thin branches. Flat-topped clusters of white flowers in May give way to red berries through much of the summer. The berries eventually turn dark bluish black when they are ripe (see Trip 46 for more on hobblebush). Sharp-leaved aster is another particularly abundant plant along the trail.

The Carter Lakes are an unexpected visual treat when you first see them below you from the height of land. Your reaction is likely to be something like, "Wow, there are actually ponds here!" The upper Carter Lake supports a number of interesting aquatic plants, including yellow pond lily, bur reed, and quillwort. Yellow pond lily has large attractive yellow flowers and heart-shaped floating leaves. Bur reed has long strap-like leaves that flop over on the surface of the water. Look for its bur-like fruit. Quillwort is a strange underwater relative of club moss (nonflowering plants somewhat akin to ferns). Its thin grasslike leaves are arranged in circular clusters along the bottom.

The upper lake is stocked with trout, so fishing is a possibility with the proper New Hampshire license. Spring peepers are also there.

Carter Notch is a glacially carved valley. Its walls are the steep slopes and cliffs of Carter Dome (4,832 feet) and Wildcat Mountain (4,422 feet). The 1,000-foot cliffs on Wildcat that loom over Carter Notch are particularly impressive. Boulders crashing down into the Notch from these two

**Carter Notch Hut.**

**The Rampart.**

mountains formed the Rampart. Look for caves hidden within the Rampart where ice can remain late into the summer. The two Carter Lakes owe their existence to the Rampart, which serves as a natural dam. The outlet of the lower lake flows under the boulders.

The boulders of the Rampart contain some large quartz crystals. Mountain cranberry, Labrador tea, and red spruce grow around the boulders.

The Nineteen Mile Brook Trail offers a number of swimming possibilities. The brook has a number of small pools deep enough for a nice stop on a hot day even if you do not make it all the way to the notch. Upper Carter Lake is swimmable, although you should wear water shoes to protect your feet from rocks and mucky bottoms.

# 9

# NATURAL ATTRACTIONS AND NATURE WALKS

**THESE DESTINATIONS ARE PARTICULARLY INTERESTING** natural features. All require short, mostly easy walks, but a few involve an uphill climb over a rough trail. We also include some self-guided nature trails. Choose one of these ten walks if you have extremely limited time or if you are hiking with very young children.

## 1. CRYSTAL CASCADE

> **DISTANCE/ESTIMATED TIME:** 0.7 mi round-trip; 30 min
> **MAP:** AMC's *White Mountain National Forest Map and Guide*, F9

Crystal Cascade is a 0.4 mile, fifteen-minute walk from the AMC's Pinkham Notch Visitor Center (PNVC—see Trip 31 for directions). You can combine a short walk to this beautiful waterfall with a visit to the visitor center or a hike up to Tuckerman Ravine (Trip 37). From PNVC, follow signs for the Tuckerman Ravine Trail and start uphill. After about ten minutes, the trail crosses the Cutler River on a solid bridge and then ascends more steeply. The viewpoint for the waterfall is on the right, a few steps up from the trail. A stone fence

**Enjoy ferns and falls at the Crystal Cascade overlook.** Photo by Jerry Shereda.

will give a feeling of security for those worried about the steep drop-off.

Crystal Cascade tumbles over a volcanic vent that formed much later in time than the surrounding schist that make up much of the Presidentials. The volcanic rocks are basalt and are black in color even when dry. They also are more "lumpy" edged than the surrounding schist. There is a small outcropping of the same black volcanic rocks just downstream of the bridge. Look near the old abandoned bridge abutment.

The persistently damp environment created by the spray of a waterfall is perfect for ferns, an ancient group of plants that first appeared on earth even before the debut of the dinosaurs. The fronds of long beech ferns (typically about 6 inches long) are roughly triangular in outline, with the two bottom-most pinnae on each side pointing backward. This fern is common throughout the White Mountains in damp woods and along the sides of waterfalls—several grow at the corner of the barrier to your left as you face the falls. Another fern growing just on the other side of the stone barrier is oak fern. This small (about 1 foot in height), delicate fern has a horizontally oriented frond that is divided into three parts. The spinulose wood fern, common along the path to the falls, has fronds up to about 2 feet long and divided into pinnae and pinnules. A distinctive characteristic of this fern is the brown scales on the stipe (stalk) of each frond.

A bird whose energetic, bubbly song can often be heard even above the din of rushing water is the winter wren. It is a small, rather nondescript brown bird that usually remains out of sight, but its true calling card is its voice. It's hard to believe that such a loud and cheerful succession of notes can emanate from something so small. This bird can clearly hold its own against the sound of the Crystal Cascade.

## 2. GLEN ELLIS FALLS

**DISTANCE/ESTIMATED TIME:** 0.6 mi round-trip; 30–40 min

**MAP:** AMC's *White Mountain National Forest Map and Guide*, F10

Glen Ellis Falls is a 64-foot waterfall on the Ellis River in Pinkham Notch. The parking area is on the west side of NH 16 0.7 mile south of the AMC's Pinkham Notch Visitor Center and about 9 miles north of the village of Jackson. There are rest rooms, an information board, and a picnic area. A tunnel underneath NH 16 leads to the 0.3-mile path to the falls.

Glen Ellis Falls is one of the most impressive falls in the White Mountains. It's worth a visit even if you have an aversion to "tourist" spots. Several signs along the trail describe the geology of the area. The falls were created when avalanches blocked the flow of the Ellis River, causing it to change its course and tumble over the glacially carved bowl in the side of a mountain. The flow over the cliff, a minimum of 600 gallons a minute, is equal to 10 gallons a second, even during late summer when other waterfalls are just a trickle.

Three lookouts at the top, middle, and bottom of the falls provide distinct perspectives. The shape of the falls pouring over the brink may remind you of water pouring out of a pitcher, and, in fact, Pitcher Falls was the original name given to Glen Ellis Falls. The pool at the bottom is bounded by lots of flat rocks that invite exploration. When the water levels aren't too high, you will find children and their parents scrambling around these flat rocks. Use caution because mist from the falls keeps everything damp.

According to Native American legend, if you look hard into the mist created by the falls, you can see the shapes of two people hand in hand. These were lovers from different tribes who plunged to their deaths together over the falls when the woman, the daughter of the chief, was promised to someone else.

**Glen Ellis Falls.** Photo by Carrie Loats.

## 3. KEDRON FLUME

**DISTANCE/ESTIMATED TIME:** 2.0 mi round-trip; 1–1.5 hr

**MAP:** AMC's *White Mountain National Forest Map and Guide*, G8

Kedron Flume is a series of small cascades carved into the side of Mount Willey. It is reached by a 1-mile uphill hike from the Willey House Historical Site off US 302 in Crawford Notch. The historic site is approximately 3 miles south of Crawford Depot and the AMC's Highland Center. Do not confuse it with the Willey House Station Site, which is 1 mile farther south.

The Kedron Flume Trail is a moderately steep hike (600-foot elevation gain) with a few rough spots on the trail, so good hiking shoes are a must. Plan for at least a one-hour outing. Walk through the picnic area on the south (left) side of the historic site.

The trail crosses the railroad tracks of the Conway Scenic Railroad at 0.4 mile and reaches Kedron Brook at 1.0 mile. The flume, a small canyon carved into the rock by flowing water, is to your right (uphill) and a waterfall to your left. Be careful when exploring along the brook because the rocks are slippery in this shady spot. Flat rocks make good seats for lunch or a snack. After visiting the flume, cross the brook and walk about 50 yards farther for a great

view of across Crawford Notch to Mount Webster. You will see several streams plunging down the glacially carved steep slope of this mountain. Note also a very large red spruce that somehow escaped the loggers just across creek from the flume.

After enjoying the falls and views, retrace your steps back to the parking area. Those seeking a longer outing could continue farther along the Kedron Flume Trail for another 0.3 mile to where it ends in the Ethan Pond Trail (Trip 30). This section of the trail is substantially steeper and rougher than the hike to the flume.

**Kedron Flume.**

# 4. TRIPLE FALLS

**DISTANCE/ESTIMATED TIME:** 0.4 mi round-trip; 40 min

**MAP:** AMC's *White Mountain National Forest Map and Guide*, E10

It takes about as long to hike this trail as to say, "Take the Town Line Brook Trail to Triple Falls." The walk is short (0.4 mile round-trip, 40 minutes) and steep, dead-ending after passing three scenic waterfalls. The banks of the brook are heavily forested and dark and, combined with the mythological names of two of the three falls, create a mysterious atmosphere. The area has some impressively large rocks and a steep gorge with passageways and holes. Large fallen hemlocks create natural bridges over a narrow gorge.

Like many waterfalls in the White Mountains, Triple Falls is best visited early in the season or after a rainstorm. This is not a trail to allow children to run off unsupervised, since there are some steep drop-offs without any protective barriers.

The Town Line Brook Trail starts at Pinkham B (Dolly Copp) Road. From the Twin Mountain area or points north, Pinkham B Road goes right off US 2 approximately 0.8 mile east of the Appalachia trailhead parking lot. The trailhead, marked with a sign, is 1.4 miles south of the railroad crossing, on the right just past the bridge over Town Line Brook. From Pinkham Notch, Jackson, and North Conway, Pinkham B Road goes left off NH 16 at the Dolly Copp Campground (not the picnic area) about 6.5 miles north of the AMC's Pinkham Notch Visitor Center (PNVC). The trailhead will be on your left just before the bridge over Town Line Brook, less than a mile past the Pine Mountain Road Trail.

Triple Falls is really three separate waterfalls. It takes only five minutes to reach Proteus Falls. Proteus, a Greek god associated with water, is often pictured as an old man. He has prophetic powers and can change into any shape he wants. Erebus Falls, a few minutes beyond, is the most vertigo-inducing of the three falls because of the steep drop-off at a point where you overlook the gorge. Erebus, the father of the Three Fates, is the dark place where souls pass on their way to the underworld. Look for a dike of white quartz running across the base of Erebus Falls, an intrusion in the darker metamorphic rock of the Northern Presidentials. The trail ends at Evans Falls, a lighter spot that is a good place for a picnic. From there you retrace your steps back to your car.

## 5. DIANA'S BATHS

**DISTANCE/ESTIMATED TIME:** 1.0 mi round-trip; 45 min

**MAP:** AMC's *White Mountain National Forest Map and Guide*, I10

Diana's Baths is a pleasant spot to relax and hang out on a summer afternoon. A short, level half-mile walk along the Moat Mountain Trail brings you to this former mill site where you can wade in one of the many pools among numerous picturesque cascades or explore the ruins of the old mill. It is a popular family destination, suitable for the youngest hikers. The combination of shady forest and cool water make this an ideal place to visit during the summer.

From North Conway, turn west on River Road, which leaves NH 16/US 302 at the traffic light just north of the Eastern Slope Inn. Cross the Saco River and bear right at the next two intersections. You are now headed north on West Side Road. A parking area, well-marked with a sign, is on the left about 0.9 mile past the road to Cathedral Ledge (2.4 miles from NH 16 in North Conway). If you are traveling from the south, pick up West Side Road in Conway Village by turning left from NH 16 onto Passaconaway Road at the intersection where NH 153 goes off to the right. Continue north (straight) as the road turns into West Side Road. About 5 miles past Conway, bear left where River Road comes in from the right. Pass the road to Cathedral Ledge and follow the above directions. From Crawford Notch, travel east on US 302 and turn right on West Side Road about 4 miles east of the turnoff to Bear Notch Road in Bartlett. The parking area is about 0.3 mile south of the Conway–Bartlett town line.

Leaving the parking area, the Moat Mountain Trail parallels Lucy Brook, a tributary of the Saco River. In about ten to fifteen minutes it reaches a clearing. The mill site is immediately to the left, and Diana's Baths is just a little ahead, also to the left. The Moat Mountain Trail continues beyond the baths, but it becomes very steep.

Numerous cascades will immediately catch your attention. Even with the crowds, you will still be able to find a flat rock and an interesting stretch of water that you can claim for several hours. Kids will enjoy meandering up the granite terraces to see the wonderful assortment of waterfalls, pools, and rocks upstream. Look for the numerous small, round potholes carved into the flat granite. These were formed by the scouring action of small stones and sand carried around by spring floodwater. Some are perched high above the current level of the water and were probably formed during the melting of the last glacier when water levels were much higher than they are now.

Some gears, pipes, and stone walls from the old mill are still present. This was a gristmill that used the waterpower of Lucy Brook to grind flour.

Diana's Baths are named for the Roman goddess of the hunt, who was often pictured in woodland settings surrounded by animals. Enjoy your swim, and watch out for the water sprites that legend has it used to inhabit the area.

## 6. THE BASIN AND CASCADE BROOK

**DISTANCE/ESTIMATED TIME:** Mileage and time vary by route
**MAP:** AMC's *White Mountain National Forest Map and Guide*, H4

The Basin is one of the largest, most impressive glacially carved potholes you will ever see. It is a short (ca. 0.1 mile), easy walk from the parking lots on either side of I-93 (Franconia Notch Highway) and is wheelchair-accessible. If you approach from the south, the clearly marked exit for the Basin is about 4 miles north of the Lincoln/North Woodstock exit and 1.5 miles north of the Flume Gorge. After parking your car on the cast side of the highway, follow the signs to the Basin via a walkway under the highway. If you are heading south through the Notch from the Franconia or Twin Mountain area, the exit for the Basin is about 1.5 miles south of the Lafayette Place Campground, and the parking area is on the west side of the highway. This popular destination has rest rooms but no other facilities.

The Basin is located in a curve of the Pemigewasset River. About 30 feet in diameter and 15 feet deep, it was scoured out and polished into a smooth, round surface by sand and small stones thrashing about in water rushing from snowmelt around the time the last continental glacier departed the region (within the past

The Basin Cascade Trail is a delightful walk along the water.

25,000 years). Take a moment to read the sign describing how it was formed. (After his 1858 visit Thoreau wrote in his journal, "This pothole is perhaps the most remarkable of its kind in New England.")

If you want a longer outing, pick up the Basin Cascade Trail a short distance beyond the Basin. This trail should be on every waterfall-lover's list. It follows Cascade Brook past Kinsman and Rocky Glen falls and a whole series of smaller waterfalls, rapids, potholes, and small gorges. Many large flat, sunny rocks are perfect for family picnics.

## 7. THE FLUME GORGE OF FRANCONIA NOTCH

**DISTANCE/ESTIMATED TIME:** mileage and time vary by route
**MAP:** AMC's *White Mountain National Forest Map and Guide*, H4

If you like the idea of strolling along rushing water on a boardwalk through an extremely narrow gorge bounded by straight, vertical cliffs then you should not miss the Flume Gorge. The Flume is a popular tourist destination at the south end of Franconia Notch State Park and is a perfect half-day outing. You can combine the 800-foot boardwalk through the Flume with an easy, 2-mile loop trail that takes you past waterfalls, a giant pothole, huge boulders, and two covered bridges. Before setting out, you can pick up a trail map at the Flume Gorge Visitor Center, which also has interpretative exhibits, a cafeteria, picnic tables, snack bar, gift shop, and rest rooms.

The parking area for the Flume is off Exit 34A of the Franconia Notch Highway, the extension of I-93 through Franconia Notch. The exit is very well marked and is about 4 miles north of the exit on I-93 for North Woodstock, Lincoln, NH 112, and the Kancamagus Highway. From early May to late October, there is a charge for admission to the Flume (in 2005, $8 for adults and $5 for children six to twelve).

There are a number of overlooks with steep drop-offs, so parents should keep an eye on younger children, especially those who like climbing on split rail fences.

Starting from the visitor center, you pass a huge glacial erratic after 200 yards. Follow the path through the Flume Covered Bridge and the Boulder Cabin for 0.7 mile to the Flume. The walk through the Flume to Avalanche Falls is mostly on boardwalks, stairs, and more bridges. At this point, you can take a shorter loop back toward the visitor center on the Rim Trail or continue to the Pool on the Ridge Path (the Pool is as spectacular as the Flume). The Ridge Path leads to the Pool and the Sentinel Pine Covered Bridge over the Pemigewasset River in about 0.7 mile (mostly downhill). From there it is 0.6 mile back to the visitor center, through a forest laced with boulders.

Why are the walls of the Flume so straight? The Flume was formed by erosion of a basalt dike within the granite. Two hundred million years ago the granite, which tends to crack in straight lines, fractured vertically at the Flume. Lava from deep within the earth then flowed into the fractures, forcing the granite apart and solidifying to form a seam of basalt

**The Sentinel Pine Covered Bridge spans the Pemigewasset River.**

from twelve to twenty feet wide. Eventually water began to flow over the granite and basalt, eroding the softer basalt and leaving the steep granite sides of the Flume. The narrowness of the gorge reflects the width of the original basalt dike. The straightness of the walls shows the fracture planes of the granite. In some places, you can still see remnants of the black basaltic rock.

From overlooks 130 feet above the Pool you look down on a giant pothole 150 feet wide and 30 to 40 feet deep within the Pemigewasset River. The Pool was formed by the scouring action of sand and small stones blasted against the rock over millennia of winter snowmelts and floods.

The Sentinel Pine Covered Bridge crosses the river right at the Pool. Make sure you see the fallen 175-foot white pine that forms the base of the bridge. The best view of the tree is from a short spur trail to the left after you pass through the covered bridge.

The Roaring River Nature Trail is a quieter experience than the walk through the Flume. Here you can learn about the forces of destruction and renewal that shape the northern hardwood forest. Pick up the pamphlet from the visitor center. A gazebo provides a place to listen quietly to the sounds of the forest while looking out at a view of Mount Flume and Mount Liberty, two 4,000-foot peaks of the Franconia Range.

## 8. SABBADAY FALLS

**DISTANCE/ESTIMATED TIME:** 0.6-mi loop; 40 min
**MAP:** AMC's *White Mountain National Forest Map and Guide,* J8

The short (0.6 mile) walk to Sabbaday Falls off the Kancamagus Highway has been one of the most popular in the White Mountains ever since tourists first started to frequent the region. A flat trail with minimal elevation change, it is an ideal walk for families with very young children. At the falls, it's easy to spend a long time watching the patterns of water rushing over granite ledges, through a narrow flume, and into deep, clear pools.

The trailhead for Sabbaday Falls is on the south side of the Kancamagus Highway roughly 15 miles west of NH 16 near Conway and about 19 miles east of I-93 in Lincoln. For those coming through Crawford Notch or Bartlett, the trail is 3 miles west of the junction of Bear Notch Road with the "Kanc." The parking area has picnic tables, rest rooms, and an old hand pump for water.

Walk along the Sabbaday Brook Trail until you see the sign for the falls at 0.3 mile. The loop goes off to the left, passing a pool and an interesting small pothole. The loop then ascends stone stairs into the gorge created by the falls. The loop crosses a bridge, goes past the upper pool, and then returns to the

main trail. Turn right for the short walk back to the parking area.

Sabbaday Falls contains a number of interesting geological features described on interpretive signs. The gorge, the pools, and the small rounded potholes in Sabbaday Brook were carved out by sand and small rocks carried by meltwater from the last continental glacier about 12,000 years ago. The floods that accompanied the melting of the glacier must have been tremendous, far surpassing anything we see today. Not only did the glacier unload vast volumes of water on the landscape, but it also

**Basalt dike and Sabbaday Falls.**

unloaded sand and gravel that, in combination with the fast currents, acted like sandpaper to grind down rocks, creating waterfalls, new stream channels, and pools.

The narrow, straight gorge, or flume, at Sabbaday Falls was formed by the same processes that created the Flume Gorge of Franconia Notch (Natural Attraction and Nature Walk 7). A layer of basalt that had intruded into a crack in the granite wore away during the last Ice Age, leaving steep-sided granite walls 50 feet or so above the water. You can still see some remnant of the gray-black basalt within the flume at its lower end where it enters the lower pool.

Initially, the falls tumbled into the lower pool, but they eventually carved their way back through the basalt dike to form the flume and are now really several falls. At the deep upper pool you can get a feeling for the powerful erosive action of the grit-laden water by observing how the rock underwater has been carved away in a neat curve, creating an overhanging ledge. Keep in mind that the geological processes that created these marvels are still going on today, albeit at a slower rate than in the past because there is no glacial meltwater.

## 9. RAIL 'N RIVER NATURE TRAIL

**DISTANCE/ESTIMATED TIME:** 0.6-mi loop; 30 min
**MAP:** AMC's *White Mountain National Forest Map and Guide*, I8

The Rail 'n River Nature Trail is an short nature trail off the Kancamagus Highway at the Passaconaway Historical Site. The trail is a flat, wide path through a forest with some very tall trees and includes a short section on the banks of the Swift River. Past logging activity and the old logging railroad that used to run here are major themes of the nature walk. Intepretive signs along the trail describe the logging history of the area.

You can combine this walk with a visit to the Russell Colbath House, where people in period dress describe how the early settlers lived. The house also serves as a National Forest Information Center. A new post-and-beam barn at the site is used by the Forest Service for programs and has picnic tables under a porch (very handy on a rainy day!)

The Passaconaway Historic Site is just west of the junction of the Kancamagus Highway (NH 112) and Bear Notch Road (closed in winter). From NH 16 in Conway, it is about 13 miles west on the Kancamagus Highway. From the Crawford Notch area, take US 302 to Bartlett, turn right on Bear Notch Road,

**Remnants of the logging railroad bridge over the Swift River.**

then right on the Kancamagus Highway for 0.5 mile. From Franconia Notch and Lincoln, the historic site is about 22 miles east of I-93 on the Kancamagus Highway. The parking area is on the north side of the Kancamagus Highway.

The Nature Trail is a 0.5 mile loop that is wide and easy. You walk past a number of embankments that were beds of logging railroads. Their present overgrown appearance makes them look natural until you realize that no geological process would have made them so straight. There are also depressions where gravel was dug to build up the railroad grades. At the Swift River you see old log pilings that are all that is left of a former railroad bridge of the Bartlett and Albany Railroad. This railroad hauled logs to Bartlett in the late nineteenth century. In the early twentieth century, the Swift River Railroad brought lumber from this area to mills in Conway.

The short section along the Swift River is a treat. If you are there during dry periods in summer, the river won't be very swift. The water meanders by slowly, allowing you to see reflections of trees and sky. The bottom is covered with a lush growth of aquatic vegetation. In spring when the snow melts, however, the Swift River can be a raging torrent and live up to its name.

## 10. FOREST DISCOVERY TRAIL

**DISTANCE/ESTIMATED TIME:** 1.5-mi loop; 1.5 hr
**MAP:** AMC's *White Mountain National Forest Map and Guide*, 16

The Forest Discovery Trail is off the Kancamagus Highway 2.3 miles east of the White Mountain National Forest's visitor center at the Lincoln Woods Trail and 7.4 miles east of Exit 32 (Lincoln NH 112) off I-93. It is 0.2 mile beyond the Big Rock Campground.

Along the Forest Discovery Trail you will learn different techniques the White Mountain National Forest is using to manage the forest for multiple use. You can walk the easy 1.5-mile loop in an hour, or linger longer if you want to sit and relax in one of the many benches placed along the trail. 11 stations with interpretative signs cover such topics as natural forest succession, selective cutting, maintaining openings for wildlife, the value of riparian forest, old growth, and managing for multiple age stands. The trail provides a particularly nice view of Scaur Ridge and Mount Osceola from the sign overlooking a clear-cut. Look for pin cherries (brick red bark with pores), trembling aspen (smooth grayish green bark), and young American beech (smooth pure gray bark) coming up in this clear-cut. A loop through a riparian forest is also particularly interesting. The hobblebush leaves in the understory of this forest are especially huge.

# Appendix A

# HIKING WITH CHILDREN

**HIKING WITH CHILDREN REQUIRES FLEXIBILITY,** a sense of humor, and patience. You need to slow down and encourage children to explore the natural world around them—the sights, the sounds, and the smells—even if it means you might not make it to that scenic overlook or waterfall. You have a wonderful opportunity to enjoy nature as your child sees it.

Our recommendations are based on our experiences and those of many AMC staffers and friends, but please keep in mind that it's difficult to generalize about what a child can handle at a given age. Some precocious and energetic five-year-olds are ready for a 4,000-footer. Some ten-year-olds may not be willing to hike very far at all.

Don't be afraid to start your kids early. Our daughter slept through her first hike in a front carrier at two months of age. Hiking with a one-year-old in a backpack actually is much easier than negotiating with a toddler. Pack diapers, baby food, and other items just as you would on any daylong outing, and be prepared with extra clothes.

## WHAT KINDS OF HIKES DO KIDS LIKE?

With the right spirit, every trail can be fun for adults and children alike, but some will engage children more easily than others. In our hikes with children, we've noticed a few especially winning features.

Children love to be around water. The White Mountains have an abundance of waterfalls and lakes that are popular destinations for family hikes. You can go swimming or wading, look for small critters, throw stones in the water, or have a picnic or snack on big, flat boulders while dangling your feet in the water. It is much more fun to hike along a river or a small babbling stream than through a monotonous woodland.

Children also love to walk on wooden plank bridges that cross streams and wetlands and on split logs that traverse muddy areas. Covered bridges are even better, but there are only a few in the White Mountains.

Kids like to stop and look at little things, such as an odd-looking bug crossing the path, a colorful leaf in autumn, or a brightly colored fungus. It is hard to predict what will strike their fancy. One friend remembered her nephew's fascination with small conifer trees that were his own height. Take the time to enjoy those things with them rather than hurrying off to the next destination.

Young hikers like to climb on rocks and explore the big boulders so common along many trails in the White Mountains. Especially intriguing are those that form caves or overhang the trail. Beginning hikers will proudly show you how they have "conquered" even a small rock in the middle of a trail.

Kids love scrambling around rocky ledges, particularly after they have been hiking through a dense forest. At a ledgy scenic overlook, the scenery itself is likely to play second fiddle to the scrambling. (Of course, if their parents ooh and aah over enough views, children will eventually start oohing and aahing too.) Rocky ledges are like a substitute jungle gym. Just keep your eyes on them, since there are no railings on most trails.

Most kids love picking and eating blueberries. They may not persevere long enough to collect a stash for tomorrow morning's blueberry pancakes, but they will certainly enjoy it for a while. The summits of many of the smaller mountains listed in this

**Big boulders invite exploration.**

book are loaded with ripe blueberries toward the end of July and in August. Huckleberries, blackberries, and raspberries are also there for the picking.

Some kids love wildflowers and brightly colored mushrooms, although others may not notice them. Keeping children from picking flowers may be the hardest job you'll have on the trail, but once they get into the habit of just looking, they'll keep it for life.

Kids like to see animals. Insects, fish, tadpoles, and mammals are usually the most popular animals in a child's bestiary. Trees riddled with woodpecker holes, bark stripped by moose, or trees scarred by bear claws are great things to show them.

Birds are hard for children to enjoy because they are much more often heard than seen in the White Mountains. Encourage children to listen to the beautiful bird songs in the forest, but don't push it. You'll likely be more successful if you show them either big birds in open spaces and wetlands such as hawks, herons, and ducks, or sassy, tame birds like gray jays and chickadees.

Before we had children many of us sought out quiet, backcountry trails to get a refreshing break from our hectic work lives and our urban or suburban existence. Children are less likely to feel the need for such a wilderness experience than their parents. In fact, they may rather enjoy the crowds at such places as the Flume Gorge or Glen Ellis Falls.

Few people enjoy walking through an endless tunnel of trees with no scenic or watery breaks. Adults can tolerate those kinds of trails in anticipation of a reward at the end in the form of a summit or a waterfall. When you are hiking with children, however, there is no guarantee that you will make it to the end, so pick a hike that won't be disappointing, even if you turn around before completing it.

Navigating can be a fun challenge. Some younger kids will be motivated by the responsibility of spotting the next blaze. Older kids may want to learn how to read trail maps and use a compass. They may enjoy helping to plan the hike as well.

## FAVORITE DISTRACTIONS

Inevitably the kids will hit a low point while on a hike. Here's where you need to be creative and prepared.

Some children love singing songs on the trail. Camp songs and songs they have learned in school are great when the trail seems never ending. Let them pick out the songs, but be ready with your own.

Stories and tales of what you did when you were their age work wonders at distracting children. Ask them a nature question they can answer along the hike—look at the hike descriptions for suggestions. Often there's something close at hand that can be made into a game, such as balsam blisters, spruce gum, or jewelweed.

Make the hike into a scavenger hunt. Have a list of items kids can search for and be ready to pull it out at a strategic moment. Possible items are mushrooms, spider webs, Indian pipes, pine cones, maple leaves—whatever you can glean from reading the Nature Notes section of the particular hike. In keeping with the "Leave No Trace" philosophy, have the older kids take pictures (digital cameras are great for this), but encourage them to leave things as they found them.

## ADDITIONAL THOUGHTS

Be flexible and allow plenty of extra time. Be ready to change your plans mid-hike and always encourage the kids to investigate the natural world. Time spent watching a moose feeding on water plants or a moth caught in a spider web likely will be remembered much longer than whether they made it to that last waterfall.

Be ready to bail out if the hike isn't working or if the children get engrossed in little things they see along the trail and time runs out. The idea is to have fun, not to make this into a forced march. On the other hand, don't necessarily turn back at the first complaint either, particularly if there is something you're sure they'll really enjoy with just a little more effort. Children have an amazing ability to do a complete 180-degree recovery just after they have insisted that they can't possibly move their legs another inch. We've been saved many times by something like a toad magically appearing on the trail and stimulating a great mood change just when it seemed all was lost. Sometimes picking them up, clowning around, and carrying them for a short period will get them back on track. And be liberal with praise for how well they are doing.

Just about all the trails described in this book have interesting things for both adults and children to see along the way so that the trip will be worthwhile, even if you do not complete the entire hike. The text suggests logical places at which to turn around before reaching the end, such as a nice view or swimming hole.

Remember, it is much more important for you to instill an appreciation for the natural world in your kids than to impart facts about nature. Sooner or later a kid will ask something that even the most expert naturalist can't answer. Make it into a game and help them look it up in a field guide. Bring pad and pencil to record field notes and questions.

Your own enthusiasm for the hike will rub off on them.

# Appendix B

# NATURAL HISTORY OF THE WHITE MOUNTAINS

**THE WHITE MOUNTAINS ARE A SPECIAL PLACE,** not only for their scenery and outdoor recreational opportunities, but also for their wonderful diversity of natural history. A brief description of the region's geology, plants, and animals hopefully will enrich your hiking experience. Look for additional information in the individual hike descriptions. A complete guide to the natural history of the White Mountains would take up several volumes, so check the bibliography (page 281) if you want to know more.

## GEOGRAPHY

The White Mountains of north central New Hampshire and western Maine are the largest expanse of mountains in New England. Forty-three peaks exceed 4,000 feet in elevation and seven exceed 5,000 feet. Most of the region is included in the White Mountain National Forest and several state parks. The area has an extensive network of hiking trails maintained by the national forest and volunteer organizations such as the AMC and Randolph Mountain Club.

Because of their elevation, the White Mountains have a cooler climate and a more "northern" ecology than one would expect at their latitude. Snow remains in some mountain ravines into June, and trees generally do not grow above 4,500 feet. The higher peaks are notorious for damp, misty weather that, on the positive side, contributes to the lush, almost rain-forest-like aspect to some slopes and makes you particularly cherish a great summer day when there are extensive views.

A major geographic feature is the north-to-south-running valleys (called notches) that separate the major mountain ranges. From west to east these are Franconia Notch, Zealand Notch, Crawford Notch, Pinkham Notch, and Evans Notch. All except Zealand are traversed by roads.

## GEOLOGY

Where did the White Mountains come from? The story is one of enormous collisions and rifts of ancient continents drifting across the earth. Eons ago there was a sea here instead of mountains. About 400 million years ago, the thick layers of sand and mud at the bottom of this sea were squeezed between two colliding continents, North America and an ancient island continent called Avalon. Under this immense pressure these layers hardened to form the schist, gneiss, and quartzite of the Presidential Range and then were uplifted. A second major geologic event occurred 230–180 million years ago when the granite that is the bedrock of much of the rest of the White Mountains solidified from molten rock deep within the earth as ancient continents split apart. Subsequent uplift and erosion of layers of softer, overlying rocks brought the granite to the surface. Volcanic eruptions at that same time created additional rocks.

The rocks along the trails in the White Mountains are almost all granite or schist. Both have a salt-and-pepper appearance because they are comprised of different-colored minerals. Granite is composed primarily of crystals of feldspar (whitish or pink) and quartz (translucent white or gray). Usually there are smaller amounts of mica flakes (biotite if brown or black; muscovite if white or silvery) and hornblende (black). Schist was formed originally from sand and mud that accumulated under the sea before the mountains rose. The mineral crystals in schist are smaller than those in granite.

Gleaming white quartz and glossy mica flakes are evident along just about any trail. Rock hounds will especially enjoy a visit to one of the abandoned mines, such as those on Lord Hill or on North Sugarloaf. At these mines you can find large crystals of mica, feldspar, and, if you look hard enough, topaz, garnet, beryl, smoky quartz, and even amethyst.

When hiking through White Mountain forests, you will undoubtedly come upon some monstrous boulders. Jumbles of boulders at the base of mountains—or Ethan Pond Trail at Whitewall Cliff or on the Boulder Loop Trail—probably tumbled down during landslides. Isolated boulders may be erratics carried to their destination by glaciers and left behind when the glacier melted.

You'll find large glacial erratics at the Flume Gorge, the Trestle Trail, "the Boulder" near the Cascade Path in Waterville Valley, and Glen Boulder near Pinkham Notch.

Many of the hikes take you past huge outcroppings of exposed bedrock. Famous profiles such as the Indian Head near Franconia Notch and the Elephant Head at Crawford Notch are outcrops of bedrock visible from highways.

On most outcroppings of bedrock you can find narrow bands of white or black rocks, called dikes, crisscrossing the grayer granite. Dikes form when molten rock, heated by forces deep within the earth, flow into cracks in the granite and then cool. Pegmatite dikes are typically white and contain relatively large crystals of feldspar and sometimes other minerals. Basalt dikes are black and do not appear to have any crystalline structure at all, because the magma (molten rock) flowed near the surface of the earth and cooled rapidly, not allowing time for crystal formation. Narrow, steep-sided gorges called flumes form where flowing water has eroded the softer dike and left the relatively harder granite walls.

The erosive action of glaciers had a profound effect on the White Mountain landscape. Mountain glaciers high up on the sides of peaks carved the famous bowl-shaped ravines (called cirques) in the Presidential Range. These include Tuckerman, Huntington, and King ravines and the Great Gulf. Mountain glaciers also carved the sharp, narrow ridge of the Franconia Range.

The continental glaciers that covered much of North America during the Ice Age had an even more widespread impact than the mountain glaciers. Four separate advances and retreats of glaciers occurred between 1 million and 12,000 years ago. The last glacier covered even Mount Washington with several thousand feet of ice. Its erosive action smoothed out the summits of the Presidentials and carved out U-shaped valleys such as Crawford and Zealand notches. Pine Mountain is a good place to see scratches in the bedrock etched by stones dragged along by the movement of ice.

Recent investigations by the New Hampshire Historic Preservation Office has shown that people inhabited the area around Jefferson, New Hampshire, about 11,000 years ago, indicating that the glaciers were no longer covering the White Mountains by then. Archaeological investigations since 1995 have uncovered tools, fluted spear points, and other artifacts.

## FORESTS

The White Mountains are densely forested, a fact many easterners may not appreciate unless they have spent time in the Sierra Nevada or other western ranges. Many walks described in this book pass through two different types of forest: the northern hardwood forest at lower elevations and the boreal forest higher up.

Northern hardwood forests are dominated by three broad-leaved trees: sugar maple, American beech, and yellow birch. Canadian hemlock, a needle-bearing tree, is very abundant along streams in shady gorges. Hobblebush and striped maple are common in the understory. Northern hardwoods cover a wide band of the northern United States and southern Canada from Maine through Minnesota. This forest glows with beautiful colors in autumn—a great, bug-free time to hike.

As you ascend above 2,000 feet, you will notice an increasing number of co-nifers—cone-bearing trees with needle leaves. The two most common species are red spruce and balsam fir. Spruce and fir, along with pine, are often called evergreens because they keep their needles year-round; however, conifer is a better term because some broad-leaved shrubs, such as rhododendrons, are also "evergreen."

Above 2,500 to 3,000 feet, a dark forest of conifers, the boreal forest, com-pletely replaces the northern hardwoods. Boreas, the Greek god of the north wind, was portrayed in mythology as blowing a cold wind across the land, and, indeed, the boreal forest occurs in colder places such as the middle lati-tudes of Canada and Russia. An ascent of several thousand feet in the White Mountains is ecologically equivalent to driving several hundred miles north of Montreal. The summit of Mount Washington, the highest point in the White Mountains at 6,288 feet, is roughly equivalent to the environment of northern Labrador.

The boreal forest, also called the spruce-fir forest, is a fantasyland of dense Christmas trees with a soft, dark, mossy understory. Red spruce tends to be more abundant in the lower part of the boreal forest (below 3,500 feet), while balsam fir predominates higher up. Scattered throughout the forest, particu-larly in clearings, are a few broad-leafed trees and shrubs such as paper birch and mountain ash. The upper part of the boreal forest grades into dwarf trees and scrub near treeline.

Humans have had a major impact on the character of White Mountain for-ests. Red spruce at lower elevations was logged heavily in the late nineteenth and early twentieth centuries. Since then, northern hardwood forests have grown up in many places where spruce once dominated.

Fire has been the other major human impact. The most famous fires oc-curred during the logging era in the Zealand and Wild River valleys, but very few areas were not touched by fires at one time or another. Many of the lower-elevation summits below 4,000 feet are now "bald" because the forest cover

**Flag (banner) trees show the effects of wind.**

was burned off. (The true alpine zone, where weather conditions are too harsh to support the growth of trees, begins between 4,200 and 4,800 feet in the White Mountains. The Alpine Garden Trail is the only hike in this book that takes you into that realm.)

On summits trees are often contorted into odd shapes. This is the result of wind exposure. Flag, or banner, trees with branches on one side occur only when the combination of ice and wind kills the branches that attempt to grow into the prevailing winds, which are generally from the west or northwest. The surviving branches point away from the wind, just like a flag rippling in a stiff breeze.

# Appendix C
# LEAVE NO TRACE

**THE APPALACHIAN MOUNTAIN CLUB** is a national educational partner of Leave No Trace, a nonprofit organization dedicated to promoting and inspiring responsible outdoor recreation through education, research, and partnerships. The Leave No Trace Program seeks to develop wildland ethics—ways in which people think and act in the outdoors to minimize their impacts on the areas they visit and to protect our natural resources for future enjoyment. Leave No Trace unites four federal land management agencies—the U.S. Forest Service, National Park Service, Bureau of Land Management, and U.S. Fish and Wildlife Service—with manufacturers, outdoor retailers, user groups, educators, organizations such as the AMC and the National Outdoor Leadership School (NOLS), and individuals.

The Leave No Trace ethic is guided by these seven principles:

- Plan ahead and prepare
- Travel and camp on durable surfaces
- Dispose of waste properly
- Leave what you find
- Minimize campfire impacts
- Respect wildlife
- Be considerate of other visitors

The AMC has joined NOLS—a recognized leader in wilderness education and a founding partner of Leave No Trace—as a national provider of the Leave No Trace Master Educator course. The AMC offers this five-day course, designed especially for outdoor professionals and land managers, as well as the shorter two-day Leave No Trace Trainer course, at locations throughout the Northeast.

**For Leave No Trace information and materials, contact:** Leave No Trace Center for Outdoor Ethics, P.O. Box 997, Boulder, CO 80306; toll free: 800-332-4100, or locally, 303-442-8222; fax: 303-442-8217; www.lnt.org.

# GLOSSARY OF FLORA AND FAUNA

## COMMON TREES

Identifying different types of trees can seem intimidating at first, but there is a logical way to proceed. Here are some simple steps that will help you narrow down the possibilities. These steps are also helpful for shrubs and wildflowers. It really is like solving a puzzle.

1. Determine if the tree has needles or broad leaves. This will distinguish the two main groups of trees, conifers and the broad-leaved deciduous trees.
2. Examine the shape of the leaves. Do the leaves have lobes like maple and oak? Are they rounded at the base like paper birch, or heart shaped at the base like yellow birch, or do they taper at both ends like beech? Are the edges of the leaves distinctly toothed like beech, or smooth like a rhododendron?
3. Closely examine the needles of conifers. If the needles are relatively short (less than 1.5 inches) and are attached singly to a branch, then it is a spruce, balsam fir, hemlock, or yew. If the needles are longer and attached to branches in clusters of two, three, or five, then it is one of the pines. If the needles are in bunches of twenty or so, then it is a larch. If the needles are tiny scales along the branches, it is a juniper or white cedar.

4. The bark on some trees is a good key to identification. The white peeling bark of paper birch and the smooth gray bark of beech are two examples.

5. Check the descriptions and illustrations of the common species in the next section and in selected hikes. If a tree or leaf does not fit any of the descriptions, refer to one of the comprehensive field guides listed in the bibliography.

**Sugar maple** is one of the major trees of the northern hardwood forest. Its leaves have three or five lobes, somewhat like the palm of a hand, and are attached to branches in pairs (opposite-leaved). Maple seeds are winged "keys" that delight children as they spin through the air like little helicopters. If you are interested in distinguishing sugar maple from other maples, see page 184.

**Striped maple** (moosewood) is common in the understory of the northern hardwood forest, although it can occasionally grow up to be a tree. Leaves often are quite large and have three lobes that end in narrow points (resembling a goose's foot, hence another name, goosefoot maple). Branches and young stems are distinctly marked with beautiful green and white stripes.

**American beech** has distinct smooth gray bark. The combination of smooth bark and long, pointed buds makes this an easy tree to identify, even in winter. Leaves are tapered at both ends and are toothed along the edges, with prominent parallel veins running to each tooth.

**Yellow birch** has yellowish brown or gray bark lined with distinct horizontal pores called lenticels. The bark peels in horizontal layers. Leaves are heart shaped at the base and serrated along the edges. Its small twigs taste like wintergreen when chewed for a while.

**Paper birch** has unmistakable white bark that peels into horizontal strips. Please resist the temptation to peel the bark, since the scar may never heal. Leaves are toothed and rounded at the base. Paper birch is often the first tree species to colonize an area clear-cut by loggers.

**Canadian hemlock** is a sprawling conifer of cool ravines and stream sides at lower elevations. It has short, half-inch needles with two white lines underneath. The needles are flat, a trait they share with balsam fir. Hemlocks produce small cones at the tips of branches.

**Balsam fir** is one of the two major trees of the boreal forest. Like hemlock, balsam fir has needles that are flat, have two whitish lines underneath, and occur individually on branches. Balsam fir needles are longer (up to 1.5 inches) than hemlock's and emit that wonderful balsam fragrance when crushed. It is the only conifer with cones that sit upright on branches. The trunk is covered with balsam blisters, which if popped are sure to leave a sticky, sweet resin on hands and clothes. Dwarfed balsam fir is a major component of the scrub forest that occurs near treeline.

**Red spruce** is the other major tree of the boreal forest. Its 0.75 to 1.5-inch needles are attached singly to branches and are square in cross section. If you can roll a needle between your thumb and forefinger, it is a red spruce. If you can't (because the needles are flat), it is a hemlock or balsam fir. Spruce needles are sharp to the touch, so remember that to "spruce up is to look sharp."

**White pine** has needles in bunches of five. The three- to five-inch needles are soft and flexible so they won't prickle you. White pine can grow up to 150 feet tall, making it one of the largest trees in the White Mountains. It's a great tree to snooze under, since its soft needles make a comfy bed on the forest floor.

**Larch,** also called tamarack, is a tree of open boggy areas. It is less widespread than the other trees in this list, but it is a personal favorite. Larch is a beautiful, distinctive conifer with lacy, curved branches. The one-inch needles grow in clusters of ten to thirty. The larch is unique among conifers in that it drops its needles in the fall after they turn a beautiful bright yellow. This again illustrates the point that "conifer" is a better term than "evergreen" for this group of trees. Look for larch on Blueberry Mountain or Mount Avalan, or around Ethan Pond.

## COMMON SHRUBS

**Blueberry** is probably everyone's favorite White Mountain shrub. Several species occur on open, low summits and ledges, where they are often less than a foot high. During July and August the tasty berries are a great focal point for several hikes described in this book. Delicate white clusters of small, bell-shaped flowers in May and June precede the berries. Lowbush blueberry, the most  common species, has leaves that are edged with tiny teeth (use a hand lens if you have one). Leaves of sour-top blueberry lack toothed edges and are somewhat hairy underneath.

**Hobblebush** is the most abundant shrub in the forest understory of most hikes. It is easy to identify. Rounded, paired leaves with toothed edges and heart-shaped bases run along straggling stems. The thin, often horizontal stems form impenetrable tangles in the forest, giving rise to the name hobblebush and other names: tanglelegs and witch-hobble. Hobblebush produces flat-topped white clusters of flowers in May and clusters of inedible red berries during the summer.

**Raspberries** and **blackberries** may be as delicious as blueberries, but picking them can be a scratchy affair. These plants grow as thin, arching "canes" covered with thorns and prickles. White flowers appear in June and the fruits in July and August. Raspberry and blackberry are colonizers of forest clearings, roadsides, and recently logged areas.

**Labrador tea** is a small (1-to-2-foot) shrub of bogs and boggy shorelines of ponds. Its dark green, leathery leaves are rolled underneath at the edges and remain on the plant all year. Turn the leaves upside down for a surprise: the bottoms of the leaves are covered with dense rust-colored hairs (sometimes white on new leaves). In June Labrador tea produces spherical clusters of white flowers at the tips of its branches.

## WILDFLOWERS

The White Mountains abound with wildflowers. The peak time for seeing the greatest variety of native woodland wildflowers in the mountains is in May and early June. This great floral display also coincides perfectly with black-fly season, a time when even hardened natives of New Hampshire avoid journeying in the woods. As a result most people miss the best wildflower time.

Why does this springtime schedule of woodland wildflowers coincide so poorly with that of human visitors? Many wildflowers produce new leaves and flowers before tree leaves come out and block the sunlight. Once they are under the dark canopy of the forest, some wildflowers, such as trout lilies, completely shrivel up.

Do not despair, however, if you cannot get to the White Mountains before July 4 or if you really can't stand the thought of black flies. Attractive summer wildflowers grow in the woods and fields and on open summits. Some of the spring wildflowers also produce showy berries in midsummer. And remember that flowers bloom later in the season at higher elevations, so you just might catch that last goldthread in bloom if you are willing to hike up.

If you are interested in identifying wildflowers, don't forget to take note of the habitat in which they grow. Some plants are characteristic of wetlands, others occur only in the northern hardwood forest, and still others are partial to the mossy understory of the boreal forest. The flowers of fields and roadsides grow well in direct sunlight and do poorly in the shade of woodlands.

Here's a brief description of some wildflowers you are most likely to encounter on just about any hike in the appropriate habitat and season. Additional flowers are mentioned in the trail descriptions.

## Spring Wildflowers

**Clintonia** is a lily with large, shiny, smooth-edged leaves that hug the ground. A single stalk produces several yellowish green flowers with six "petals" in late May through June. Summer visitors are more likely to see the glossy blue-black berries that give rise to its other name, blue-bead lily. Do not eat the berry.

 **Painted trillium** is one of the grandest of the White Mountain woodland wildflowers. It is unmistakable, containing a whorl of three leaves on a one-foot stem. The stem is topped with a single white three-petaled flower with a purple center. In summer the flower is replaced by a large red berry.

The petals of red trillium are completely wine red. If you take a whiff of red trillium, you'll find out why it is also called stinking Benjamin. Its foul odor attracts certain flies as pollinators.

**Canada mayflower**, a small plant, is abundant in many wood-lands at both low and high elevations. It has two or three smooth-edged, heart-shaped leaves. Its white, fuzzy spike of small flowers develop first into a white-and-red-speckled berry and then into a red berry by late summer.

**Pink lady's slipper** is another eye-catching flower. Its single flowering stem arises from two large, wide, smooth-edged leaves. You might mistake its leaves for those of clintonia but for the distinct parallel veins running lengthwise. The hanging flower is shaped like a shoe or moccasin. In the White Mountains the flower of the "pink" lady's slipper is as likely to be white as pink.

**Goldthread** is a small flower of shady, mossy woods. For most of the year it is recognizable by its three small, rounded leaflets, each with scalloped edges. In spring a single delicate white flower with five to seven petals arises from a separate stem. Goldthread is named for the bright yellow underground stem that connects different individual plants. Before the ad-vent of modern medicines, goldthread was used to relieve  the pain of toothache and to combat dyspepsia (what our great-grandparents called indigestion) and the "drinking habit."

**Starflower** is an easy one for kids to guess since its delicate white flowers really do resemble stars. Typically, two white "stars" with six to eight petals each are on top of a whorl of five to seven narrow, pointed leaves on a four-to-eight-inch stem.

**Wild strawberry** grows along roadsides and power line rights of way and in sunny clearings. Their three leaflets with sharply toothed edges form dense colonies. Flowers have five white petals surrounding numerous yellow stamens. The tiny berries, ripe around July 4, are much more delicious than their larger, cultivated relatives.

**Alpine wildflowers** have always been a key enticement for climbing to higher elevations in the White Mountains. There are a number of showy species that bloom in early to mid-June. (See the description in the Alpine Garden, Trip 38.)

### Summer Wildflowers

**Bunchberry** is a cheery white wildflower that usually occurs in large colonies on the forest floor. The flower is also called Canada dogwood. As with the flowering dogwood tree, the four white "petals" of the bunchberry are not true petals but modified leaves that surround a cluster of tiny green flowers. Bunchberry produces a whorl of four or six smooth-edged leaves. Six-leaved plants almost always produce flowers, and four-leaved plants hardly ever do. A good game to play when they are in bloom is to see if you can find any exceptions to this six/four rule. Bunchberry blooms in June at low elevations and early July at higher elevations.

**Mountain wood sorrel**, another wildflower of the forest floor, will remind you of a shamrock. Its three leaflets, notched at the apex, are a common sight in cool woods. Despite the resemblance, wood sorrel is unrelated to clovers. Mountain wood sorrel has attractive, delicate white flowers with five petals inscribed with thin pink lines and (usually) a pink circle surrounding the center. It blooms in late June through August.

**Twinflower** is a small plant with rounded, paired leaves on a stem that trails along the ground. The plant is named for the two pink flowers that bloom from a single stem in late June and early July. This small, delicate flower was a favorite of Carolus Linnaeus, the Swedish biologist who devised the system of using two Latin words, the genus and species names, to denote each type of organism on earth. Twinflower was given the Latin name *Linnaea borealis* in honor of Linnaeus, who was often pictured holding this plant.

**Indian pipe** grows in isolated small groups in the forest. It is odd looking, easily mistaken for a fungus because of its ghostly white appearance and lack of green leaves. Drooping white flowers are produced on top of six- to eight-inch stems. Indian pipe gets its nutrition from organic matter on the forest floor and therefore has no need for green leaves.

**Bluet** is a small plant, less than three inches high, which seems to reflect the color of the sky. Individual flowers have four light blue petals surrounding a yellow center. They are less than half an inch in diameter but grow in dense colonies that can be quite showy. Bluet sometimes occurs in sunny areas along trails but is more likely to be found along roadsides and fields.

**Sharp-leaved aster** is a very common flower in the northern hardwood forest from mid-August through September. Its leaves are tapered at both ends, coming to a long point at the tip. The plant is also called whorled wood aster because the coarsely toothed leaves appear to be whorled around the stem. Its flower heads are daisylike, consisting of white (occasionally light purple) rays and a brown center. Blue asters you may encounter in the forests in late summer include heart-leaved aster and large-leaved aster. Both have heart-shaped leaves, but those of the latter are especially wide.

**Goldenrods** are showy late-summer flowers of fields, roadsides, and occasionally sunny spots in forests. Distinguishing the many species is challenging, but it is not hard to enjoy the bright yellow color they add to the landscape in August and September.

**Turtlehead** is a tall plant (two to three feet) common around the edges of wetlands. Just about every swale crossed by a bog bridge at low elevation in August or September has least a few stems. Its white, oddly shaped flowers, named for their resemblance to the head of a tortoise, are in clusters. Paired, toothed leaves attach to the stem opposite each other.

**Orange hawkweed** looks like a small orange dandelion. It is not native to North America but provides a striking splash of orange color along roadsides and in cultivated areas such as ski trails and around AMC huts. It is also called devil's paintbrush. King devil, another nonnative plant, is a yellow hawkweed that often grows in the same places as orange hawkweed. Introduced species like these two, although attractive to look at, often push out native plants.

## FERNS, CLUB MOSSES, AND MOSSES

**Ferns** have attractive, feathery leaves called fronds that are divided into leaflets called pinnae. Most pinnae are further subdivided into pinnules. Spores used for reproduction occur in clusters, which are fun to examine with a hand lens. A number of species are abundant in the forests of the White Mountains:

**Long beech fern** is very common in moist forests and on damp ledges around waterfalls. It is roughly triangular in shape, with its two lowest pinnae pointing downward.

**Rock fern**, also called Virginia polypody, grows right on rocks wherever enough soil has accumulated. It is a small (one foot) evergreen fern whose fronds are divided only once. Look at the underside of a frond to see the round spore clusters.

**Interrupted fern** is a large (three to four feet) fern. It gets its name from the brown, spore-containing section of fertile fronds that occurs between the green pinnae along the stem. This fern grows in wet areas, often in clearings and along roadsides. A similar species, cinnamon fern, has dense tufts of rusty hairs where the pinnae join the stem.

**Hay-scented fern** is a lacy, medium-sized fern that grows in dense colonies in small clearings such as those created by falling trees. It gives off the sweet smell of freshly mown grass when the fronds have dried out in late September and October.

**Bracken fern** is a robust fern with a triangular frond divided into three parts. Unlike most ferns, it grows in sunny, weedy locales, such as along roadsides.

A number of species of **wood ferns** are common on the forest floor. These have finely cut fronds and brown scales along the stem.

**Club mosses** are not really mosses but plants whose ancestors were the size of trees in the time of the dinosaurs. Modern club mosses are usually less than eight inches tall. They grow on the forest floor in extensive colonies where individual stems are all linked by underground stems. Ground pine looks like a tiny six-inch tree. It is used as a Christmas decoration because it resembles a conifer. Others, such as the shiny club moss, have upright or horizontal unbranched or occasionally branched stems covered by small, needlelike leaves. Most species have conelike structures on top of their stalks for reproduction.

**Mosses** are small, primitive plants that provide a beautiful cover of greenery in damp forests. In the boreal forest they cover rocks, logs, and old stumps, often being the only understory vegetation.

**Haircap moss** is one of the most common woodland mosses. Its upright branches are covered with small, needlelike leaves. This moss gets its name from the hairy cap that covers its spore-containing capsules. The capsules, located on stalks on top of its branches, are often quite obvious, even to the casual observer. The spores are shot out of the capsule as it dries.

**Fern moss**, also called piggyback moss, is feathery and fernlike. Smaller plants grow by piggybacking on top of larger ones.

**Sphagnum moss**, or peat moss, is the most economically important moss. It covers bogs with green or red colors, depending on the particular species. Sphagnum mosses have a tremendous capacity to hold water, which is why they are useful as a soil conditioner.

## FUNGI

**Fungi** come in an assortment of odd shapes with occasional vivid colors. They are like icebergs—what you see above ground, their reproductive structures, is only a small part of the whole. Below ground or within a decaying log myriad fungal filaments break down dead plant matter, helping to create soil. Without these decomposers all the trails in the White Mountains would be knee-deep in dead leaves and logs. Other types of fungi penetrate plant roots, where they aid plants in the essential process of taking nutrients up from the soil.

Mushrooms, with their classic umbrella-shaped cap are the best-known fungi. Most types have gills on the underside. These radiate around a central axis, like myriad spokes of the umbrella. Another group of mushrooms, the boletes, have pores rather than gills on their undersides. Typically a mushroom first appears as a "button" on the ground. As it develops, the button grows upward on a stalk and expands. Eventually the mature, open mushroom releases its spores from the gills or pores.

The best time to find a variety of mushrooms in the White Mountains is in late summer. Russulas are among the most common. They have a stout stem and a broad, brightly colored cap that may be red, yellow, or white, and six inches across. Mycenas are much smaller and delicate, with a conical grayish brown cap on a thin stem. They tend to grow in clumps. Amanitas are intermediate in size between russulas and mycenas. They are usually white, although some have colored caps or turn brown with age. The base of the stem is enclosed with a cup (you may have to dig through leaf litter to see it) that may be quite ragged at the end of summer. Virtually all amanitas are deadly poisonous.

Mushrooms are eye-catching, but can be dangerous. They are a challenge to identify, often changing shape as they develop. Leave picking and eating wild mushrooms to the experts.

**Bracket fungi** form massive horizontal, dull white lumps on dead trees and fallen logs. Their bottom surfaces are covered with small pores rather than gills.

**Puffballs** look like balls made out of brown paper. Each ball contains billions of spores. The spores come out in a brown dusty cloud when they reach maturity.

**Witch's butter** is a bright yellow-orange, jellylike fungus that grows on decomposing logs.

**Coral fungus** looks like someone dropped a piece of coral on the forest floor. They are typically yellow or white and have upright, fingerlike bodies that are often branched.

**Lichens** are fungi that have the trapped cells of algae within them. The tiny algal cells produce food for the organism, and the fungus provides the alga with some nutrients and with protection from the environment. Lichens can live in harsh places, such as the bare rocks above treeline, because they provide for their own nutrition and have an amazing ability to resuscitate after being almost completely dried out. These symbiotic organisms grow so slowly and live so long that individual ones can be used to track the slow, frost-induced movement of the rocks upon which they live.

Lichens are abundant on rocky ledges, summits, and drier forests of the White Mountains. They come in three general shapes: crusty, leafy, and bushy.

**Map lichen** creates green and yellow splashes of color with a black background on boulders on open ledges and summits. These brightly colored lichens grow as flat crusts in patches that resemble the patterns of rivers, oceans, and islands on a map (thus the scientific name for map lichen, *Rhizocarpon geographicum*). Because the lichen is so flush on the rocks, it appears to be part of the rock itself rather than an independent, living organism.

**Rock tripe** is a leafy lichen abundant on boulders in the forest. It looks like overlapping pieces of black or dark brown rubber, each one to two inches across and irregular in shape. Each piece is attached to rock by a central stalk.

**Reindeer lichen** is bushy, with many pale yellow-green entangled branches arising from individual stalks. It grows on open, scrubby ledges, often in large patches that look so neat and well manicured that you might think a gardener deliberately planted them there. Farther north, these lichens are consumed by caribou and reindeer.

 **British soldier** lichen is named for the bright red tips located on top of thin, upright, pale-green stalks. Each stalk arises from a leafy mass covering a rock or log. The red tips are its reproductive structures.

## ANIMALS
### Insects, Spiders, and Related Invertebrates

Insects and spiders often grab your attention, whether it is a colorful damselfly darting over a pond or a brown bug ambling across a trail. Take the time along the trail to stop and enjoy this fascinating group of animals.

There might be many admirers of the insect clan were it not for the two most notorious insects of the White Mountains, black flies and mosquitoes. Knowing something about their lives won't make their bites any less annoying, but they do have an interesting story. Both lay eggs in or near water and have aquatic larval stages. Black fly larvae attach their hind ends to rocks in flowing waters and feed by filtering small organisms from the water. Sometimes the larvae are so dense, hanging on in the swift current, that they darken the rocks over which a riffle or cascade flows. After they pupate into adults and mate, female black flies search for a blood meal to ensure the optimal development of their eggs.

**Blackfly** season runs from early May through mid-June, a time when only the brave or the foolish dare go into the woods without a liberal dousing of repellent or long sleeves and a head net. Generally, open summits  are good places to escape from black flies but only if there is a breeze. Black flies are less likely to be out on damp, cool days but, unfortunately, so are we.

 Just when the black flies are tailing off, **mosquitoes** pick up the slack. Mosquito breeding areas are typically stagnant, isolated pools of water. These could be temporary pools of water created in small depressions in the woods, permanent shallow swamps, or even water that has collected in tree holes. Mosquitoes can be a real annoyance along swampy, lowland sections of trails in the White Mountains but aren't as bad at higher elevations.

If you can get beyond black flies and mosquitoes, you will find many attractive insects in the White Mountains. **Butterflies** are high on everyone's list. They are sometimes called flying flowers, a tribute to their lovely colors and perhaps to their affinity for feeding on nectar. Two of the most common and striking are tiger swallowtail  and mourning cloak. The tiger swallowtail is yellow with black stripes and two "tails," one projecting from each hind wing. The boldly patterned mourning cloak, yellow with a black border to the hind wings, is fun to watch as it darts from flower to flower.

 **Dragonflies** and **damselflies**, members of the same insect order, are common around the edges of ponds. They are large, have big eyes, and are often colored with iridescent blues and greens. Dragonflies are strong flyers, moving straight ahead rapidly on outspread wings like little airplanes and changing direction quite abruptly. Damselfly flight is typically floppy, like a butterfly. Dragonflies hold their wings horizontally when at rest whereas damselflies  bring their wings together over their bodies. Both are predators of other insects, which they catch on the wing. Both have long immature stages in water, where they breathe through gills before becoming adults.

**Water striders** are fascinating to watch as they stand on the surface of small pools and skate about gracefully. Like all insects, they have three pairs of legs, but only the back two are in contact with the water. Tiny hairs on their "feet" enable them to stand on the water without falling through. If the light is right, you can see that the surface of the water under  each "foot" bends as if it was elastic. The front legs are used to capture prey.

Large black **wolf spiders** are often observed scurrying across rocks on open summits and ledges. These eight-legged relatives of insects are predators of other insects. Unlike most spiders, wolf spiders catch their prey without the use of a web. Of course you can also find many spiders that spin traditional webs to snare their prey in the White Mountains.

Fallen trees often harbor a variety of invertebrate life that aids in decomposing the tree and recycling nutrients. **Ants** and **termites** create networks of chambers under bark and scatter wildly when you uncover them. **Centipedes** and **worms** of various sorts take up residence in decaying logs. Make sure you return any logs you overturn to their original positions.

## REPTILES AND AMPHIBIANS

The long, cold winters and damp summers of the White Mountains do not make an ideal climate for reptiles. These scaly, egg-laying vertebrates are more diverse in drier, warmer climates. There are no poisonous snakes in the White Mountains.

If you do find a snake, it is likely to be an **eastern garter snake**. It is brownish with three yellow stripes running along the entire length of its body. Although harmless, this snake won't like being picked up and may rub a very stinky fluid on you if you try (you can hardly blame it). Garter snakes feed on insects and small vertebrates.

**Painted turtles** are occasionally seen basking on rocks and logs in ponds at lower elevations. Their heads are marked with short yellow stripes, and their shells are bordered with red. You may not get a good look at these markings without binoculars, because painted turtles are very wary and will plop into the water if you get too close.

Amphibians, which include frogs, toads, and salamanders, are much more tied to water than reptiles. They lay their eggs and develop as tadpoles with gills in water. Many species remain in, or close to, water as adults even though they breathe air.

The **American toad** is the most wide-ranging amphibian in the region. You'll often find them along trails in the forest far from water, as high up in elevation as treeline. They blend in very well with the dead leaves of the forest floor, and your first clue to them is a rustling sound as they move about. Their leathery, warty skin allows them to wander farther from dampness than most amphibians, although they return to water to lay their eggs.

Frogs of various kinds inhabit ponds and wetlands of the White Mountains. It is much easier to identify them by their sounds than it is to see them. In early spring the birdlike chorus of **spring peepers** is a familiar sound. Since early spring is a relative term in the White Mountains, choruses of spring peepers can be heard in April at low elevations and in July in high-elevation ponds. **Green frogs**, which sound like someone plucking a string of a banjo, are heard in midsummer.

Salamanders are creatures of damp woods, mountain streams, and ponds. They generally remain hidden and are difficult to see unless you look under dead logs in the woods or flat stones by water. Despite their secretive habits, the abundance of some species makes them very important to the ecology of the soil and leaf litter of White Mountain forests.

The **red-backed salamander** is an extremely abundant woodland species that lives under dead logs and leaf litter. It is long and thin with dusky sides, a rusty red back, and small legs. If you examine the underside of fallen logs in damp woods, you will likely run into quite a few of them.

The only salamander bold enough to cross a trail out in the open is the **red eft**. This bright red salamander with greenish spots can afford to be more brazen than other salamanders because it is very toxic. The red color is a warning to predators to keep away. The red eft is actually a juvenile, land stage of the **red-spotted newt**, an aquatic salamander common in some ponds in the mountains. Red efts often are quite abundant in the mountains, particularly after a summer rain.

## BIRDS

Birds are more often heard than seen in the White Mountains. Nonetheless, a few will catch your attention. Young and old alike should stop periodically to enjoy the lovely songs of thrushes, winter wren, white-throated sparrow, and other birds in June and July.

The handiwork of woodpeckers is evident in dead trees riddled with holes. A softball-sized hole in a tree is probably the doorway to the nest of the largest woodpecker in the White Mountains, the pileated woodpecker. The **pileated woodpecker** is the size of a crow and is black and white with a flaming red crest. Look for large chips of wood under a tree it has chiseled as it probes the bark for insects. The little **downy woodpecker** is the woodpecker you are most likely to see. It is about the size of a cardinal and is speckled with black and white. Downies produce a lively descending whinny when they land.

Woodpeckers are essential to the ecology of the forest because their holes are used as homes by many different kinds of birds and mammals. Because of this, the Forest Service has a policy of protecting "wildlife trees."

The **black-capped chickadee** is a favorite of children, because it is perky, relatively tame, and is constantly saying its own name. You'll see them on most hikes.

A **dark-eyed junco** is a small, sparrowlike gray bird with a white belly and white outer tail feathers. It spends much of its time on summits and ledges.

Many different kinds of birdcalls and songs fill the forests and summits of the White Mountains, but a few are particularly characteristic and easy to identify:

The **white-throated sparrow** sings a number of clear, sweet-whistled notes varying in pitch followed by several wavy notes. Its song sounds like "See old Sam Peabody, Peabody, Peabody" and is very easy to imitate.

The **winter wren** has an amazingly extensive, bubbly song that varies in pitch. It makes a lot of noise for such a small bird.

The song of the **hermit thrush** is flutelike and ethereal. It starts with a single long note and then gradually modulates up the scale. Usually it sings from shrubs or the lower branches of trees.

The **ovenbird** belts out a raucous, booming two-syllable "t'cher, t'cher, t'cher" that increases gradually in volume. This warbler sings from the ground.

The **raven** makes a hoarse "caw caw" or a series of piglike snorts as it flies overhead.

## MAMMALS

In the White Mountains it is not easy to see large animals. Unlike western mountains, there are no large herds of antlered animals that prance across alpine meadows. Nonetheless, you will see ample signs of mammals in the holes in trees, scratch marks on bark, and beaver dams. Other than the ubiquitous red squirrel and chipmunk, consider the sighting of mammals an extra treat.

The **beaver** is abundant here. Many of the trails take you by beaver ponds, where you can see their wooden lodges, dams of sticks and mud, canals, and chewed trees. The animals themselves can sometimes be seen around dusk or dawn. Lost Pond in Pinkham Notch has been a good place to see beaver in recent years.

The **red squirrel** is the most frequently encountered mammal in the White Mountains. It scolds hikers entering its territory with a rattling chatter usually delivered from a red spruce or balsam fir. It can be a little thief at campgrounds.

The **chipmunk** is also a popular campground rodent. It chirps like a bird and scampers on the forest floor over fallen logs and into holes in the ground much more than squirrels.

A **snowshoe hare** looks somewhat like a cottontail rabbit with slightly larger ears and feet that appear a bit too big and gangly for its body. Its large feet act as snowshoes, helping it to stay on top of deep snow in the winter. The snowshoe hare is also called the varying hare because it turns white in winter and is brown in summer.

**Moose**-watching is becoming a popular pastime in the White Mountains as their population has increased. This largest member of the deer family occasionally can be seen along roadsides around dusk. It is not as timid as a deer but may slowly amble off into the forest if too many cars stop. The wetlands along the Kancamagus Highway near the Passaconaway Historic Site are particularly good places to look for moose. In the fall rutting season males can be ill tempered, so give them a wide berth. Moose leave characteristic stripe marks on trees with their teeth.

**Black bear** is rarely encountered by hikers on the trails, but you may see the claw marks it leaves on trees to mark its territory. Bears are omnivores, feeding on a variety of mammals, insects, fruits, and nuts. In recent years one of the most reliable places to see a black bear is on the open ski trails of Cannon Mountain, where it browses on berries.

# SELECTED
# BIBLIOGRAPHY

## NATURAL HISTORY GUIDES

Appalachian Mountain Club. *AMC Field Guide to Mountain Flowers of New England*. Boston: Appalachian Mountain Club Books, 1977.

Arora, David. *Mushrooms Demystified*. Berkeley, CA. Ten Speed Press. 1986.

Bliss, L. C. *Alpine Zone of the Presidential Range*. Edmonton, Canada, 1963.

DeGraaf, Richard M., and Mariko Yamasaki. *New England Wildlife: Habitat, Natural History, and Distribution*. Lebanon, NH. University Press of New England. 2000.

Johnson, Charles W. *Bogs of the Northeast*. Hanover, NH: University Press of New England, 1985.

Jorgensen, Neil. *A Guide to New England's Landscape*. Barre, MA: Barre Publishers, 1971.

Marchand, Peter. *North Woods: An Insider's Look at the Nature of Forests in the Northeast*. Boston: Appalachian Mountain Club Books, 1987.

Newcomb, Lawrence. *Newcomb's Wildflower Guide*. Boston: Little, Brown, 1989.

Pease, Arthur Stanley. *A Flora of Northern New Hampshire*. Cambridge, MA: New England Botanical Club, 1964.

Peterson Field Guide Series. Various titles and publication dates. Boston: Houghton Mifflin. (The Peterson Field Guides cover all aspects of natural history—birds, trees and shrubs, wildflowers, reptiles and amphibians, etc. —and are an invaluable resource to professional and amateur naturalists alike.)

Phillips, Roger. *Mushrooms of North America*. Boston: Little, Brown, 1991.

Raymo, Chet, and Maureen Raymo. *Written in Stone: A Geological History of the Northeastern United States*. Chester, CT: Globe Pequot Press, 1989.

Sibley, David Allen. *The Sibley Guide to Birds*. New York: Alfred A. Knopf, 2000.

Slack, Nancy G., and Allison W. Bell. *AMC Field Guide to New England Alpine Summits*. 2nd ed. Boston: Appalachian Mountain Club Books, 2006.

## NATURE WITH CHILDREN

Cornell, Joseph. *Sharing Nature with Children*, expanded edition. Nevada City, CA: Dawn Publishing, 1998.

Gertz, Lucille N. *Let Nature Be the Teacher*. Lincoln, MA: Massachusetts Audubon Society, 1993.

Sheehan, Kathryn, and Mary Waidner. *Earth Child: Games, Stories, Activities, Experiments and Ideas about Living Lightly on Planet Earth*. Tulsa, OK: Council Oak Books, 1991.

## WHITE MOUNTAINS GUIDES AND HISTORIES

Appalachian Mountain Club. *White Mountain National Forest Map and Guide*. Boston: Appalachian Mountain Club Books, 2005.

Belcher, C. Francis. *Logging Railroads of the White Mountains*. Boston: Appalachian Mountain Club Books, 1980.

Billings, Marland P., Katharine Fowler-Billings, Carleton A. Chapman, Randolph W. Chapman, and Richard P. Goldthwait. *The Geology of the Mt. Washington Quadrangle, New Hampshire*. Concord, NH: State of New Hampshire, Department of Resources and Economic Development, 1979.

Bolnick, Bruce, Doreen Bolnick, and Daniel Bolnick. *Waterfalls of the White Mountains: 30 Trips to 100 Waterfalls.* Woodstock, VT: Countryman Press, 1999.

Daniell, Gene, and Steven D. Smith. *AMC White Mountain Guide.* 27th ed. Boston: Appalachian Mountain Club Books, 2003.

DeLorme Publishing Company. *Trail Map and Guide to the White Mountain National Forest.* Freeport, ME: DeLorme Publishing, 1992.

Monkman, Jerry and Marcy Monkman. *Discover the White Mountains of New Hampshire.* Boston: Appalachian Mountain Club Books, 2001.

Morse, Stearns. *Lucy Crawford's History of the White Mountains.* Boston: Appalachian Mountain Club Books, 1978.

Mudge, John T. B. *The White Mountains: Names, Places, Legends.* Etna, NH: Durand Press, 1995

Randall, Peter E. *Mount Washington: A Guide and Short History.* Woodstock, VT: The Countryman Press, 1992.

Reifsnyder, William E. *High Huts of the White Mountains: Nature Walks, Natural History, and Day Hikes around the AMC's Mountain Hostels.* Boston: Appalachian Mountain Club Books, 1993.

Smith, Steven D. *Ponds and Lakes of the White Mountains: A Four-Season Guide for Hikers and Anglers.* Woodstock, VT: Backcountry Publications, 1998.

Waterman, Laura, and Guy Waterman. *Forest and Crag: A History of Hiking, Trail Blazing, and Adventure in the Northeast Mountains.* 2nd ed. Boston: Appalachian Mountain Club Books, 2003.

Wight, D. B. *The Wild River Wilderness.* Littleton, NH: Courier Press, 1971.

Willey, Benjamin G. *Incidents in White Mountain History.* Boston: Nathaniel Noyes, 1856.

# INDEX

# ABOUT THE AUTHOR

**ROBERT BUCHSBAUM** has both a professional interest in and a passion for the natural history of New England. He received a Bachelor of Science degree in natural resources from Cornell University and a Ph.D. in marine ecology from the Boston University Marine Program at Woods Hole. A native New Yorker, he moved to New England in 1978 and has since spent many of his free weekends and vacations exploring the White Mountains. As an AMC Volunteer Naturalist since 1986, Buchsbaum has presented programs in the huts and elsewhere in the Whites on a wide variety of topics, including botany, alpine ecology, birds, and geology.

Buchsbaum resides in Beverly, Massachusetts with his wife Nancy Schalch and their children, Alison and Gabriel. He works for the Massachusetts Audubon Society as a conservation scientist, carrying out research related to conservation initiatives. He has written numerous magazine articles on natural history and has published extensively in technical journals and books.

# The Appalachian Mountain Club

Founded in 1876, the AMC is the nation's oldest outdoor recreation and conservation organization. The AMC promotes the protection, enjoyment, and wise use of the mountains, rivers, and trails of the Northeast outdoors.

## People
We are nearly 90,000 members in 12 chapters, 20,000 volunteers, and over 450 full time and seasonal staff. Our chapters reach from Maine to Washington, D.C.

## Outdoor Adventure and Fun
We offer more than 8,000 trips each year, from local chapter activities to major excursions worldwide, for every ability level and outdoor interest—from hiking and climbing to paddling, snowshoeing, and skiing.

## Great Places to Stay
We host more than 135,000 guest nights each year at our AMC Lodges, Huts, Camps, Shelters, and Campgrounds. Each AMC Destination is a model for environmental education and stewardship.

## Opportunities for Learning
We teach people the skills to be safe outdoors and to care for the natural world around us through programs for children, teens, and adults, as well as outdoor leadership training.

## Caring for Trails
We maintain more than 1,400 miles of trails throughout the Northeast, including nearly 350 miles of the Appalachian Trail in five states.

## Protecting Wild Places
We advocate for land and riverway conservation, monitor air quality, and work to protect alpine and forest ecosystems throughout the Northern Forest and Highlands regions.

## Engaging the Public
We seek to educate and inform our own members and an additional 1.5 million people annually through AMC Books, our website, our White Mountain visitor centers, and AMC Destinations.

## Join Us!
Members support our mission while enjoying great AMC programs, our award-winning AMC Outdoors magazine, and special discounts. Visit www.outdoors.org or call 617-523-0636 for more information.

**THE APPALACHIAN MOUNTAIN CLUB**
Recreation • Education • Conservation
www.outdoors.org

# AMC BOOK UPDATES

**AMC BOOKS STRIVES** to keep our guidebooks as up-to-date as possible to help you plan safe and enjoyable adventures. If after publishing a book we learn that trails are relocated or route or contact information has changed, we will post the updated information online. Before you hit the trail, check for updates at www.outdoors.org/publications/books/updates.

While hiking or paddling, if you notice discrepancies with the trail description or map, or if you find any other errors in the book, please let us know by submitting them to amcbookupdates@outdoors.org or in writing to Books Editor, c/o AMC, 5 Joy Street, Boston, MA 02108. We will verify all submissions and post key updates each month.

AMC Books is dedicated to being a recognized leader in outdoor publishing. Thank you for your participation.

AMC BOOKS & MAPS

**EXPLORE THE POSSIBILITIES**

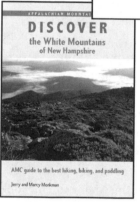